Shree Shree Ma Anandamayee

My Mother ANANDAMAYEE

Vishuddha

Allied Publishers Pvt. Ltd.

NEW DELHI • MUMBAI • KOLKATA
CHENNAI • BANGALORE • HYDERABAD

ALLIED PUBLISHERS PRIVATE LIMITED

1/13-14 Asaf Ali Road, **New Delhi**–110002
Ph.: 011-23239001 • E-mail: delhi.books@alliedpublishers.com

17 Chittaranjan Avenue, **Kolkata**–700072
Ph.: 033-22129618 • E-mail: cal.books@alliedpublishers.com

15 J.N. Heredia Marg, Ballard Estate, **Mumbai**–400001
Ph.: 022-42126969 • E-mail: mumbai.books@alliedpublishers.com

No. 25/10, Commander-in-Chief Road, Ethiraj Lane (Next to Post Office)
Egmore, **Chennai**–600008
Ph.: 044-28223938 • E-mail: chennai.books@alliedpublishers.com

P.B. No. 9932, 1st Floor, Sunkada Chickkana Complex,
Loop Lane Off Race Course Road, Next to Hotel Maurya,
Gandhi Nagar, **Bangalore**–560 009
Ph.: 080-22262081 • E-Mail: bngl.books@alliedpublishers.com

Sri Jayalakshmi Nilayam, No. 3-4-510, 3rd Floor (Opp. State Bank of India)
Barkatpura, Telangana, **Hyderabad**–500027
Ph.: 040-27551811, 2755 1812 • E-mail: hyd.books@alliedpublishers.com

Website: www.alliedpublishers.com

ISBN: 978-93-87997-83-7

Introduction to Cover

The background of the cover photograph is of the Varanasi Ashram which includes Kanyapeeth and Annapurna temple. Below left shows Smt. Indira Gandhi arriving at the ashram ghat and being received by the 'Kashi Naresh'.

Foreword

Om Jai Ma

In this holy land of ours people of outstanding stature manifest themselves in all ages and times to revive spiritualism. In our age such an outstanding manifestation is Shree Shree Ma Anandamayee. She was a miracle for two reasons: for one, She revealed Herself in the form of a woman–a typical housewife hidden behind the veil. Secondly, Her revelation in public was not prompted by any conscious effort in the form of any kind of penance. The whole thing was a spontaneous outburst proclaiming Her coming like a tempest that carries everything in its wake. She is the embodiment of the declaration made in Devi Sukta, Rig Veda:

"Ahameva Vata Iva Pravami"

(I blow like air)

At the vital contact of that flow, lives of many have been revived into a second birth. One of them is the writer of "My Mother Anandamayee"–Brahmacharini Vishuddha. Everything about her, right from the naming up to moulding of her life is the doing of the Mother.

The sole aim of Ma Anandamayee was to motivate the lives of human beings Godwardly. Specially due to Her divine vision She evoked the spirit of Gouri within a woman. "*Yatra nari, tatra Gouri.*" 'Wherever there is a woman, there is Gouri.' With the same goal in view, Gurupriya didi, who served Mother whole heartedly and was an inseparable associate in Her divine Leela, founded a Kanyapeeth at holy Varanasi Dham. Vishuddha having her lodging in that Kanyapeeth from her infancy was initiated into the means of elevating her life to a divine existence.

As a resident of the Kanyapeeth, she had the rare opportunity of direct participation in diverse divine modes (leelas) of Shree Shree Ma. Here she has recorded them with the highest pitch of commitment and sincerity. While reading this book, those who were acquainted with the Mother would be gratified by having once more a direct view of Her in an incarnate form. They would be able to realise in what diverse ways the Mother inspired those who came directly under Her aegis–sometimes by Her indulgent affection and sometimes influencing them by the regulating power of Her strict discipline–to mould their lives into ideal form. Vishuddha was able to have the rare fortune of serving the divinity embodied in the Universal Mother by bathing Her, cooking food for Her consumption, massaging Her feet and lying down near those very feet. In this way she was able to purify and gratify herself.

Many would be able to know from this book the detailed account of the Savitri Maha Yajna performed by the kheyal of Ma at Varanasi. Besides, many miraculous divine incidents have been recorded in it. Shree Shree Ma laughed and played with celibates like Vishuddha. Ma was dressed as they liked to dress Her and sometimes even wept profusely while detecting some lapses in them. She, prostrating Herself at their feet, crying effusively with eyes moistened with tears would say, "Forgive me, forgive me thou Goddess in the kumari form".

Once, finding Her bathed in tears and repeating the same words in a state of trance, Gurupriya di was struck dumb with surprise, She said, "Ma, why are you asking for forgiveness? We are the perpetrators and are at fault at every step." Ma replied, "Didi, the faults committed by those who are called upon to gather around this body, are part and parcel of this body."

In this way the Mother identified Herself with all. When we realise it, we would be alert and try to do no wrong lest it should go down to Her and bring tears to Her eyes. The responsibility of keeping the Mother free from tears, rests with Her children.

We can get these wonderful instructions from these anecdotes of Vishuddha. I hope that all would read this book and be gratified by deriving inspiration towards the life divine. I for one am gratified and these few lines are just to unlock my heart, for I am too humble to write an 'introduction' to this wonderful book. Only fellow celibates like Vishuddha, or her teachers at Kanyapeeth, are competent for the task. Only a teacher, striver or a fellow student of Vishuddha, her contemporary at Kanyapeeth is entitled to this task.

Kolkata
March, 2000

Mahamahopadhyaya
Dr. Govinda Gopal Mukhopadhyaya

Ma with Her mother Swami Muktananda Giriji

Ma with Kanyapeeth girls and teachers
after Savitri Mahayajna 1950, Varanasi Ashram

Sitting from left to right
Bindudi (Swami Shantananda), Minati Chakraborty (Banerjee), Gangadevi Panchateertha, Juthika Guha (Bunidi), Swarna K. Jaspal (Billojee), Shree Shree Ma, Didi Gurupriya, Udasjee, Ratna Mitra and Shraddha Chakraborty.

Standing from left to right
Madhuri Bhattacharya, Puspa Sen (Swami Bhajananada), Tara Kar, Nirmalya Chakraborty, Sarba Chakraborty, Ganga Chakraborty, Chandan Bhattacharya, Jyoti Chakraborty, Vishuddha Chakraborty and Kshama Mitra.

Shree Shree Anandamayee Sangha
Kankhal (Haridwar)

Ma always used to say–"This body has a spiritual relationship with all." Moreover, She said, "Nobody can love you as much as this body does."

After going through the book, "My Mother Anandamayee," written by Vishuddha, I feel that how minutely Ma observes Her children's every step–minor or major.

During the period of Ma's secluded life. She chose only one to stay with Her. She was Virajmohini Didi an inmate of domestic life. She was very pious and devoted to Ma. Virajmohini Didi on her own, chose to keep a record of Ma's daily life of this period in the form of a diary. When the duration of Ma's isolation from public life was nearing its end, one day, Ma threw away the diary in the river and said to her, 'Let the unknown remain unknown'. Ma always tried to maintain a low profile and turned away any form of publicity.

Just like a movie in Vishuddha's book, we can visualize Her before our very eyes in myriad form and we stand awe struck.

Kankhal
4th December, 2004

Swami Bhaskarananda
General Secretary
Shree Shree Anandamayee Sangha
Kankhal (Haridwar)

Ma on a swing during Jhulan in Kanyapeeth, Varanasi

Om Ma

Why this attempt

This book is a modest attempt at depicting the beauty, simplicity, magnificence and glory of Ma's Leela. I pray the readers will be able to experience joy and draw upon the essence and sublime spiritual significance of the "Leela".

Some of Shree Shree Ma's most loyal devotees who dedicated their lives only to serve Her–our beloved Dadabhai Gurupriya Devi, respected B.K. Shah, Swami Shivanandajee, our teachers at Kanyapeeth Renu di, Sati di and others insisted on my putting in print my recollections of Mother. I had the rarest privilege of having Her as my mentor. Since then began my trepidation as to whether I would be true to the task and my pen would be able to reveal a sacrosanct portrait of the Supreme Mother. It took me years to make up my mind. My diffidence finally gave way and I mustered strength following an incident. It came upon my life as Mother's boon. It was and incredulous story–a kind of miracle indeed.

A few years ago, I was down with serious meningitis. On recovery, I discovered I had forgotten much about my recent past. However, through the infinite mercy of Ma, I still do remember clearly many old incidents about Her. I felt that these should be on record as long as they are still a fresh in my memory otherwise, one fine morning they might sink into in oblivion. So I started writing.

The fact is, I had the good fortune of growing up in the loving care of the Mother. Due to Her infinite grace She guided us affectionately as part of Her Divine Leela. In writing about Mother, I can hardly avoid personal references. I would like to say in the words of Tagore:

"O Mother, let me not display
myself through my actions,
may Thy supreme will be realised
in the midst of my life."

Professor Niraj Nath Das Gupta (Manikda), the eldest son of Shree Gangacharan Dasgupta, a committed devotee of Ma, went through my humble account of Mother. He said, "Vishuddha, you must have it printed lest it would be lost. This is the only narrative on Ma which brings alive Her homely aspects." This statement of Manikda gave me courage and I resolved that–it should be done. The idea of publishing this immature effort of mine never came to my mind. There was also the question of money to meet the cost of printing. My younger brother Shree Keshabananda Chakraborty offered a donation in the name of Late Shraddha, my eldest sister, by way of a stipend towards research to be conducted at Shree Ma's Kanyapeeth. With the consent of my brother, I proposed to print the book out of this fund with the approval of the secretary of Kanyapeeth.

The rare opportunity of my growing up at Ma's ashram and serving Her was entirely due to the will of Dadabhai (Gurupriya didi). In 1955, when she was lying ill in Mumbai, I used to look after her. It was she who first inspired me to write about Mother as I had seen Her. It is my misfortune that it could not be written in her lifetime. Today by the grace of Mother, the book is about to see the light of the day. Accordingly, I wish, to dedicate it respectfully to our most affectionate Dadabhai, my Preceptor and Instructor. Dadabhai's absolute surrender at the feet of Ma is beyond question. I hope what is dedicated to Dadabhai, in a way will be an offering to the lotus feet of the Mother.

I am grateful to Mahamahopadhyaya Dr. Govinda Gopal Mukhopadhyaya, the renowned scholar and philosopher, an ardent devotee of Ma, who was kind enough to write a foreword for the Bengali version of this book on my request. This I accept humbly as a token of Mother's blessing.

I offer my cordial thanks to all those who helped me in translating the Bengali book into English–Mother's devotees Km. Aruna Pandya and Smt. Shanti Devi (Ghosh), a blessed child of Mother and like my elder sister. I am thankful to Dilip Guha for his labour and love for this book. He not only took pains to go through the manuscript but also corrected the proofs. He went a long way in matters of printing and promoting this book among the devotees of Ma. I would like to thank the nephew of Brahmachari Kamalakanta da, Dr. Binoy Banerjee, who was initiated by Shree Ma for patiently correcting the book.

I would be failing in my duties without thanking the staff of Allied Publishers who brought out this book in such a nice way.

Jai Ma.

Vishuddha

Dedication

In memory of my Guru Gurpriya di (Dadabhai), the Preceptor and Instructor of my life.

My Preceptor—Gurupriya di (Dada bhai), daughter of Dr. Shasanka Mohan Mukherjee (Civil Surgeon of Noagaon), her name at home was 'Adaroni' and lovingly called 'Khukini'—referred as such by Ma in the initial days. She was christened as 'Gurupriya' by Ma when she began her ashram life. Later Ma started referring to her as didi (The lore goes that she was born in Ma's family in her previous birth). Due to her manly demeanour Mauni Ma named her Dada bhai (elder brother) and was referred to as such by the girls of Kanyapeeth.

My Mother Anandamayee

1

A few days before my birth, Shree Shree Ma, Baba Bholanath, Bhaiji, Khukuni di, my grandmother (maternal) Virajmohini Devi and others had visited Naogaon in Assam. My father Shree Nagendranath Chakravarty, one of my uncle Shri Dharanimohan Bhattacharya, elder brothers and local devotees brought Ma directly from the Naogaon railway station to our house in a procession chanting holy names. Ma had stayed there for two or three days. Ma left my grandmother with my mother. Bhaiji said to her, "Viraj di, Ma has come on a visit before the birth of a child, you must write to me about the new born, whether it's a boy or a girl."

On my birth in September 1935, my grandmother wrote about the time and particulars. Bhaiji studied my horoscope and informed my grandmother what it foretold. There were five good points and three evil portents. The evils could be averted if my name has the initial 'A'. Bhaiji named me 'Ambika'. At the 'rice eating ceremony', my father named me 'Gayatri'. Later when I came to Kanyapeeth, it appeared that there was another girl by the name Gayatri, So Ma called me Vishuddha. That is another story.

My father was a disciple of Swami Shivananda (Mahapurush Maharaj), a direct disciple of Shri Ramkrishna Dev. My father was very fond of Kirtan, Satsang (holy discourse), etc. Every evening, he recited holy names and read holy books before us at night. One night he read from the 'Udbodhan' (A journal published by the Ramakrishna mission) what Shri Sarada Ma had said to a devotee. Even if a fly happens to die at Kashi, it is liberated. That led my father straight to Kashi. At that time he had a good job in the Imperial Bank of India, big house with gardens, while we the little ones were in the best schools. Learning that my father was about to start for Kashi leaving everything behind, the neighbours suggested that he should first go to Kashi alone to make necessary arrangements and then let others follow. My father said, "Religion is not compatible with backwards pull." He was determined to leave for Kashi with the entire family.

My father was very much fond of the ancient Vedic system of education. So he sent my eldest brother to the Ramakrishna Vidyapeeth at Deoghar, second and third brothers to Shree Anandamayee Vidyapeeth at Dehradun and elder sister to Shree Anandamayee Kanyapeeth at Raipur (Dehradun). When we left Assam for Kashi, our family consisted of our parents, me and two of my younger brothers.

It was the year 1944 and the Second World War was on. I remember that it took us 14–15 days to reach Kashi from Naogaon, as the trains were packed with military personnel exclusively. Ordinary passengers could be accommodated only if some trains happened to be empty or space was available in any train. Due to the uncertainty, it couldn't be ascertained who would reach where, when and how. However, when we finally reached Kashi we had no place to put up. Initially we stayed at Harasundari Dharmashala and then shifted to a rented apartment at Pataleshwar.

Ma's ashram at Kashi had not yet come into being. Swami Akhandanandaji, Swami Umeshanandaji, Shri Nishikanta

Mitra, Shri Sachikanta Ghosh and his sister Manorama Devi (Mejdi) and others were in a rented house near Dashwamedh Ghat. Every other day my father took me there. There were discussions on Ma and many other religious topics and subjects. Before taking sanyas Swami Akhandanandaji was a civil surgeon at Naogaon hospital. He knew my father. Sachidadu had also been to our house there for a few days. He took a great liking to the religious environment of our house and remarked "Nagenda, your house looks like a hermitage. You have brought up your children in a religious atmosphere. It would be better still if you send them to an ashram."

Akhandanandaji asked me, "Do you know why your father has brought you here? He would have sent you to a forest (a place of seclusion) or to an ashram." He knew very well of my father's liking for ashram life. They treated me with the affection that knew no bounds.

During that period, Shree Shree Ma was a frequent visitor to Kashi. As the ashram was not yet built, She stayed either at a dharmashala or in a barge on the river Ganga. Shri Nalini Kanta Bhattacharya (Nanida), a committed devotee of Ma, was residing in a bungalow near Varanasi railway station. At times, a tent was arranged for Ma on his spacious lawns. Ma used to stay there for a few days and then move somewhere else. I saw Shree Ma for the first time in those tents. I remember that we were in the lawn outside the tent, when Ma came out moving aside the flap of the tent. I had seen Ma's photograph at the altar of our worship room. But at the first sight of Her in person, I was captivated and could hardly take my eyes off Her. Near the pillow on Ma's cot was a beautiful red rose.

beside Ma, the rose paled into insignificance. Ma looked at me and smiled sweetly. After paying homage to Her we left.

While at Kashi, my father used to bathe thrice in the Ganga. I too accompanied him. Often I saw Ma moving in a big barge on the Ganga. Occasionally, I caught a glimpse of somebody walking on the other side of the river carrying a parasol in hand. It indicated that Didi with a parasol in hand was escorting Ma to the toilet. Kashi being Baba Vishwanath's place, many eminent Mahatmas' like Swami Harihar Baba and others used to cross the Ganga for toilet purposes.

Ma lived mostly in a special barge owned by the royal family of Vijayanagaram. Whenever we learnt about Ma's arrival at Kashi, we left instantly for the barge. The middle portion of the barge was covered with a nice thick square screen. Inside this was a room for Ma to relax. Around it was a verandah running along the four sides for the devotees.

There was an arrangement for holy discourses (Satsang) in the morning and evening, right on the barge. At noon, the barge was anchored at a high ground or at a landing place. Khukuni di, Matori aunt or Paramananda Swamiji cooked Khichri (a rice and pulse mixed preparation). There Khukuni di fed Ma and then served hot Khichri on leaf plates for those who were present there. The taste of the food was excellent.

After we had our meal, we threw away the leaves into the Ganga and washed our hands and faces. When Ma rested, the screen around Her would be drawn. We too rested wherever we could, sitting or lying down. In the afternoon, the barge was afloat again. On the banks of the river, most of the ghats were crowded with people sitting in groups around a spiritual singer or a learned man giving religious discourses. Slowly, the lights on the ghats and bridge were aglow. To us, seated in the barge on the Ganga, these lights presented a rare sight of the divine.

Many devotees came in the afternoon to have a glimpse of Shree Shree Ma. I remember that respected Mohanananda Brahmachari ji was then living somewhere near 'Kedarghat'. Every evening he remained in meditation on the roof of a small barge anchored at 'Gauranga Ghat'. When Ma was at Kashi he came to Ma's barge and sang some melodious songs and kirtans with accompaniment of a 'Manjira'. Another visitor Shree Govinda Gopal Mukhopadhyaya used to come to Ma and sang devotional songs with unalloyed devotion. Besides, there were Abhay da and Shobhan da who made the place quite vibrant by modulations of music of kirtans while Kamal da (Virajananda ji) recited from the religious texts. There was an unceasing flock of devotees from Kolkata.

2

Swami Akhandananda ji and Swami Umeshananda ji started living in a rented house at Devnathpura, Varanasi, where the Kanyapeeth girls were also lodged. Vivek di, Bindu di, Kshama di, Surobala di, Tara di and others were in-charge of the younger girls. Then Ganga di, Jamuna di, Chandan di, Pavitra di, Anjali di, Roma di, Shuddha di, Shraddha di and others joined the Kanyapeeth. We lived nearby. We used to visit the ashram every day. Once we learnt that Ma would rest at Mughalsarai railway station's waiting room the next day for 4–5 hours at noon to board another train. Many of the elders from the ashram went to see off Ma. Next day my parents, both younger brothers and I set off for Mughalsarai railway station on time. Among the local devotees, Swami Shankaranandaji, Nepal da, Haralal da, Patal da and many others went there.

I remember that Ma was resting in an armchair of the waiting room reclining half length. All of us paid our respects to Her and stood by. It was very hot, but Ma was not in a habit of using the electric fan. Someone was trying to comfort Her using a hand fan. Ma asked me with a smile, "Well friend can you fan?" I answered in affirmative. She asked for the fan to be handed over to me. I began to fan her briskly. Previously I had observed my mother wetting the fan before fanning so, after a while I too went to the bathroom, put the fan under the tap and after wetting it resumed fanning Ma. I failed to notice that Ma's clothes had become drenched as a result. When Khukuni di and my mother tried to stop me, Ma asked them to keep quiet. Then She asked me, "Can you massage hands and feet?" Though I could not massage, but by nature I was incapable of saying 'no' to anything. With a broad smile I said, "Yes". Ma stretched out her right hand to me. I started massaging as far as I could. Ma waited a little and said, "No friend, this is not the way." She took my hand and massaged it properly with both hands to show the right process of doing it. I then started pressing Her hands in the same way. All present there were highly amused at Ma's ways. Finding Khukuni di so amused, Ma said, "Do you know why Khukuni looks so happy? Because you are going to be a Kanyapeeth student." Strangely there was no talk yet, of my enrolment in Kanyapeeth.

Ma came to Kashi over and over again. For Dadabhai also Kashi was a very blissful place. She was unhappy as there was no ashram for Ma yet. All the efforts to find a suitable site were in vain. Later I heard from Dadabhai that Ma was going somewhere via Lucknow. She had to change the train there. Arrangements were made for Ma to rest in the railway station waiting room. Dadabhai went to the bathroom for a bath. When she came out a little later, she found Ma standing on a table and gazing at a map of Uttar Pradesh hanging on the wall. As soon as Dadabhai entered the room, Ma placed Her finger on the map and declared, "Khukuni look, this is the site for your ashram." Dadabhai leapt in joy and standing beside Ma on the table she marked the place adjoining the river Ganga near Assi Ghat. Then again while travelling by boat along the Ganga, Ma pointed with Her finger and showed the place. She revealed that whenever She passed that place by boat, many divine forms had raised their hands and invited Her to the site.

Next, at the divine will of Ma, the present site of the ashram was purchased. As far as I remember, on the day the foundation stone was laid, a puja was performed in the centre of the present courtyard of the Kanyapeeth building. Bricks were laid by Ma. She and others sang kirtan around the place. There was a continuous chanting of holy names for 8–10 days at the site. Arrangements were made for the lodging and boarding of all at several houses near the ashram. A few days later, Ma left.

Swami Paramanandaji stayed back for the construction work of the ashram. We used to go towards the Assi ghat while walking along the bank of the Ganga in the afternoon. There we saw Swamiji standing at Imlighat in front of the ashram site. He would smile and pat us whenever he saw us. Near the landing place of the Ganga, there was a big tamarind (imli) tree. So the ghat came to be known as 'Imlighat'.

The first festival at this ashram, Vasanti puja, was celebrated in a temporarily erected mandap (marquee), on a big scale. I recollect that during that puja, I was, for the first time worshipped as a kumari. Bithu di (Dr. Bithika Mukherji) draped me with a saree, put sandal paste on my face, garlanded me and used liquid vermillion for beautifying the edges of my feet. Bishu da (Shree Bishweshwar Bhattacharya), a great devotee of Ma conducted the Vasanti puja. I was taken to the Chandi mandap and seated on a cushion. My feet were put on a big copper plate meant for the worship of Devi (Goddess). Bishu da worshipped me and later bowed before me. He was like my father to me. I was overcome with embarrassment that he paid respect to me by touching my feet. After the worship I too did pranam to Bishu da. Ma exclaimed, "Such an action wasn't seen before."

On the morning of Mahashtami, a large crowd gathered at the courtyard of the ashram. My mother was standing a little away from the crowd. I was standing next to her. All of a sudden Ma emerged from the pavilion and approached us rapidly. She had a garland of red Jaba (Hibiscus) hanging around Her neck to her feet. She took off the garland and put it around my mother's neck.

Then touching her repeatedly from head to toe, She kept saying "The goddess incarnate, the goddess incarnate, the goddess incarnate." Then She went back to the Chandi mandap just the way She had come. This was the last meeting between my mother and Shree Shree Ma. After one month my mother passed away at Kashi.

At noon, after the Bhog we all sat down with leaf-plates in the ashram courtyard. Khukuni di came with buckets full of Khichri, vegetable preparation and kheer (rice milk sweet dish). Ma served all of us with ladles full of prasad. Hundreds of devotees were gratified to have prasad from the holy hands of Goddess Durga Herself. All ate with great joy and loudly uttered 'Jai Ma' again and again. At times Ma laughed heartily. When all had finished their meals, Ma covered Her body with prasad and then rushed to the Ganga and jumped into it. She was followed by all devotees. It was a splendid sight.

Ma left Varanasi after Vasanti puja. The girls of Kanyapeeth went back to the rented house at Devnathpura and the devotees to their residences with unearthly delight.

3

The memory of Vasanti Puja reminds me that while leading the Kanyapeeth girls to the mandap through the crowd, a girl named Shuddha screamed as Kshama di, the in-charge of Kanyapeeth then, touched her waist by chance. Kshama di could not what notice it. Later, when Kshama di questioned her, she kept silent. Through sheer shyness she even refused to show her the spot. She was of course obliged to do so under collective pressure. Then it appeared that there was a red mark and swelling on her waist. It was too painful to touch. On examination, the doctor suggested an immediate operation. The patient was so weak that anaesthesia was ruled out. The doctor operated on her at the ashram itself after consulting Swami Akhandananda ji, the retired civil surgeon. On the day of the operation, we went to the ashram. At noon Shuddha di was in a large room on the first floor. At her request, a tulsi plant was placed before her head. Below it, there was an image of Gopal which was visualized by her in a dream and she got the same by the grace of Ma. Vivek di sat by the side of her head, Kshama di at her feet and Akhandananda ji was in the front. Outside the door, the girls of Kanyapeeth were chanting the name of Ma. The Doctor conducted the operation without anaesthesia. It took about 3–4 hours. After a big incision on one side, putrid matters were removed by hand and a big gauze was put inside. To the wonder of wonders, Shuddha di lay quietly from the beginning till the end. She forced her hands up towards Gopal without the slightest sign of pain over the long time her body was being tampered with. Either it was an incredible tolerance or the grace of Gopal.

Meanwhile Shuddha di's parents (my maternal aunt and uncle) came and accompanied their daughter to Kolkata for treatment. There she was admitted into the Campbell Medical Hospital. She underwent several operations by an English surgeon and was convalescing. But due to some carelessness on the part of the doctor, Shuddha di finally expired. As long as she was in the hospital, she took all other food and medicines only after my uncle had brought her Gopal's Prasad. Her piety was exemplary.

When Shuddha di was 5–6 years old, (she was named Vasanti by her father) she had gone to Ma's ashram at Vindhyachal with my grandmother Virajmohini Devi. My grandmother lived there at that time. Ma was also there. Many devotees came to have a glimpse of Ma and some of them used to have a private conversation with Ma. One day the little girl Vasanti said, "Grandma, I too want to talk privately with Ma." When she repeated it a number of times my grandmother rebuffed her, "Keep quiet". But the simple girl kept insisting. So grandmother was obliged to take her to Ma once. There, what she confided to Ma took everyone by surprise. Vasanti told Ma that she had seen in her dream a roly-poly infant Gopal sucking his right big toe. She must have such a Gopal.

God readily responds to His devotees. He couldn't but satisfy this innocent demand of a child. Ma went to a jeweller at Mirzapur with Vasanti and her grandmother. She asked Vasanti to be in the posture of Gopal as she had seen in her dream. Looking at her a craftsman made a sketch. Ma asked him to make a large sized Gopal out of an alloy of eight metals. Once the idol of Gopal was made, Ma duly married her to Gopal and directed how to serve her divine husband daily. This took place when Vasanti was six years old. She died at the age of 16–17 years. She didn't take anything before offering food to Gopal as long as she lived.

The Kanyapeeth was located in Raipur at Dehradun. My father went to meet Ma at Raipur with my elder sister Savitri and my maternal cousin Vasanti. There they made obeisance to Ma when two words, "Shraddha and Shuddha" came out of Her holy lips. Thus through the inspired fancy (kheyal) of Ma they got their new names. They were at Kanyapeeth for about a year and a half. Later Shuddha di was taken away by her parents for treatment. My mother wanted my elder sister back home as there wasn't adequate arrangements for education at Kanyapeeth for them. After all means to persuade her to leave, failed. She was finally taken away by sheer force.

She came home dressed in a frock and wrapper. She wore the frock washing and drying it on her own refusing to wear a new frock when one was brought. The girls at Kanyapeeth lived a life of strict purity. They did not eat food cooked by others. She refused to take anything cooked by her mother. Being too young, she did not know how to cook, she wouldn't lie on the bed and slept only on the wrapper spread on the floor. Seeing this, my mother, took her to the ashram one day hoping it would improve her mood. Good Gracious! At the ashram she entered into a small room, stayed there with the doors and windows shut and did not open the door even when people knocked. At last we came back home crestfallen. At night we woke up hearing Khukuni di knocking at the door. We found her standing outside the door with my elder sister. She said, "Nagen da, here is your daughter". Then she left. Later we came to know that on her return to the ashram at night, Khukuni di learnt everything, awoke my sister and escorted her straight to us. It was also heard that Khukuni di's father Swami Akhandananda ji rebuked her saying, "Is this the kind of training you are giving these children that they don't obey their parents?" Khukuni di also said that Ma is of the view that Shraddha should observe discipline in her meal, she could take meals cooked by her own mother. Since then the 'Shuddhacharies' are allowed to partake food cooked by their mothers.

My elder sister Shraddha resumed studies at home. A few days later, after a brief illness my mother left for her heavenly abode at Kashi at the early age of 35. My father was very fond of holy men and attending religious discourses. Thus, at Kashi my father was acquainted with a few sadhus and brahmacharies of Ramakrishna Mission and Ma's ashram. They frequently came to our house for religious discussions. It so happened that on the day when my mother took her last breath, 5–6 sadhus and brahmacharies were present there. I remember that they chanted text from the Vedas in chorus. My father took part in the evening kirtan regularly with us. On that day at the end of the evening kirtan my mother found eternal peace at the feet of Vishwanath listening to the chanting of Vedas by the monks, fully conscious till the end. Shree Shree Ma was then at Vindyachal. Hearing of my mother's demise, She said, "She has attained Kashi after residing there for exactly one year, one month, one day and one hour." Later on father verified with my mother's diary and found Ma right.

After the passing away of my mother Shree Shree Ma sent our grandmother Virajmohini Devi to look after us. Grandmother told us, "Look, those who become motherless in their infancy are perpetually in sorrow, but remember, don't refuse even a glass of water given by anyone lovingly. You will find that never in your life shall you miss love and affection." It proved to be true enough as following grandmother's advice, I have reaped a rich harvest of love and affection. I accept it as an unending grace of our Ma.

About this time I was simultaneously attacked with small pox and typhoid. I was confined to bed for long. Some commented, "She loved her mother so much that this separation from her, might hasten her death." It was a close call. One noon I dreamt that Shree Shree Ma had been pacing up and down the side of a barbed wire fence along the bank of the Ganga in the ashram. I and my elder sister Shraddha were standing by while Ma came walking in front of me and with a smile remarked, "Well friend, you are perfectly well." After that I recovered gradually.

Ma's birthday celebration took place in the newly built ashram at Varanasi. At that time continuous Ma naam Japa and Ma naam Kirtan were the main programme of the celebration. On this occasion Ma's devotees used to come and sing to Her. That year Shree Mrityunjay Chakraborty and his younger brother came and recited the verses of Ramayana. Every evening on the banks of the Ganga on Ma's terrace Ramayana was being recited. We were engrossed in it. One day Shree Shree Ma was not present. On that day the topic being recited from the Ramayana was the incident when Shree Ram's two sons Lav and Kush had captured the horse sent for Ashwamedha Yajna by Shree Ram. Lakshman was ready to attack the enemies with his bow and arrow. Just at that moment two young boys resembling Shree Ram with their hair tied on the top of their heads appeared, and seeing such beautiful looking ashram boys, Lakshman stared at them without winking his eyes.

At that very moment with Her hair arranged on the top of Her head, smiling sweetly and softly treading Shree Ma entered the terrace. What is to be highlighted was the similarity between Ma and Luv-Kush's style of walking, synchronization with the music and the emotional situation. I was too young to understand the subject of Ramayana. However, the co-incidence of the situation, Ma's unparalleled expression left a deep impression on my mind.

After the first annual ritual of my mother, Krishna was married to my eldest brother on the direction of Ma. The girls of

Kanyapeeth had not yet arrived at Varanasi. I remember that my sister-in-law (Krishna) received ashirvada in the presence of Ma with durva brought from the ashram garden and a lighted lamp. Ma distributed sweets to all. While this was going on a lady arrived with a silver bowl full of kheer for Ma. Everyone present there fed Ma kheer with a silver spoon. I also came forward. Khukuni di asked, "What? You too want to feed Ma?" I nodded and smiled. Ma too smiled sweetly and said, "Do let her." Unconcerned, I put a spoon full of Kheer into Ma's mouth. Ma smiled and said, "You see her hand did not tremble at all." That was the first time I had fed Ma. I was between 10 or 11 years old at that time.

My father had gone to Shree Shree Ma at Tarapeeth for the sacred thread ceremony of my eldest brother Premananda. Baba Bholanath, Bhai ji, Swami Akhandananda ji, Gurupriya didi, Maroni di and others were present. This was the first incident when the sacred thread ceremony of the son of any devotee had taken place in the holy presence of Ma. On the instructions of Ma, Baba Bholanath ji became the Acharyaguru of my brother. After observing the ceremonial rituals in detail, my elder brother Premananda was confined in a closed room for eleven days according to the scriptural injunctions. Many years ago when Ma's Sadhana Leela was taking place, then Ma had also gone through the sacred thread ceremony. At that time Ma had 'kheyal' to arrange for the sacred thread ceremony for Dadabhai and Maroni di. Pandit Dinesh Shastri ji and Baba Bholanath were the acharya gurus of Dadabhai and Maroni di respectively. They were enclosed in a room for three days. My brother and Maroni di were both very young. So they were being looked after by Dadabhai. Maroni di looked upon my brother as her own brother.

At our home, brahmins, kumaris and the poor were fed every Monday. After the ashram at Kashi was built, Didima, Mounima, Nishidadu, Hemi di and others frequently came to our house and had their meals. For some time Maunima used to sweep the floor and took rice, pulses and curry there. It was a part of her worship as desired by Shree Krishna. Sometimes, I saw her eating rice from a napkin spread on the floor. Nishidadu used to regale with stories about Ma. Unfortunately, I couldn't recall anything about those stories.

As a child I was rather restless and naughty. I did not like doing household jobs at all and staying indoors. I preferred instead to fly kites, wrestle, swim, row boat, and romp about with my brothers. Grandmother taught me to stitch kanthas, make rag dolls and similar tasks even when I had no taste for them. It was in my habit to keep smiling. The elders rebuked me for it every now and then. It was in the midst of these circumstances I couldn't help missing my mother. Almost every day I used to go to the ashram walking along the bank of the Ganga. During this period Shree Shree Ma lived mostly at Kashi. I could address Mother as Ma, this gave me a lot of pleasure. Finding a tomboy in me and concerned about my future, grandmother asked Khukuni di to get me admitted into Kanyapeeth. I was glad to join Kanyapeeth on 20th January 1949. As a student of class VII at school, I was among the first three in the class. As there was no proper arrangement for education at Kanyapeeth, my father was little interested to put me in the ashram. It was Ma's attraction that brought me here.

My original name at home was Gayatri. As there was another Gayatri in Kanyapeeth, Ganga di who was then in-charge of Kanyapeeth, brought it to Ma's notice. Ma named me 'Shuddha'. When my grandmother came to know of the new name Shuddha, her eyes were filled with tears and she said, "One Shuddha named by Ma died prematurely, a new Shuddha again?" Ma came to know about this from Ganga di, while walking up the staircase. She clapped and said, "Whatever you may say, I will not discard Shuddha, you are welcome to add 'V' (the Bengali pronunciation would sound 'B') to change it into 'Vishuddha'." As I was naughty, Kshama di, Renu di and others called me 'Bichhu' (scorpion) affectionately, while Bimala di called me Bishu (short from the Vishuddha).

Later when Dadabhai was seriously ill at Vrindavan, Bimala di, Renu di, Gini di and myself were engaged in nursing her. One day Bimala di called 'Bishu, Bishu' for me. Ma heard her and remarked, "You do not like to pronounce the fine name, I see." Bimala di was then working outside the room. She didn't catch Ma's words, so Dadabhai said, "Oh Bimala, don't you hear what Ma says? Can't you call her Vishuddha?"

Ma sent me to Kolkata for treatment. I had pain in abdomen and went to Harrington Nursing Home for examination with Tara, another girl of Kanyapeeth. Dr. Satya Bose (the attending physician) wanted to know our names. Hearing that Ma named me, he asked, "Are you a favourite of Ma Anandamayee? She has given you such a sweet name but denied such a favour to her (Tara)." As I heard this, my bosom swelled with pride. Who doesn't want to be Ma's favourite? When I repeated Dr. Bose's remark to Ma, She smiled very sweetly.

4

When I joined Kanyapeeth in January 1949, a three year long Savitri Mahayajna was going on at Varanasi ashram. The Yajna was to be over by mid-January 1950. Over the year, ten thousand brahmins were fed. It was a grand affair. To observe the occasion, distinguished brahmins were invited from different states of our holy motherland. The strict brahmins from different states had different do's and don'ts. The brahmin cooks, familiar with their rituals and customs of different groups, cooked for their respective masters according to their tastes and rites. The brahmins had their seats (asana) in the spacious hall adjoining the Ganga, as well as on the roof. I remember that there were ceremonial drawings around the seats for the brahmins from South India. They were served in plantain leaves, ghee in leaf-cups and there were pulses, vegetables, curd, sweets, besides many other items. When all the brahmins were seated and before they were served food, Ma, accompanied by us took Her place in the hall below. The brahmins were treated to a ritualistic welcome (aarti) with incense, lamps and chowries (chamar) accompanied by songs of aarti by us and ringing of bells. At the end of the aarti, the scholars chanted Vedas in chorus. When we left after the salutations, they started eating. To observe different groups of brahmins taking their meals on different days was a rare experience. The brahmins from the Southern part of India wore multi coloured silk clothes and had tilak (holy mark) with bhasma (ashes) on their foreheads and arms which added to their grace.

During the festival, one day Shree Ma was sitting on the terrace on a wooden cot and was draped in a shawl. We were observing Ma from upstairs and we noticed a huge fat monkey approached Ma and caught hold of the shawl and was tugging at it. Ma slowly turned around and let go the shawl. I mentioned this to Dadabhai who immediately went and draped Ma with another shawl.

On the terrace of the Kanyapeeth, on Ma's prompting, a feast for the monkeys was arranged. Ma Herself stood there and asked us to arrange for eleven asanas, leaf plates, etc. On the plates before each asana were placed bananas, guavas, laddoos (sweet) and pooris. Ma asked us to stay at a distance, so that the monkeys would feel free to come. After quite some time, one big fat monkey came and smelt each of the plates and then left. Later a number of monkeys came and ate. Coincidently as a part of the festival, eleven Rudri (Shiva) recital was being held in the hall under the terrace.

At the time of Mahayajna special Ganga worship took place. Those days the width of the river was almost one and a half mile. Ganga was garlanded with huge flower garlands right across the river. One and a quarter maunds of cow milk, beautiful silk saree, fruits, sweets and dry fruits were all offered to the holy river.

Half way through the Yajna utsava a fifteen day function of Shrimad Bhagawat was held. The exponent speaker of the Bhagawat was Swami Akhandananda ji from Vrindavan. The original recitation of the Bhagawat was done by Pandit Agnishwatta Shastri (Batu da). The ashram was thronged with people who came to listen to it. And a number of people used to hear from their boats and enjoy it.

In the front courtyard of the Varanasi ashram, an old Shivalinga is installed at the wish of Shree Manamohan Ghosh

(Mana da), an ardent devotee of Ma since the Bangladesh days. His son late Saroj da with great difficulty managed to bring this Shivalinga by air from Dhaka (Bangladesh) to Varanasi.

On the day of the final offering (Purnahuti) of Savitri Mahayajna, it was installed under a bel-tree. One had never seen Mana da worshiping outwardly. One day, Ma made all the arrangement for Shiva puja and asked Mana da to do the worship. The person who was to conduct the puja was also present there on Ma's instruction. When Ma asked Mana da to do the puja, he queried twice, "Will I have to do it?" After a pause he started offering the puja items one by one on Ma's head instead of pouring them on the Shivalinga. Promptly Ma in turn placed Her head against the Shivalinga and remained in that posture till the puja was over. The leela of Bhakta (devotee) and Bhagawan (God) was immemorable. This incident was narrated to me by Mana da himself.

The Yajna Kund as Decorated for the Final Offerings of Savitri Maha Yajna

During these three years, sesame, barley, etc. for Yajna and other things for the offerings were washed, winnowed and handpicked silently and flawlessly by Kshama di as directed by Ma and assisted by Mukta di. We, the girls of Kanyapeeth also picked lovely barley, sesame, etc. silently at a particular time every day.

One day, a lot of potatoes had to be sliced for a food preparation for the brahmins. There was not much time to spare. Ma had a few bags of potatoes which She emptied on the verandah of the Chandi mandap and directed the girls of the Kanyapeeth to come with cutters. Ma asked us to keep the peeled potatoes and the peelings separately. This way I was initiated into the art of chopping vegetables for the first time in my life. When it was done, Ma asked us to ascertain the number of potatoes handled by each. It was found that Pavitra di had peeled the maximum number and I did the least, i.e., only 8–10. Ma measured the thinness of the peelings of each and said, "Vishuddha comes first." I was filled with indescribable joy. Ma's words still ring in my ears. On Ma's praise I smiled broadly. She too responded with her usual sweet smile.

Ma employed Bithu di and Renu di to make satin flags of various designs with different symbols, for displaying at the site of the Yajnashala, according to the norms and scriptures. For this work Bithu di enlisted Jyoti di and me. We started working in the basement of Kanyapeeth building. On large multi coloured flags, rectangular, triangular and square, we sewed applique of coloured satin demonstrating the mounts and weapons of different Gods and Goddesses. A large number of flags were made. Paintings were done by Renu di and me. When it was all done, we showed them to Ma. She expressed great delight. During the final offering of the Savitri Yajna, these flags were hung over the Yajnashala, as prescribed in the scriptures.

Before the final offering, there was a continuous chanting of holy names (kirtan) for a month. At this stage, innumerable saints, sages, scholars and devotees came to Varanasi ashram to attend the final offering (purnahuti). Due to lack of sufficient accommodation in the ashram quite a few were accommodated in private residences and dharmashalas, etc. The atmosphere in Varanasi reverberated with continuous chanting of holy names on the mike, sound of Vedic text by the brahmacharis (hotas) of the Yajna, religious discussions by scholars and musical performances.

On this occasion the senior most mahatma Devgiri Maharaj of Uttarkashi, Khanna Baba, Triveni Puriji–the unattached saint of Punjab, Avadhutji–personified figure of detachment, Hari Babaji Maharaj–most revered holy devotee of Vrindavan, learned speaker of Bhagawat Swami Akhandanandji, respected Prabhudutt Brahmachariji of Jhunsi, venerable Chakrapaniji, Gopal Thakur–the supreme Vaishnav of Allahabad, many mahatmas of a high order, the rulers of princely states of India and their queens, celebrated musicians and countless devotees were present. Ma Herself welcomed the Mahatmas and devotees introducing Herself as their 'little girl'. Letters were written to all, individually by Dadabhai and Kamal da dictated by Ma Herself. Sitting at the letter writing session we felt that Ma was teaching us by Her example on how to pay respect to the learned, the accomplished, the great Mahatmas and the general devotees. But alas! Have we been able to learn from Her? At that time Ma fell seriously ill. She vomited out whatever she was fed. She physically became much thinner. Dadabhai used to say that Ma has absorbed in Herself prospective diseases of all, so that the performers of Yajna (hotas) could carry out their work in good health and no problem is created by someone falling ill. In spite of Her illness She looked after the details of the occasion of final offering (purnahuti).

Finally the hour of the final offering arrived. On the preceding day, Ma called the Kanyapeeth girls and said, "Those of you, who are present at this great Yajna should know that you have been waiting for this auspicious moment over a number of successive births. You share a rare privilege by the grace of God." She presented us with a few yellow silk wrappers with holy names written all over. She took back the one She had given to me and said, "Wait, I shall give you a new one." She gave me one on which, 'Shree Ram Jai Ram Jai Jai Ram' was written. I thought that all of them were new, then why did Ma say like this? Later I observed that other wrappers had 'Hare Krishna' or 'Shiva Naam' written on them. Only mine bore the name 'Rama'. Later Dadabhai gave each of us a small amount of barley, sesame, myrobalan and pieces of gold and silver and directed us to offer them the next day at the final offering. We were also told the holy words (mantra) that should be uttered at the time of final offering.

For several days the ashram was being specially decorated. Patal da had entrusted it to Nanku Mali who was known to him. The gardener with some assistance decorated the ashram. On the roof of the big hall, garlands of marigold were heaped up like a mountain. The insides and upper sides of the Yajnashala were fully decorated with yellow and red marigold garlands by the bhramacharis (hotas). From the Annapurna temple to the roof of the Kanyapeeth hung streams of garlands in such profusion that it seemed as if a flower canopy was spread over the ashram yard. The multi coloured flags made by us were also arranged over the Yajnashala according to the scriptures. The four gateways of the Yajnashala served as the emblems of the four Vedas. The doors were decorated in golden lace. In the hall by the side of the Ganga, non-stop Kirtan could be heard the whole day and night. On the eve of the close of the three year-long celebrations, the whole ashram was echoing with jubilant vibrations.

In the meantime, we little girls of Kanyapeeth had to retire for the day and hit the bed at 10 p.m. singing *Mother is here and so are we* according to our daily routine. It was about 12 or 1 o'clock at night when Billo ji came to wake us up and said, "Ma has sent for you all." It was a winter night of January and we got up with great difficulty and stood before Ma, rubbing our eyes. Ma rebuked us saying, "One earns the good fortune of seeing such a festival by the merit acquired through several successive births and you were in deep sleep? Fie on you. Go quickly and serve your level best for the festival." We came back with dropped jaws. I fixed flags on the doors with Billo ji and later did the some work in Ma's kitchen.

Next morning we cleaned the entire ashram and after chanting the morning Kirtan we bathed in the Ganga and finished the daily worship and aarti. Then we put on the cloth and namavali given by Ma and with the articles meant for the offering, presented ourselves at the western main gate of the Yajnashala. Ma also entered the Yajnashala, clad in white silk saree and chadar. As Dadabhai, Udas ji and Maroni di were invested with the sacred thread, they and Didima stood behind Ma in the Yajnashala and we girls stood behind them.

The seats for the celebrated Mahatmas were placed in the front yard of Kanyapeeth at the Southern gate of the Yajnashala. Respected Triveni Puri ji also known as Khanna Baba, Devigiri Maharaj, Swami Sharanananda ji, Hari Baba ji, Avdhut ji, Chakrapani ji, Prabhu Dutta Bhramachari ji, Gopal Thakur and other saintly persons were on their seats. Countless devotees were at the Chandi Mandap verandah towards the Northern gate of the Yajnashala and on the terrace towards the eastern gate of the Yajnashala facing the Ganga.

Inside the Yajnashala, Shri Agnishwatta Sharma (Batu da), the learned pandit versed in Vedas, together with the brahmacharis (hotas) were chanting Veda mantras befitting the occasion. At the top of this voice, Shankar the well favoured young son of Batu da, clad in royal dress of satin, was also there chanting Vedas. Sushri Namita, daughter of Shri Adhir Bhattacharya, the elder brother of Bibhu da (Brahmachari Brahmananda) dressed in bright red Benarasi saree and gold ornaments, was worshipped as Kumari in the Yajna Mandap. After all ceremonies were duly completed at the auspicious moment of the final offering, Shri Nepal Brahmachari (later Swami Narayananda Teertha), the chief hota of this Yajna and other hotas made the final offering as Ma stood touching them. Batu da and other brahmins versed in the Vedas started uttering Veda mantras loudly. A costly red Benarasi saree was placed around the Yajna fire. The flames consumed it in no time. Gold ornaments, garlands, etc. were offered to the fire. During the final offering the saints who were present and we the girls of Kanyapeeth, at the direction of Ma, made offerings to the Yajna fire. The chanting of the Veda mantras went on and in the midst of it we with folded hands, uttered prayers to the fire God, as taught by Ma, for the well-being of the universe.

Yajna Kund in the Courtyard in front of Kanyapeeth. Shree Shree Ma sitting on the stairs of the entrance of Kanyapeeth.

Shree Shree Ma attending the Purnahuti of Savitri Mahayajna

Then something happened. During the final offering as ghee was being constantly poured into the fire, the flame flared up and in a moment started touching the top of the Yajnashala.

Ma had earlier directed someone to have at hand a large sprayer and Ganga water mixed with milk. Accordingly buckets full of Ganga water with milk mixed and a sprayer had been innocuously kept under the stairs near the western gate of the Yajnashala. As the fire rose threateningly, Ma signalled to spray water at once. As this was done readily the fire came under control. At the sight of the flame raging high, Batu da who was presiding over this vast Yajna, overcame with fear, but as the arrangement for water and sprayer caught his eyes, he with folded hands directed to Ma's feet, said, "Ma, you are omniscient, the averter of danger, so you have saved us today from this great danger. At large-scale Yajna, it is usual to arrange for milk, water and sprayers, but I had missed issuing this much needed instruction. Ma, you the seer and all knowing, you have saved your child from disgrace. A small mistake of mine might have led to a great catastrophe."

Procession after Savitri Mahayajna—Gopal Thakur, Swami Sharananandaji, Shree Shree Ma, Nepalda and Gurupriyadi

The next day, a vast procession consisting of the Yajna fire, Shree Shree Ma and the saints was taken out. Respected Hari Baba ji walked all along the route of the procession constantly playing a heavy ghanta with both his hands. The procession went around the city of Varanasi accompanied with the beating of the mridanga, castanets, conchshells and bells and chanting, *Jai Ma Gayatri, Jai Ma Savitri, Jai Ma Brahmani and Jai Jai Ma.* In this way the great Yajna came to a close according to the prescribed rites.

Procession around the city of Varanasi after the Savitri Mahayajna

One by one the saints and the devotees returned to their respective places. As instructed by Ma, Atul Brahmachari was entrusted with the task of maintaining the Yajna fire ablaze at the Yajna kunda. Since then, i.e., the year 1950, offering is performed every day. On the Yajna fire, holy food (choru) is cooked daily by a ser and a quarter of cow milk, rice, ghee and honey of specified quantity and after dedication, the prasad is taken every day by one of the ashramites only. On that day he or she would eat nothing else but milk, fruits and the holy food (choru). If one was unable to eat the whole of the holy food, the residue is to be cast into the Ganga. That was Ma's direction.

Once during the Savitri Maha Yajna at the time of daily silence (maun) at 8.45 p.m. one lady was drowning in the Ganga. As everyone was silent at that time, her pitiful cry could be heard. She was rescued and brought to the ashram. Later on she came to be known as Gopalu di since she had a Gopal. She used to serve in the Kanyapeeth. She was very kind and simple. She also served Ma for some time.

One day in my presence she was feeding Ma some sweets prepared by her. I noticed that she had fed Ma one bite and the other part of the sweet was hanging by a strand of a hair. She removed the strand and fed Ma the rest of it. We saw the strand of hair but Ma was indifferent to it and consumed the entire sweet. Generally if there was any hair found in Her food, Ma refused to take the food. But this time Gopalu di's devotion overcame it.

Once Ma had gone to Vindhyachal for 15–20 days. Gopalu di was also with Ma. Thinking of a chance of spending some time in seclusion with Ma, Mahamahopaddhyay Gopinath Kaviraj from Varanasi and Barrister Anil Ganguly from Kolkata, reached there. Over there Gopalu di was suffering from a severe pain in the abdomen. Ma immediately left for Delhi for her treatment. Gopi baba and Anil da were left stranded and surprised as they never witnessed this kind of incident before.

5

In the beginning, Udas ji took choru every day. It was because, Udas ji had decided to do 108 crore Japas for Ma's well-being. Continuously for three years she used to leave the bed every morning before sunrise, bathe in the Ganga and perform Japa sitting in the cave at Kanyapeeth. As directed by Ma, we used to prepare a pot full of whey and put it on the alcove of the window in front of the cave. Udas ji got up once at noon, drank the whey and sat down again for Japa. Completing the definite number of Japa, she ate the holy food of the Yajna (Choru) at night. After sleeping for 2–4 hours she woke up at the end of the night and after taking a bath in the Ganga she would start doing Japa. This was her daily routine. Many perform worship, Japa, Yajna, etc. for their own salvation or attainment of self, but Japa for the welfare of one's object of devotion and that too 108 crore times, is something unheard of!

We have heard from Shree Shree Ma, that even after days of doing Japa, Udas ji's determination to reach her target of 108 crore Japa in three years duration was next to an impossibility and she was considerably disheartened. At that time her heart-rendering prayer to Ma brought instant results. By the grace of 'Japa Bhagawan' she was able to complete it within the time limit. Ma said that the impossible became possible only because she was caught in a current in which she was able to complete a few lakhs in a few hours. It continued at a rapid speed nonstop. Udasji felt that this was Ma's grace.

In this context I recall that the money, gold, silver and Benarasi clothes that parents of Udasji had set aside for her marriage, were all used by her to build a room of white marble on the second floor of Kanyapeeth including a large throne of gold and silver, silver utensils for everyday use of Ma, exclusive bed of brocade and a bedcover of super fine transparent Benarasi cloth. She worshipped Ma offering these grand things on the auspicious day of Gurupurnima. It was an unprecedented event. All that Udasji did had to be perfect. Shri Manamohan Ghosh, a great devotee of Ma had helped in the construction of the fine temple while Patalda and Habulda, devotees of Ma and grandson of the renowned Chowkhamba Mitra family, the old residents of Varanasi, helped in making the gold and silver throne, ornaments and silver utensils.

When all arrangements were complete, this special festival started on the auspicious day of Guru Purnima. Udasji worshipped Ma in the morning after decorating her with floral ornaments. Ma removed the crown from Her head and made Udasji wear it and ordered her not to take it off for the whole day. Helpless she was, as nothing could be done. As ordered by Ma she performed her daily duties with the crown on. In the morning she made Halwa of kuttu atta (flour) in a large cauldron with pure ghee, plenty of almonds, cashew nuts, pistachios and raisins. This was kept in the hall of the

Kanyapeeth. Being a Kashmiri, Udasji had put so much ghee that it overflowed the cauldron and was trickling down. She washed big earthen plates with Ganga water and served in each of them a big ladleful of halwa and a big mango for everyone. Ma had asked the number of plates to be displayed. Surprisingly enough, the number of plates demanded turned out to be exactly the same, not one more not one less.

In the evening, the new throne was beautifully decorated with garlands of sweet scented flowers like Bela and Jasmine. The bed was made on the marble floor on silk sheet by covering the brocade mattress with very fine Benarasi bed-spread and with brocade pillow. Varieties of silver utensils were arranged for different uses, right from brushing of teeth and washing of mouth in the morning, drinking water to eating of Rajbhog at noon, afternoon meal and dinner. There were silver shoes (Khadau) and silver lotus to be placed under Ma's feet. Two Kanyapeeth girls were made to stand on both sides of the throne with large silver-handled chamars. Ma was clad in beautiful Benarasi saree looking like a queen of queens, with a crown and a full set of jewellery. She was led along a path strewn with petals of pink rose and placed on the throne by Udasji. Ma's feet were washed by scented Ganga water, wiped and then put on a big silver lotus. Finally Udasji offered Her handful of red lotus and bel leaves smeared with sandal paste, blades of grass and flowers. Thus she worshipped the supreme object of her devotion to her heart's content.

The puja room was small with a narrow verandah adjoining it with little space in front. For the countless devotees present at the divine celebration, the space was too small. So everyone bundled together, advanced and retired in turns. No one was satisfied with a bare glimpse or momentary sight. I was fortunate to get a place at one corner as I was entrusted with the task of decorating the place with flowers. So I continued to have a clear sight as long as I wished.

After finishing the worship and aarti Udasji was making obeisance by placing her head on the lap and feet of Ma, who in turn took this opportunity of taking out the ornament one by one and giving them to those in front of Her. Raising her head, Udasji observed this and quickly taking hold of Ma's hands said, "No, no, please don't give them away, these should be with you." Ma smilingly said, "Oh, didn't you then give them to this body? So be it." Saying this She stopped giving. Thus Ma made it clear to us that after offering something to the Divine, we cannot leave behind the sense of proprietorship. The ego lingers even after everything is given away. The idea that I am the donor cannot be readily effaced. But the kind heart of Ma would not permit the shade of egoism to stand in the way of moral progress of Her children. So She showed us a unique means to avoid such a pitfall.

In the recent past, Rani Saheba, the wife of the Maharaja of Solan, a committed devotee of Ma, died. As they had no children, she left a gift for the boys and girls of Vidyapeeth and Kanyapeeth respectively, looking upon them as her own children. Udasji had to incur some debt to make the marble room, the costly throne and other articles. So Ma arranged for the repayment of the debt with the money donated by the Rani Saheba to the Kanyapeeth. Since then the temple has been used as our daily puja room. Later, on innumerable occasions, such as worship of Goddess Lakshmi, Kali and during the festivals of Jhulan, Janmashtami, Gurupurnima, etc. the girls of Kanyapeeth persuaded Ma to sit on the silver throne in the worship room and performed worship, aarti singing and chanting the glory to Ma.

Generally, I used to decorate Ma while Ganga di or Chandan di worshipped Her. Then I was almost 13–14 years of age. I was small and short while Ma was fairly tall and well-built. I disliked asking anybody to help me in my job. Once we brought Ma to the temple. To dress Ma in a saree all by myself, I wrapped with both my hands a Benarasi saree around Ma's waist. While encircling Ma with my small hands, my head was thrust into Ma's chest. Standing gracefully and amused at my way of draping Her with the saree, Ma smiled and said, "You live within the Kanyapeeth and don't go out, then where from did you learn how to put on a saree?" At once I replied, "Why? Indeed we don't wear it, but don't we see others putting it on?" Ma said to Dadabhai, "Ah Khukuni, do you hear? Even if you lock them up, they see everything." At this there was a general outburst of laughter and while the conversation was on, I had put the saree in the reverse order and the fringe didn't come right. I bit my tongue with shame and taking the saree off, dressed Her properly. Ma noticed it and said, "You had made it right. For you brahmacharis the opposite is proper."

In those days, after her tours elsewhere, though moving about, Ma resided mostly in Varanasi. We studied in the hall and Ma walked to and fro in the verandah. In between She entered into the hall and saw what we were reading, asked us about it and had fun. Finding Ma walking in the verandah, if we went there and stayed for a while She would say, "You should do your work. If you come and stand here, this body will go away." One day while Ma was strolling, I crept from below and stood in front of Her. Ma took a good look at me and said, "You do asanas (exercise) every day, don't you? So your body looks fit."

At that time at Kanyapeeth, we used to sleep on the floor of the hall facing Ganga. Our bed consisted of only Kush asana covered with woven jute and a piece of old cloth as a bed sheet. During winters we spread a blanket on the kush asana and covered our body with another. Ma came and directed us to where the bed of each should be placed. Two beds were to be made in the first row for the grownups, in the next row below, three in order of age and again two in the third row. All the beds were to be arranged in this order. She directed the beds to be placed in such a way that nobody's head should be right at the feet of someone else. At that time we did not use pillows. Later Ma made small pillows and said, "You all should rest your heads on such pillows."

Once Ma made Her way to Varanasi at night by car via Vindhyachal, Allahabad, Jhusi, etc. We went to bed as usual at 10 p.m. After meeting every one downstairs Ma came up to our hall. She made a sign not to follow Her, took off slippers outside, entered the hall, bent Herself with folded hands at the bed of each girl, looked at the face of each and then retired to Her room. We were unaware of all this, being in deep sleep. Next morning we heard about the visit of Ma from the elder sister and tried not to think of our postures in sleep when Ma saw us. Such incidents happened frequently.

Once while Ma was in Allahabad, a devoted local lady made sweets of milk in proper way and offered it to Ma. She knew that the Kanyapeeth girls didn't take sweets bought from the market, but took only self-cooked food. At once Ma by Her kheyal sent those special sweets with Dadabhai for all of us mentioning each of us by name. Dadabhai carried the sweets with the special kheyal of Ma and reached Varanasi. Attending to her other duties she asked Kshama di at the Kanyapeeth, "Kshama, call the girls here at once." Kshama di said, "Didi, it is late night, the girls are asleep, let them be called tomorrow morning." But Dadabhai thought that Ma's kheyal should be carried out at once. She couldn't rest at ease until the sweets were given to the girls. Late hours didn't bother her. She said, "Why, it is still evening and they are asleep? You don't follow any rules, I see." Kshama di started laughing and said, "Didi, it is not evening, it is past twelve o'clock. The girls never sleep in the evening." It had no effect on Dadabhai and she insisted, "Whatever it may be, call the girls at once." So we had to get up and stand before Dadabhai. She called each of us by name and gave the sweets as Ma intended. When she called me by name and gave me the sweet, I was surprised that Ma remembered me by name. As I thought about it, I was gratified beyond measure. Dadabhai, inspired by Ma, built up the Kanyapeeth in stages out of the money donated by people. It was no wonder that she was attached to the girls. Noticing Ma's special favour for us, people said, "Well, it is Didi's Kanyapeeth, that's why Ma is favourably disposed to it."

In our small garden a white pumpkin plant grew on its own from a seed dropped by chance. Wonder of wonders, it bore a small fruit. Due to the ravages of monkeys at Varanasi, anything growing on a tree had no chance of surviving. At that time Ma was at Varanasi ashram. The pumpkin was plucked and shown to Her. Ma and Dadabhai were highly pleased to see it. Ma said, "Bring a cutter at once, I shall teach the girls how to cut a pumpkin for a special fry. On the ground floor verandah of Kanyapeeth building a wooden seat was placed for Ma. Taking the cutter and the pumpkin Ma sat decently on the seat, while we girls stood all around Her to observe. Ma peeled the pumpkin very nicely and cut it into four equal pieces. Then taking one piece, kept one side intact and cut the opposite side into thin slices. She directed us to cut the other three pieces to see how much we had learnt. Then She asked Dadabhai to mix ground mustard, coconut, green chilli and salt, stuff the mixture into the openings, dipped those stuffed pumpkin slices into the paste of rice flour and fried them nicely. That day a small white pumpkin starred in a festive atmosphere for all of us. This was the way of Ma, whatever She did was complete in itself, perfect and rejoicing.

Shree Shree Ma Cutting Vegetables in Kanyapeeth

In this context I remember that the food which was prepared daily by Dadabhai for Ma carried the imprint of her matchless skill. When Ma stayed at Varanasi, Dadabhai cooked for Her and made it a rule that each day she would be assisted in the kitchen by a particular girl of Kanyapeeth. Thus, she would teach us how to cook. A special feature of Dadabhai's cooking was that she avoided too much frying or using much spices, not even turmeric. The main spice she always used was ginger grinded fine as sandal paste and green chilli. I noticed that she cooked each item by covering it with a lid. She said that this made the vegetable well cooked and palatable with its food value intact. Pulses cooked by her were excellent to taste. Pulses were first soaked in water and then washed well after being rubbed thoroughly. If after washing, the pulses floated in the water, it meant that the washing was perfect. She put it in the oven with a small amount of water and added hot water little by little as required. Ma used to eat such thick cooked pulses.

The food for Ma was cooked on charcoal. Charcoal gets burnt up soon. If we were present, we put charcoal into the oven from time to time, but mostly Dadabhai did it herself. This blackened her hands. Before she fed Ma she washed her hands with flour. But this did not remove the black stains fully. While eating, glancing at Dadabhai's hands, She said, "Feed, feed this body with coal." Dadabhai said helplessly, "What can I do Ma? I wash but the stains sticks on." She did not use soap, lest Ma should be bothered by an offensive smell.

Once I had fever. Jyoti di and I were at the sick room. That was the first time, that three cots were placed in the sick room. At night while sleeping, I fell down from the cot. In the morning Ma while visiting us said, "Well friends, how are you?" Bhanu di was incharge of the patients. She said, "Vishuddha fell down from the bed last night." Then Ma said, "Call Kamal at once." When Kamal da came, She said, "Cut off the legs of the bedstead by six inches. Little girls sleep on them. They may fall down if the beds are so high." Many laughed hearing that I had a fall. After Ma's order they said, "Ah, here is Ma's pet. For such a big girl to fall down is a disgrace. But Ma had the legs of the bedstead cut off, that was too much."

6

When I came to Kanyapeeth the new girls were made to observe all the strict shuddhachary rules for one year (these days for three years as instructed by Ma) before they were accepted as shuddhacharis. Besides, they were to bathe in the Ganga and take 'Panch Gavya'. Then they were to do repetition of God's name, whichever they liked.

Later, they were initiated by revered Didi ma. After Diksha again ten thousand japas were to be done. Then one was allowed to cook Ma's bhog and feed Her with their own hands. Only after this procedure they were called shuddhachary. We could do Ma's special puja, cook bhog, etc. This was a special privilege.

After one year of my stay at the ashram, I was supposed to take 'Diksha' from Didima on the auspicious day of Gurupurnima. However I desired to take 'Diksha' from Dadabhai. Ganga di, then incharge of Kanyapeeth, on hearing this scolded me and said, "This is just an excuse for not taking 'Diksha' as after that, one would have to work much more like cooking, serving, etc. Everyone is taking Diksha from Didima, so why are you not taking it from her." I replied that I am very fond of Didima and she is also very affectionate towards me but as far as Diksha is concerned I would take it from Dadabhai.

Ma and Dadabhai were at some place in Punjab at that time. I do not know if any message had been sent to Ma. All of a sudden Dadabhai came to Varanasi. Next day in the morning she took me to Ma's room and gave me the mantra. She said, "Ma has sent me for this and whatever Ma has said I have given to you. You should learn the process of doing japa from Didima."

My Diksha (initiation) took place without the requisites like asana, utensils, flowers, garlands or fruits, etc. This incident occurred before Gurupurnima. Nobody came to know about it. Kshama di and Renu di were discussing that who is Vishuddha's Guru would be known on the Gurupurnima day, as she would do the Guru Puja surely. Whatever I did, I did unnoticed. Never did I worship Dadabhai outwardly. If Dadabhai ever stayed at Varanasi on Gurupurnima day and I went to do pranam to her, she always said, "Whatever you do, offer to Ma as She is the real Guru." When I went to Didima to enquire about the process of prayer (Sandhya), Didima gave me two more mantras.

A few days later, early in the morning at about 4 a.m. when I was in deep sleep, I dreamt a huge form of Ma, beautiful face radiant against the light of dawn, on the Kanyapeeth terrace, with the Ganga flowing in the background. Shree Shree Ma bent down towards me and placing Her hand over my head uttered a mantra and said, "Do this mantra daily." I heard it so clearly as if Ma was there in person. At that time Ma was not in Varanasi. Didima was present there. So I asked her about the mantra. She said, "Hush, hush, don't utter it, that is a sanyas mantra." A few days later Ma arrived and I mentioned it to Her. She said, "Yes, do this mantra first and then do the rest." After this incident Ma gave me an Alkhalla in front of Dadabhai.

A few days after the final offering of Savitri Mahayajna, Ma went to Etawah. She took with her 4–5 girls of Kanyapeeth.

Didima (Ma's Mother) in front of Kanyapeeth.
To her left is my sister Shraddha

Our luggage consisted of just a bag and a bedding for each. How happy we were travelling by train with Ma! Buni di was also with us. Dadabhai and Buni di decided where we should sit in the train and what we should eat. Buni di was quite efficient in everything. I very much liked the way she went about her business. Reaching Etawah we found that a large crowd had assembled to escort Ma singing kirtan along the way. We followed Ma in another motor car to reach Lakshmi Narayan temple. Ma was ceremoniously welcomed in the temple by giving an asana, putting sandal paste on her forehead and garlanding. Adjacent to the temple, there was a spacious hall and above the hall was a dharmashala where a large room was arranged for Ma which was done up immaculately. A white bedsheet was spread on the bed for Ma and an exclusive carpet was laid on the floor. The large windows around were covered with screens. Though there were several other rooms, Ma said, "Didi, the girls shall stay here in this one." On Ma's instruction we kept our bags and bedding neatly in a corner and came back after our bath. I found that in the store room adjacent to Ma's room, plenty of milk, fruits, homemade sweets, vegetables, rice, pulses, etc. were arranged in order. Dadabhai fed Ma some fruits and sweets and we also had food. There all the sweets were prepared in the temple cleanly for Ma, so we were told that we might have them freely.

Ma rested for a while before going down to the temple hall. That very evening was the eve of the holy Nam Yajna. The next day there would be chanting of Mahanam from sunrise to sunset. A large number of devotees arrived from Delhi and many other places. Dhiren da, Biren da and others were decorating the mancha (A decorated small centerpiece with pictures of God and Nitai Gaur, etc.). Dadabhai went to the Kitchen to cook for Ma. We girls joined to assist her. At noon Ma went for Her meal to a small room adjoining the kitchen. Dadabhai was feeding Ma and I was fanning Her. Ma sat with Her right leg placed over Her left. Her hair was coiled up over Her head and while eating She swayed a little. Dadabhai mixed rice, pulses and vegetables into a sticky consistency and fed Ma in relatively large portions. This was because there was nothing certain about Ma. All of a sudden She might declare "Enough" and would refuse to take any more. So She had to be fed quickly. Dadabhai had a mother and child relationship with Ma while feeding Her. She wanted to feed Her as a mother feeds her child.

The devotees of Etawah used to take Ma and us to many places every day in a car. The destinations were different on different days like some temple under a tree or at the bank of a river. Mats and carpets etc. were taken along. Wherever we went, carpets etc. were spread out and arrangements were made for a religious discourse or chanting of kirtans.

One day as usual the carpet was spread on the large stairs of a landing place on the bank of the Ganga. All were seated. It was close to evening. The place was infested with mosquitoes. Ma pointed towards me and said, "When this body had come here with her grandmother Virajmohini on an indefinite tour (Agyatvas), this building was under construction (She pointed out at a building in front of the landing place). The landing place was not cemented. This body and Virajmohini oblivious of everything were seated on this landing place. We were sitting there for a long time. It was about evening time. As this body showed no signs of getting up, Virajmohini felt that I meant to stay there, but where was I to sleep? A contractor was sitting on a bamboo cot, overseeing the works of the labourers. Virajmohini went to him and pleadingly said, "Baba, if it is not too inconvenient to you, can Ma lie on this cot?" He said, "Mataji, why should you lie here? You can come to my house, rest, eat and drink." Virajmohini said, "No, no, Baba, Mataji does not stay in a householder's place. We can lie here well enough." So the contractor made the cot clean and went away. The cot was sagging at the middle through day-long use.

The place was mosquito infested. Virajmohini was at a loss about how to let Ma lie amidst a swarm of mosquitoes. After some thought she knotted together the clothes that she and this body were to put on the next day and somehow improvised a makeshift mosquito net. Then she invited this body to lie down. This body said to her, "Mother, you too should lie on this cot." Virajmohini folded her hands and implored, "Forgive me. I shall by no means lie with you on such a small cot. After the day's toil I am so tired that I shall fall asleep wherever I lie down. Mosquitoes are no problem to me. If I lie with you, firstly my feet would touch yours, secondly, I shall not be able to sleep through worries. Kindly don't ask me to lie beside you." The more she objected, the more this body insisted, "You must lie beside me."

At last this body started weeping like a child. Virajmohini was helpless. She laid down on the cot beside this body. She was stoutly built and this body was not thin either. However, Virajmohini fell asleep as soon as she lay down. At midnight, she suddenly woke up wondering where she was lying that night. As soon as she recalled that she was lying beside this body on the same cot, she tried to feel with her hand where this body was? Good gracious! She was lying alone! She was overcome with anxiety and astonishment wondering where this body had gone at that hour of the night in the darkness. She did not have the courage to climb down from the cot and look for this body. She thought if Ma was lying below, she might step on Her while getting down. She recalled that Ma never went anywhere without letting her know. Not knowing where to look for this body in the dark, she lay down in the dark repeating the name of God. Towards the dawn when the sky had cleared up a little she saw this body lying by her side. She was very surprised indeed. At last when she got up she asked, "Well Ma, where were you last night? I could not find you. Ma, where were you really?" This body smiled and said, "I leave it to you to guess." The fact is that God can assume all forms on the prayer of a devotee. Virajmohini was afraid that Ma would feel discomforted if she lay on that small cot. In order to let her sleep at ease, lying on that same cot, Ma made Her body ethereal (subtle).

At Etawah we shared a room with Ma. She said, "You should carry out your daily routine of worship, reading scriptures and singing kirtans, etc. in due time." She pointed out where each should lie near Her bed. At 10 p.m. we spread our beds and after singing our night prayer–"*Ma is here and so are we...*", we laid down. Ma also seemed to be transformed into a girl of Kanyapeeth and said to Dadabhai, "As the girls are in this room, so no outsider should be allowed herein." When Ma took Her seat in the hall next to our room, the visitors might come. Getting up at 4 a.m. we recited in chorus–

"Asato Ma Sad Gamaya
Tamoso Ma Jyotir Gamaya
Mrityor Ma Amritam Gamaya
Aviravir Mayedhi."

(May my journey be along the path of honesty
avoiding dishonest one;
May the supreme kindness
lead me towards, the light Divine.
Oh! Thou Omniscient divine
lift me up towards the glorious heavenly rejoice
releasing me from the inevitable end in death
Oh! Thou omnipresent infinite
Let this humble self be absorbed in thee.)

With this incantation, we made obeisance to Ma and left our bed. I found that Ma was also seated on Her bed. Through the large windows of the room the early glow of the dawn made Ma's face radiant–it was a splendid sight. Sitting there we completed morning kirtan and got up. It was our daily practice to maintain silence till quarter past seven in the morning. So moving up the beds silently we arranged them in array in their proper places and went to bathe. Next we went through our daily worship, Japa and aarti, etc., had breakfast of milk, fruits and sweets given by Dadabhai and finally went with her to attend to the preliminaries of cooking for Ma.

On that day in the temple hall below, a continuous chanting of Mahanam started from early morning. Last evening after ceremony, lamp was lit to burn continuously. In the morning Ma came down and took Her seat. We were looking on from the floor above. I remember Biren da's way of performing kirtan. Sometimes he was immersed in a rapturous recital of

Kirtan and if there was a slight lapse in sounding of the cymbal, he ran to the culprit and landed a few blows on his back. He was a strange person in kirtans. He addressed Ma as 'Karta' meaning the boss. At noon after Mahaprabhu's food offering prepared in big earthen pots was over, Ma was also fed. Many people had the sacred prasad. In the afternoon again, Ma accompanied by us, went down. After going around the city singing kirtan, Moni da, Biren da and others completed recital of the name and asked Ma to sing. With great bhava Ma started singing–*Nitai dake aay aay, Gour dake aay aay...* (Nitai beckons come all, Gour beckons come all). We too joined Her in singing. All were immersed in a divine ecstasy beyond description. After a sweet, melodious and continuous kirtan by Ma the Nam Yajna came to an end marked by 'Hari loot' of Batasa (puffed sugar) in the name of Hari (God). Thus after enjoying Ma's company for a few days, we returned to Varanasi.

During Savitri Mahayajna, Mrs. Kamla Mohanlal, the committed devotee of Ma, arrived at Varanasi and stayed at Kanyapeeth for quite some time. She was expert in knitting. Ma asked her to adopt us as her pupils. We attended her knitting classes regularly. Now and then Ma came to see how we were doing. After a few days we were knitting in the hall when Ma came and touching my knitting asked, "What are you knitting?" I answered, "A four-needle stocking." Ma said, "Is it? Let me see." Saying this She took the stuff from my hand and started putting Her foot in it. I had completed only up to the ribbing and as the wool was insufficient I made it small. Good gracious! Ma put Her foot into the small thing with four needles on, and sitting on the swing began to show it to everyone by moving it around and said, "Well done, it is really nice." Ma's foot was small and well-shaped and with the maroon coloured stocking on, it looked fairly well. Seeing what Ma had done, I felt delighted no doubt, but was praying in heart that Ma should take it off quickly. If Dadabhai came and found Her stuck in stocking with so many needles, she might rebuke that I let Her wear it with the needles on which could prick Her. However, before Dadabhai came in, Ma Herself took it off carefully.

According to our regulation, we had a fixed schedule from morning to night. Within it whenever we were free we knitted even while chatting, so that no time was wasted. Ma was very pleased to see us so eager to learn. Then by the kheyal of Ma, handicraft institute (Shilpa Pratisthan) was set up at Kanyapeeth. Here besides knitting, sewing was taught. Renu di, Bithu di, Tara di, Buba di, Sati di and Kshama di also knitted a lot. These knitwears and sewing were sold. People (men) in general were not permitted to enter Kanyapeeth. So Ma instructed to build a few showcases on the lower verandah of Kanyapeeth to display the handiworks of Kanyapeeth girls. Ma was so pleased to see our handicrafts as a worldly mother would be to see her child's work. Kshama di looked after the handicraft institute. The eastern portion of the lower verandah of Kanyapeeth was partitioned into house, office and store of the handicraft institute.

In this connection I remember an incident. It occured when a flower bloomed in our little garden. Even if it was a grass flower, it was my inclination to pluck it and give it to Ma if She happened to be in the ashram of course, without anybody's notice. Following this, Ma and I both exchanged a smile. It was not always that I made an obeisance after handing over the flower.

Once in the month of April/May (Vaishakh) it was very hot in Varanasi. The festivities of birth anniversary of Ma were going on. Ma had gone to Punjab at the cordial invitation of the Mahatmas like Khanna Baba, Hari Baba and Avadhut ji, etc. It was either Jalandhar or Hoshiarpur where Ma's birthday festival was being celebrated with pomp and splendor. I was as usual wandering around in the morning looking for some flowers in the garden at Varanasi ashram. I found a small flower blooming in the new Gandharaj plant which was only a few months old. That was its first bloom. I plucked it at once and thought of the ways to send it to Ma. In the morning we remained silent (maun). I didn't know the whereabouts of Ma, nor could I ask anybody about it. Suddenly, it struck me that Kshama di would know Her address and I could get an envelope too from her. I made signs to her to tell that I wanted to send the flower to Ma. Kshama di supplied me with the paper, envelop, etc. I wrote to Dadabhai, "This flower has bloomed in our garden for the first time, so please give it to Ma."

A few days later I received a lovely letter from Dadabhai. She wrote, "Ma is very pleased to get the flower sent by you. Being Ghandharaj, it gave out a sweet smell as soon as the envelope was opened, though it had dried up in the intense heat. Ma smells the flower a number of times and has put it by the side of her pillow. She has showed it to saintly Mahatmas like Hari baba, Avadhut ji and others and said, "Look fathers, this has been sent by a small friend of this body." Dadabhai also wrote, "I am happy to see your devotion to Ma. I pray to Ma's feet that you should always remember Her the same way."

Regulation of the Kanyapeeth required that all letters sent and received are first read by the elders. At that time Billo ji was incharge so all the letters reached her first. When she came to know that I had sent a letter to Dadabhai without informing her, she scolded me severely. But I was least affected by her rebukes for two reasons. One, I did not break the law as Kshama di sent the letter to Ma. Secondly, Ma was pleased to accept my flower. Later on I explained to Billo ji the reason for which I could not show the letter to her. That was my Ma's acceptance of the gift of a tiny flower from a small friend. I was so happy, full to the brim of my heart.

In Kanyapeeth puja room bhog is given to Ma five times from the early morning aarti, i.e. Mangala to Shayan at night and the proof that Ma partakes of the bhog has been confirmed by Ma Herself. At the time I came to Kanyapeeth the economic condition of the institution was not very good. For Mangal aarti and morning Puja only 'batasha' (puffed sugar) was offered to Ma. One day, when she was in Varanasi, She asked Dadabhai, "Khukuni, bring some kishmish (raisins) from the worship room of the Kanyapeeth." Dadabhai was wondering from where would the girls get raisins, but since Ma was saying, it must be so. My duty was in the worship room those days. When Dadabhai asked me to bring raisins I brought them. After giving Ma the same Dadabhai asked Ma, "The girls offer only batasha, how did you know there were raisins today?" Ma laughed and said, "Didi, the girls offered me raisins in their worship and I accepted them."

One day in the morning aarti the girls forgot to offer Her bhog. Ma was away from Varanasi. Over there Ma Herself asked for 'Nakuldana' and ate it and said, "Today the girls have forgotten to give bhog to this body."

Sometimes Ma was in Varanasi. One day she was moving around and examining everything. The girls were eating in the dining hall. Ma entered the store. On one side a heap of spinach was kept. Ma looked at it and said to Bani di, who was the storekeeper, "Clean and wash the 'Saag' (spinach) well. This body also eats."

After the construction of the Varanasi ashram, Ma arrived. She was climbing down the stairs with Renu di, She noticed some grains of rice near the drain. Probably someone washed rice there and left those. When Ma saw the waste, She said, "See how they waste 'Bhiksha Anna' (the grains bought by the money donated by others). Collect them, wash them and put these grains inside my mouth." Saying this She opened Her mouth wide.

Shree Ma gave us a number of lessons like these. Oh! Only if we could learn them!

7

After the Savitri Mahayajna a enclosure was built over the Yajna kunda with a thatched roof. Inside, Yajna fire was constantly burning and offerings were made. One day Ma asked us to clean the surroundings of that enclosure in Her presence. Barley and sesame were scattered during the Yajna, so plants and weeds had sprung up. Even after the general cleaning, Ma insisted on to digging and looking up the soil and look beneath. I was continuously digging on at the southwestern corner and wondered why Ma wanted to dig even though the work of cleaning was over. After digging little deeper I discovered a sapling overlaid with earth. As soon as I saw it I shouted, "Ma look, it is out." Ma seeing it smiled, caught my words and said, "It is out, out. Did I not tell you to dig? The plant was covered and this body was out of breath." I was wrong to say 'It is out' so corrected–'It has come up', Ma also repeated this in fun. In this way She taught us in many subtle ways. Later, that plant grew up well. It yielded big rounded fruits (Ber). When Ma was in Varanasi we fed Her those tasty fruits with salt and chilli. We also enjoyed a good measure of it. Afterwards the tree was cut off for fear of monkeys as they might bite the girls of Kanyapeeth for fruits.

Since the ashram was set up at Varanasi, most revered Gopal Thakur with his family, disciples and devotees used to come every year during Geeta Jayanti, at Ma's request and performed a week-long festival with great pomp. The festival was arranged in the big hall on the bank of the holy Ganga. Firstly, the Shrimad Bhagwat Geeta was placed on a low table decorated with flowers and garlands. After it was worshipped, six chapters of Geeta were read every day jointly, led by Shri Gopal Thakur and followed by Brahmacharis, Brahmacharinis and devotees. At the end of each chapter and at the beginning of the next chapter there was an interlude singing, "*Govinda Govinda Govinda Jai*". Vani di and Kalyani di, both daughters of Gopal Thakur sang occasional songs as directed by their father. Three hours from 8 a.m. to 11 a.m. passed easily. Gopal Thakur and his followers started this programme after breakfast, so reading, singing and chanting were delayed. Shree Shree Ma also remained present for the whole duration.

Gopal Thakur took handful of flowers and showered them over Geeta and Shree Shree Ma. We were charmed by the divine looks of Gopal Thakur and his fine and Joyous ways. All the time Ma's face was beaming with joy, as if drops of nectar (amrit) were constantly trickling down.

After the recital and chanting was over, lunch for Ma and Gopal Thakur was arranged in the hall of the Kanyapeeth. Dadabhai cooked many of her preparations specially for them. Apart from all, the items cooked at Kanyapeeth and Annapurna temple's kitchen were also served to them. While having lunch Ma and Gopal Thakur, both of them being from East Bengal, enjoyed their affinity and anecdotes. We were also present there and enjoyed the conversation.

One day Ma recalled Her experience as a bride. She had gone to see Her elder brother-in-law. His wife prepared mango shake and served it to Ma. In East Bengal, owing to excessive rain, ripe mangoes sometimes contain worms. Ma, who was veiled, noticed that while mixing the milk with mangoes, one worm dropped in. Ma was observing without even mentioning anything to her sister-in-law who was preoccupied with joy. The elder sister-in-law was supposed to be like a mother, so She could not utter a word. Also, this is a fact that God accepts whatever the devotees offer lovingly. Hearing this story, Gopal Thakur smiled and said, "This universe with living beings is constantly entering into the mouth of Ma Kali. For Ma everything is all the same."

In the afternoon, Gopal Thakur gave a lucid interpretation of the Geeta. While in the three days eighteen chapters of Geeta were read at the rate of six chapters per day, on the fourth day the entire Geeta was read. On the fifth day all the copies of Geeta were reverently placed on the low table and were decorated with flowers and garlands. Then eighteen brass plates filled with eighteen varieties of dry fruits, fresh fruits, bowls of kheer, decorated with flower garlands were offered to Geeta. Since Gopal Thakur liked flowers and garlands very much, Ma used to arrange plenty of flowers. The hall was beautifully decorated with leaves, flowers and garlands. The worship performed by Gopal Thakur was also unique. With recital and incantations, he put two handful of flowers on the Geeta and then on Ma, who was the Geeta personified and at times on his own head. In a trance like state he danced and sang like 'Bal Gopal' (infant Krishna). In between his daughters Vanidi and Kalyanidi sang appropriate songs.

All were lost in joy, not conscious of their individual existence. Ma, the supreme emotion incarnate and expression of supreme delight also seemed to be identified with this worship. I have no words to express the perfect beauty that I experienced in Ma at that time. It is known only to those who witnessed that sight. The obeisance that followed the worship was equally striking. Gopal Thakur lay prostrated on the ground and Ma rolled on the ground in a trance. The devotees present raised their voice in '*Jai to Ma, Jai to Govinda*'. After the obeisance, arrangements for Geeta Yajna followed. While in the background the Ganga, Goddess from heaven flowed past, in the forefront Ma Anandamayee, the Mother of the universe was on Her seat. Pronouncing each shloka of the Geeta, Gopal Thakur and the devotees present made offerings to the Yajna Kunda. It was about afternoon when the Yajna was over. After the final offering, the prasad was distributed and then everyone had their meal.

Next day, implored by Gopal Thakur, Ma sang as if a little girl couldn't disobey her father. Dadabhai sat by Her and prompted on lyrics of the songs when required. Bibhu da played on the harmonium and Ma in Her sweet voice sang many songs one after another–

Mother have pity on me and let me be as child...

The mother does not respond...

Who knocks at the door of my heart, whose sweet voice I hear...

So Ma went on singing too many songs for me to remember. It is a pity that there was no tape recorder then for recording Ma's songs. After that there was to be a session of Ma's songs regularly. Once when Ma was singing, in the lane in front of the ashram, an ass brayed at which Ma was convulsed with laughter. She laughed so hilariously that tears ran down Her eyes. While laughing She said, "All sounds are the same, so the ass also joined by braying."

This joke reminds me of something else. On the terrace of the Varanasi ashram, after the evening kirtan the bell for silence struck at quarter to nine. Every one fell silent. Ma was also there. The lights were switched off. The tap in the yard of Kanyapeeth was not in order and the water ran down continuously. There was a pin drop silence in the ashram and the sound of the dripping water was clearly audible. It was heard by Ma also, and even in the midst of silence Ma was laughing silently. After fifteen minutes, when the bell sounded the end of silence, all made their obeisance to Ma and went to their respective places.

Dadabhai brought Ma to Her room. She saw that Ma was laughing without making a sound. She asked Her, "Ma, what is the matter?" Ma did not reply. She only went on laughing. During the spell of silence She was laughing silently, but once She reached Her room, Her laughter was quite loud. Dadabhai asked Her several times, but caught in a fit of laughter, Ma could not utter a word. The laughing mode continued up to two or half past two a.m. That night Ma could not have Her dinner. When Her laughter abated a little at the dead of night, Ma said to Dadabhai, "You see Didi, as the water was flowing down the tap in your yard, this body heard it in silence and fancied that when the Kulakundalini becomes active and the knots are loosened, everything goes beyond control, like the gushing of a fountain. There is no stopping them by any means. That was the play going on in this body for so long. Then there was no room for any question or response. You see, even repeated questions evoked no reply."

Dadabhai made obeisance to Ma and said, "Blessed are you, Ma. It is a wonder that we are with you."

With the Yajnakunda in its place, by Ma's kheyal, a nice garden was made around it. The entire place was fenced with a network of wire to keep the monkeys out. As the space was rather inadequate, wooden steps were made to keep the flower pots. Beautiful flower plants such as rose, dahlia and chrysanthemum were planted. An expert gardener was employed to look after them. That year before Geeta Jayanti celebrations, the yard became beautiful due to the multi-coloured flowers in full bloom. Seeing this Ma and Gopal Thakur were very delighted. In the morning of Geeta Jayanti worship, Ma asked me to get a pair of scissors and a large basket. She entered the garden and taking hold of each flower told me, "Cut". I cut the same and put it in the basket. Almost all big sized flowers were plucked. At last She laid Her hand on a small yellow chrysanthemum and said, "Go for worship of God." This was a signal for cutting and I did that. The sight still flashes across my mind–the clear blue sky above, the wonderful collection of multi-coloured flowers below and the unprecedented divine glamour of Ma's presence. I remember that a snap of this sight was captured in the camera by a devotee. Next, Ma arranged the flowers in a number of baskets, handed them over to Gopal Thakur at the time of Geeta worship and said, "Baba, these flowers are from your garden." The delight that Gopal Thakur expressed at the sight of the flowers is beyond description.

During Durga puja Ma went to Ranchi. Dr. Gopal Dasgupta of Varanasi went there with his family. I sent through them a paper garland of Shefali, Aparajita and Jaba. I directed Radhu, the daughter of Dr. Dasgupta to hand over the box of garlands to Buni di and tell her to offer the garland to Ma on the auspicious Mahashtami day.

The Durga puja was performed with great pomp and show in the presence of Ma. Many devotees came from Kolkata and other places. The store room was packed with various articles for worship, fruits and sweets, etc. Buni di was in charge of the store room. The Mahashtami puja was over by then. Ma entered the store room. The articles for worship were kept on and under a large cot. Ma wanted to arrange the articles properly. She asked to take out all things from under the cot. Even after everything was taken out Ma said, "Look for what else is left there." Bahadur, the Nepali boy went under the cot and repeatedly said, "There is nothing else." Still Ma insisted. At last Bahadur said, "A paper box is stuck to the wall behind." When it was taken out and opened, there was a garland made of paper flowers found in it. Then Buni di remarked, "Oh Ma, I forgot about it completely. This was sent by Vishuddha for Ma, to be offered to Her on Mahashtami." Saying this she took the garland and tried to put it around Ma's neck. Ma stopped her and said, "No, you will have to wait, you can do so at mid night when this body would go to the mandap during Sandhi puja. This body had the kheyal of this garland."

I heard later from Buni di that, she could not tell Ma about the garland before, as she was preoccupied with many duties and had completely forgotten about it. At midnight during Sandhi puja Ma was dressed in a white silk saree and when She was entering the mandap, Buni di garlanded Her with that most ordinary paper garland sent by me. After sandhi puja Ma came to Her room and hung that garland on the stand. The next morning She showed the garland to whoever came to Her room and said, "Look at the garland of flowers from Didi's garden at Kashi." Hearing this Shri Anil Ganguly, bar-at-law, Rahul Chatterjee and others wondered what was so special about the garland to deserve Ma's attention. To them it was just an ordinary garland. Afterwards, they too praised it when they learnt that it was a paper garland. When Dadabhai heard about it, she said, "Yes Ma, the Varanasi ashram has little space to spare, so the garland is so small." Ma and all the others present there broke into a loud laughter on this comment. Dadabhai had no time to spare to think as to how that fresh flower garland from Varanasi came to Ranchi without being dried up. Ma thus had fun over that garland.

After Durgapuja and Lakshmi puja in Ranchi, Ma came to Varanasi on the occasion of Kalipuja and Annakut. I made a three-fold garland out of Shefali flowers of our garden and put it around Ma's neck. Ma smiled sweetly and said, "Where will you find jewels and precious stones? A flower garland from you is beautiful instead." She also said, "Do you know that your garland of paper deceived Didi, the barrister and many others?" Then I heard the whole story from Buni di.

8

Respectable Gangadevi Panchatirtha, the disciple of Vaishnavacharya Vrajavidehi Santadas Babaji, came to take charge of Kanyapeeth. At her humble request, Ma used to come to Varanasi during the Jhulan (swing festival of Lord Krishna) and Janmashtami (birthday ceremony of Lord Krishna). It made us very happy to have Ma in our midst over five or six days, beginning from Jhulan Ekadashi to Rakhi Purnima. We decorated the large swing at our hall in a new mode every day and made Ma swing on it.

At 9 p.m. every night, after the evening kirtan and maun, Ganga di brought Ma and let Her sit on the swing. This large swing was perhaps the gift of Shri Kantibhai Munshaw, an ardent devotee from Gujarat. With Ma on the swing, Ganga di performed aarti, after offering garlands and sandal paste. As men were not allowed in the Kanyapeeth, only local ladies and we the girls of Kanyapeeth were present at this exclusive divine Leela (drama/enactment). After aarti we staged different devotional dramas. Renu di, Bithu di, Pushpa di and others trained us to act. According to Ma's instructions we had to follow certain rules, such as, whatever roles we enacted, men or women, king or beggar, there was no change in our clothes.

Our acting was emotion-oriented, i.e., we had to make the character come alive mainly through emotions and dialogues. Only little girls were made to wear colourful sarees received by them during Kumari Puja and appeared as deities or doing special aarti by a dance performance.

This reminds me of few memories. The Varanasi Ashram was just founded. Ma stayed there most of the time then. She sat on the spacious terrace facing the Ganga in the midst of devotees. Songs, recitals and religious discussions were going on. Now and then Abhay da, Bibhu da and others enacted the mystic ways of the divine devotees in the presence of Ma. Once Kamal da, Kantibhai and Bibhu da were dressed as hermits in ochre dyed clothes and performed some devotional plays. At the end of it Ma said, "There should be no playing with ochre." Once one has worn ochre clothes even while acting, he cannot discard it lightly. One must at least have his wrappers ochre-dyed. Later, they completely dressed themselves in ochre and became committed brahmacharis and monks. Then their respective names were Swami Virajananda, Swami Bhagavatananda and Brahmachari Brahmananda.

Once during Jhulan at Kanyapeeth a drama depicting some miracles from Christ's life were staged. As far as I remember, Billo ji played the role of Jesus Christ. Even Jesus being crucified was played out. The girls were acting and Ma saw it lying or sitting on the swing. After the drama was over and all lights were switched on, it was found that Ma was in a trance. Dadabhai and Ganga di had to raise Her. Blood was found on Ma's tongue. As there was no blood on Her teeth, the question was where did the blood come from? It was later realised that Ma had the 'bhav' of Christ on the cross. Many scenes from the lives of La Milarepa, Shankaracharya, Ramanujacharya, Mahaprabhu and other characters from Upanishads and Bhaktamal were staged. When the role of Nachiketa was being staged, Ma said, "The episodes from Upanishad may be viewed by all." On that day, male spectators had also attended. The verandah of our hall was simply overcrowded. I played the role of Nachiketa. In the course of acting for two-three hours I had a unique experience under the influence of profound philosophical discussions between Yama and Nachiketa.

Besides serious philosophical scenes, light subjects were also staged. I had learnt one comic act while in school and staged it before Ma. She and others who were present laughed and enjoyed to see it. Ma said to Dadabhai, "Didi, she revealed everything–both exterior and interior." Dadabhai was delighted and told me later, "Do you know what She has said? She has seen both your outer and inner selves."

During interval when the screen was dropped, Ma came out in the darkness from behind and hidden by the screen said in whispers to call out a few with a physique like Her. When they came She made them sit on the dias in meditation and covered them with a wrapper. Then She directed for the screen to be raised. Ma stood in our green room and looked at the fun. In the meantime when Ma was not found on the swing, it was assumed that one of the sitting figures was none other than Ma. Then at the signal from Ma, the spectators were asked, "Please tell us, which of these is Ma?" All pointed their fingers at one figure but when the cover was removed they were found to have guessed wrong. Everyone had a big laugh. Ma was standing in the green room and laughing silently and we too followed Her. Again sometimes Ma sat at full stretch in a meditational pose with Her body fully covered. When all were puzzled vainly trying to identify Ma, She came out from Her cover bursting into laughter. This was an amusing play of Ma.

One day Ma had a 'kheyal' of staging a play in which all of us, both young and grownups should take part. It consisted of an assumption that Ma was on a pilgrimage with Bithu di as Her companion. She would see different modes of worship by devotees at different places and made some gifts to the group of worshippers. Ma said to Bithu di, "You will address this body as maidservant." Bithu di was shocked and said, "No, no, I shall not be able to address you like that, forgive me." Thus Ma said, "Then call me 'Tirthavasini' as my grandmother had named this body." So it was settled that Bithu di would call Ma 'Tirthavasini Mai'. Jhulan festival was on. At night the celebration was over for the day. Ma seated on the swing, instructed all the girls of the Kanyapeeth, both young and grown-ups along with Dadabhai, Ganga di, Maunima, Renu di, Sati di, Pushpa di, Buba di and the rest, each what she should do. I was standing by Her side touching Her swing. She then asked me to go down on my knees in front of the swing. Ma folded Her hands, with eyes half closed and head inclined upwards in an emotionally surcharged expression showed how to pray and repeat the name of Rama in an undertone. Her pose and expression defy description.

Next day at noon Ma came with Bithu di to our hall and made room by placing a stool and a desk. As I tried to peep, Ma closed the doors and windows and laughing naughtily said, "You do not let this body see when you decorate the hall, so you also will not be allowed to have a look beforehand." At night after the spell of maun at 9 p.m. Ma stayed at the small balcony behind the hall. As directed by Ma, Bithu di made all of us sit at our respective places. As taught by Ma on the previous night we were absorbed in our own modes of worship, meditation, japa, recital, reading of text and prayers. Then Ma entered the hall followed by Bithu di. Ma was attired in a white, long loose-fitting garment (Alkhalla) with a white long bag suspended from Her shoulder. Her expression was of such a state that cannot be written in words.

She stood before each group and asked the name and their mode of worship. Bithu di informed Her briefly. Tirthavasini Mai took out gifts from Her bag in accordance with the worship of each sect. As for example She gave Dadabhai–the chief of Shiva sect, a Damaru, a Rosary to Ganga di–the chief of Vaishnava sect, a Mandira to chief of Shakta sect, an Upanishad to Maunima–the chief of Adwaita sect and a Ramtal to me acting as Mahavir Hanuman–a staunch devotee of Rama. Thus we, the dramatists of this drama became spectators and were charmed and gratified at the sight of the unique form of Ma, charged with great bhava.

Maunima (Swami Krishnananda ji) used to have darshan (vision) of Lord Krishna and used to talk to Him daily. Though unlearned, Maunima had written a book of poems (named Kanikamala) on Lord Krishna. Sometimes on Ma's request she used to dance the way Lord Krishna taught her. Surprisingly, she had never learnt how to dance. Still the dance steps were amazing. Dance beats according to the different mudras (postures) were shown by her.

On Jhulan Purnima, Gangadi used to dress Ma beautifully and make Her sit on a Jhula (swing). Once Ma was dressing up and we were watching Her. Maunima was sitting close to Ma and commented, "No matter how nicely You dress up now, we have never seen how we had seen You in Dhaka, in an ordinary householder's dress without any make-up." Hearing Maunima's opinion suddenly Ma covered Her head with saree and taking Her face close to Maunima, She said, "See, if you can see the bahu (bride) of those days." By the glimpse of Ma's young face Maunima was dumb struck. I also saw that scene and was astonished.

One day Ma was sitting on the swing and watching us enacting a leela. Suddenly She had the kheyal to enact a certain leela. Immediately She called Bithudi and asked her to stage that leela with the girls. The story goes like this–Krishna and Balaram, both the brothers come to Yashoda to eat butter. Krishna is younger, so Yashoda serves him first. On this Balaram becomes angry. Yashoda said, "From tomorrow I shall give butter first to him who arrives first." Next day both the brothers left for butter. On the way Balaram had a dip in the river and got engrossed in 'Maya'. A lot of time passed away. All of a sudden Krishna called out–"Dada!" Then he became conscious and remembered that he had to go to Yashoda to get butter. Hurriedly he came out of the river and ran back to his mother where he saw Krishna sitting on the lap of Yashoda and eating butter. He got very angry and said, "Again you have given Krishna butter before me?" Then Krishna said, "Dada, shall I tell mother that you had a dip in the river and got lost in Maya." Embarrassed, Balaram replied, "No, no, there is no need to tell anything. You eat butter first every day."

Bithu di made me Balaram and Minu (Grand-daughter of Matori aunt–the younger sister of Baba Bholanath) as Krishna and Mana da's daughter Agamoni as Yashoda. The play was immediately enacted by us and Ma was very pleased with the performance.

One day Ma was seated on the swing. After our acting was over, when Ganga di was about to raise Ma from the swing, she found Her to be too heavy to lift Her alone. Dadabhai, Maunima and others went to her assistance, but even their combined effort failed. Ma sat heavy as the universe and was smiling sweetly. We were around the swing witnessing Ma's leela. When Ganga di, Dadabhai and others gave up their effort to raise Her after several attempts, Ma extended Her right arm towards Ganga di and sweetly said, "Now raise me up." As soon as Ganga di took Her by the hand She was as light as a cork and stood up with a jerk.

Another day, after the regular programme was over, we stood surrounding Ma's swing. All of a sudden Ma caught hold of Maunima's hand and made her sit on the swing beside Herself. Then she took Didima, next Ganga di, then Dadabhai and the girls one by one. She made us sit beside Her and swang us each separately.

On the full moon night Ma was dressed as Lord Krishna and was seated on the exclusively decorated swing. After special bhajans and kirtans at midnight we all sat in meditation in the memory of Ma's self-initiation leela. That night I made paper jasmines and hanged them in the middle of the swing in the form of a canopy. When meditation began all lights in the hall were put out. Ma was in a half-lying state on the swing. The bright light of the full moon had found its way through the eastern windows to the swing. Due to soft breeze from Ganga, the festoon of the jasmine canopy was moving to and fro. I was at Ma's feet looking at Her. Ma was throughout looking at the flower. My decoration was rewarded, so my heart was filled with joy. Whatever we did was centered around Ma. Our acting as well as decoration, everything raised us to the height of delight, as they met Ma's appreciation.

Next day was Rakhi Purnima. We tied Rakhi on Ma's hand and Ma also tied Rakhi on everyone's hand present there. In the first year of this festival, Rakhis were brought from the market. Since financially Kanyapeeth was still limping, we were not permitted to buy Rakhis from the market. However, from next year, we ourselves made them. Every year I made five special Rakhis for Ma, Didima, Dadabhai, Ganga di and Haribaba. Rakhis were also prepared by others. All Rakhis were arranged in a big tray to be placed before Ma and She tied them on our wrists. One year, I remember that nearly two hundred Rakhis were made and Ma was very pleased to see our hand-made Rakhis. That year, the swing was decorated with fruits and leaves. After tying Rakhis, Ma stood on the swing and She took off the fruits and threw them at us. Thus the week long Jhulan festival ended.

A week later Janmashtami followed Jhulan Purnima. Some episodes from Shree Krishna's life were played in our hall. Renu di and Bithu di assisted by us, made up many things– Vrindavan, Mathura, Jamuna river, the prison of Kansa where Lord Krishna's birth took place, etc. After a close look Ma seemed highly delighted. At midnight, at the time of Shri Krishna's avirbhava (appearance), we prayed to Ma, made Her sit on the silver throne in our worship room and worshipped Her. After the arrival of Gopal His abhishek and full-fledged worship were performed.

Once Ma suggested that let Krishna's various leelas be displayed in the yard in front of Kanyapeeth, in the garden and around the Yajnashala. Ma Herself told us to cut out long piece of tin and cover it with soil and to scatter barley on it. A few days later small barley sprouts came out and it looked like a crop field. Placing slices of the field at different points, it seemed like green fields. We arranged plants, houses, dolls and cows on the bank of an artificial river Jamuna. It was a grand show. In it was shown Ma sitting in the verandah of our Vrindavan ashram. The sight pleased Ma and all others.

On the day following Janmashtami, Nanda festival was due. In our hall, we tied pieces of cloth on our foreheads, put hangers on our shoulders and thus dressed as cowherds, danced around Ma. Once on the day of Nanda festival, Ma asked Buni di to call a maid servant with her new born baby and to wait in the verandah. She told us to dress up as cowherds and proceed towards the village of king Nanda, Krishna's father, adding that a baby was born in the house of Nanda baba, "Let's go to see him and wish him a happy birthday." In the meantime Ma had already sent a word to Mukti–the maid servant, through Buni di that if her child did not cry at the appropriate time she should pinch the baby to make it cry. As I heard the cry of the baby, I said, as taught by Ma, "Listen, the child of Nanda baba is crying. Speed up, we must congratulate him." After that having Ma as the central figure, we started dancing merrily and singing, *"Brahma dances, Shiva dances, Indra dances in Gokul, the milkmen dance having Govinda."* Ma also danced freely in Her joyous mood, sometimes raising Her hands with us and sometimes placing Her hand on our shoulders. Thus She played the leading role in Nandotsava–the festival of joy, on the birth of Lord Krishna. In the meantime curd was taken out of the earthen pot and put into Ma's mouth. Ma also started feeding curd to us.

Since this festival occurred from morning to noon, generally at that time Dadabhai remained busy in the kitchen, cooking for Ma. So Ma sent for her and when she came and asked, "Ma, did you call me?" and as soon as she opened her mouth Ma threw a good lump of curd at her mouth. Her face was besmeared with it. Obviously there was a great laughter. After playing with us in our hall, Ma went on the roof. Male devotees, who were not supposed to enter Kanyapeeth, were getting restless on the courtyard looking upwards for Ma. We followed Ma roofward singing kirtan. From the rooftop, Ma threw down curd aiming the devotees, who were just looking like hungry birdlings who open their mouth to have food from the mother bird. It is noteworthy that Ma threw curd from the second floor roof to the yard below, but each and everybody received curd straight into their mouth, although obviously curd scattered on their faces and heads too. This Nandotsava continued from morning up to the noon. All of us and Ma were smeared with curd. After taking a good bath Ma had Her lunch (bhog) and we too had a grand feast. We all felt as if we had a drift in the sea of delight.

Once during Nandotsava Ma Herself staged a drama (leela) named "Yogi in disguise". She was the director and actress both. The previous night was Janmashtami festival, so Ma and everybody were busy. I noticed that inbetween Ma was seriously whispering something to Bithu di, Buba di and Buni di. Later I learnt that those were the instructions to them, about the drama to be staged. Ma asked a few elder girls, who lived outside the ashram to bring colourful sarees. Next morning Ma and those girls entered the room, adjacent to our hall. Everybody dressed up as per Ma's choice.

We heard that Ma was going to do something in our hall in the morning. So we got ready. When the screen went up it was seen that a very sad Radharani being abandoned by Krishna was sitting encircled by her friends. Then entered Ma, covered with a tiger skin as a yogi in disguise. At first, She blew a conch. She was holding the conch in a style as if She was blowing it, but actually it was Chabi di who blew a conch hidden behind Ma.

After blowing the conch the yogi started pacing to and fro and uttered, "I am hungry, I am hungry" in great emotion. Listening to the sound of the conch Radharani asked her friends, "Look, who has come. Is it my bosom friend?" One of her friends came out and guided the yogi to Radha. Overwhelmed Radha who was in great bhava could not speak. The friends started gossiping who was he. He might be our Shyam Sundar. Everyone said something different when Bithu di as Vrinda declared, "Oh! He is Krishna in disguise of a yogi–Our 'Ma', nobody else."

At once Ma threw away the tiger skin and came out in the beautiful blue saree. We were prepared with our hangers with curd on our shoulders and started dancing around Ma singing, "*Nanda dances, with joy he dances...*" And in this way the Nandotsava started.

Later Bithu di told me that Ma had said that Radharani's plaited hair should be seen under the transparent veil. She was not satisfied with the saree as it was not transparent at all. Ma said to Buni di that feed me breakfast on the stage when this body would say "I am hungry." But Ma was then in such a bhava that feeding was not possible.

That year Chitra di came back from America and brought a good camera. She was present there and tried her best to take a snap of Ma while acting as a yogi but failed. It must be not in Ma's kheyal, so the failure.

9

During one winter Ma came from Allahabad to Varanasi bringing with Her baskets full of guava. Dadabhai sent the guava to Kanyapeeth. Next day the girls were given guava for tiffin. After offering them to Ma in our worship room, I was distributing guava in small bowls for the girls. Suddenly I saw that Ma had got up by the staircase and was standing just in front of me. She said, "What is this you are distributing? Ah! The guava from Allahabad. Did didi give all of it to you? You see, she has not left any for this body." I asked, "Ma will you eat?" At once She opened Her mouth like a child and I put one piece into Her mouth. Ma exclaimed, "How sweet!" As the pieces were big, to make them small pieces I instantaneously used the edge of our used plate to cut and put the pieces into Ma's mouth. All the girls came and surrounded Ma. She was laughing and relating Her childhood days how She used to have guavas and mangoes. We also joined Ma in the laughter. While eating Ma asked, "Where is didi? Call her." At that time Dadabhai was having her lunch downstairs. After her daylong hard activities she had just sat for her lunch at 4.30–5 p.m. Realising that she will leave her food instantly after call, and come up at once, Ma said, "Call her little later." Ma was present there among us for a pretty long time. She was standing throughout but it did not strike us that we should offer Her an asana to sit on. As Ma asked to call for Dadabhai it struck me and I asked one girl to bring one asan for Ma immediately. An asan was brought and was placed and I requested Ma to sit on that. But with a naughty and mischievous smile Ma remarked, "I shall not sit as the asana has been put for me only after hearing Didi's name. Now let her come." But She took the seat before Didi's arrival and saved us from the rebuke of Dadabhai.

Once Ma was in Vindhyachal and we were expecting Her in Varanasi any day. Whole Kanyapeeth was cleaned by us so that Ma would be pleased. Six, seven days passed and Ma did not come. One day I remarked jokingly, "We have cleaned so well and that's why Ma is not coming, leave it untidy and you will see Ma will definitely come." When Ma came She went all around and was pleased to see everything all clean and tidy. Ma also rubbed Her finger on the windowpanes to see whether there is any dust or dirt on them. Ma was walking around the building and praising us. Naturally, we followed Her fully satisfied. When She reached the small roof near the library, She wanted to go to the bathroom. There was an unused bathroom under lock and key. Dadabhai said, "Ma, why don't you use this one?" When it was opened it was found that after cleaning the building the girls had kept all the rubbish together with brooms, baskets, etc. in that very bathroom. Seeing this Ma remarked seriously, "You girls work like this?" Hearing this, our proud heads at once bent down. Ma said, "When you work, work perfectly so that not a single corner is left untouched."

When I joined Kanyapeeth, there was no proper arrangement of teaching. Only Gangadi and Billoji used to teach us Sanskrit and English respectively. Elder ones used to go to Kolkata accompanied by Gangadi for their examination in Sanskrit known as Adya, Madhya, etc. In those days Ma used to be in Varanasi mostly and the ashram used to be thronged with disciples and devotees. Everyday there was some kind of function in presence of Ma.

I never liked studying. The whole year used to be spent in religious functions and festivals. In the sacred company of Ma, we were engrossed in kirtan, decoration, preparing special food and other various functions of the ashram. Under such circumstances, I enjoyed my ashram life very much.

On the other hand, my father was highly concerned for the studies of his children. While seeing that my studies were not satisfactory here, he wanted to take me home. About this I had no knowledge. One day we went to pay our obeisance to Ma. She said to me, "Do you know your father wants to take you home for studies. What will you do? Here there is no proper arrangement for teaching yet." I smiled and answered, "I am not going home. Father has got other children, let him educate them. If one child remains uneducated, what is the harm?" After hearing my remark, Ma laughed and said to Dadabhai, "Listen Didi, what Vishuddha is saying." Dadabhai also was pleased to hear that I did not want to go home. I repeated the same to my father and elder sister and refused to go home. My elder sister Shraddha said, "Yes I know why you prefer to stay in the ashram, as all the time there is some festival and no regular classes, you are enjoying the ceremonies in the ashram. Here there is too much fun and no studies."

It was going on like this. Suddenly Ma had a kheyal and asked Dadabhai to arrange for Chandan di and me to appear in high school examination. Somehow Billo ji, Sati di, Renu di, Kamal da and my father helped us in the preparation of the coming exam. We were busy in cooking for a great feast (Bhog), when Kamal da (The Gen. Secy. of the ashram at that time) came and told us to be ready to get photographed at once, as it was required for the examination form. The same night the forms were filled in and dispatched, as that was the last day for submitting forms.

Before going to Kolkata for the examination we did pranam to Ma and made Her touch our pens. Ma said smilingly, "Study well, pass well." We were excited to go to Kolkata but not sure enough about the preparation. We went to Kolkata with Sati di, Vimala di and my father. Those days there was a small ashram at Ekdalia in Kolkata. Ma's devotee Avani Mohan Sharma was in-charge of the ashram. Muktibaba, an old monk of the ashram had fractured his leg and was admitted to P.G. hospital. Kusum da was in the ashram to look after Muktibaba. He told Avani da that Didi's Kanyapeeth girls have come, proper arrangement should be made for them. Avani da made special arrangement for us. Kusum da also used to look after us. Ma's devotee Shri Shashadhar Bhattacharya made arrangement for our commutation to the examination hall.

When we went for the examination we found that the syllabus had changed. Somehow we attempted, but when the result was declared it was found that both of us had failed. Next year we appeared again and passed. After the school final examination, Ma asked Chandan di to prepare for oriental studies i.e. Madhyama, Shastri and Acharya in Sanskrit and asked me to study for the Intermediate examination. At that time Maunima's son Shri Shishir Kumar Dutta (Rakhal da) was engaged to teach me for Intermediate and Ganga di for Matric exam.

Just after my school final exams Ma went to Puri for a few days. Ma took me with Her. Before starting for the station, I went to offer my pranam to Ma. Dadabhai was also there. She solemnly asked me, "You are going with Ma, will you be able to manage? (do Ma's seva)." Ma looked at me with a sweet smile and told Dadabhai, "Didi, why are you belittling her? I see that her forehead is shining." As I did pranam, Ma patted my head with great affection. Parul di and myself boarded in the third class and Ma and Dadabhai were in the first class compartment. When the train halted at stations, Ma's devotees came for Her darshan and offered fruits, sweets, food, etc. to Ma. She sent prasad for us through Dadabhai.

Next morning we reached Howrah station. Lots of devotees were present to have darshan of Ma. Mr. Aptap Mitra took us to his place in Dumdum. He had made very nice arrangements. On the lawn under a canopy, Ma's seat was placed for satsang and public visit. Renuka Mitra, Mr. Aptap's wife, welcomed Ma with blowing the conch and made Ma sit on the beautifully decorated seat. Then she washed Ma's feet, put garland around her neck, offered flowers with sandal paste at Ma's feet, fed Ma some sweets and fruits and did aarti with incense and panchpradeep, etc. Ma distributed the fruits and sweets among those present there and asked everybody about their well-being. Then Aptap da and his wife took Ma to Her new room. They had prepared a nice room for Ma. Next to the staircase a small kitchen was made. There was an almirah, which contained utensils, rice, pulses, oil, spices and many homemade pickles, etc. neatly arranged for Ma's use.

It was summer, so Dadabhai spread a special mat (shital patti) on the floor for Ma to rest. Then she took me with her to cook for Ma. So many things were there in the kitchen still she asked me to bring rice, pulses, oil, etc. rather everything from Ma's basket. The basket was in Ma's room. Dadabhai asked me to bring many things one by one from the basket neatly and without making any sound since Ma was resting there. Several times I entered Ma's room silently. Ma was lying in a relaxed posture with Her eyes closed and Her hair was spread over Her head. She looked like Goddess Durga and her body was full of jyoti, i.e., illuminated.

Ma stayed in Dumdum for three days. Spiritual discourses and kirtans were carried on satisfactorily. With Ma's permission my eldest brother took some of us to see the aerodrome and aeroplanes. We also visited several devotees' houses with Ma. Then along with Ma, we started for Puri.

Next morning we reached Puri. At the station one black station-wagon was waiting for us. Ma sat in the front seat. Dadabhai, Parul di and I took the rear seat. On our way towards the ashram Ma showed us different places where She stayed for the first time at Puri. She said, "Look at the lovely blue sea. On the seashore is the ashram." We reached the ashram. Some devotees of Puri welcomed Ma blowing with the conch and putting garland around on Ma's neck. The ashram was small. On the first floor was a small room for Ma. Our luggage was kept in the next room. Dadabhai took Parul di to the kitchen to prepare food for Ma. I was with Ma. I arranged the luggage in that room as instructed by Ma.

From Kolkata Swami Paramananda ji, Binu da and Aravinda Dadu came with Ma. In Puri ashram Kshama di's father Dr. Girindra Mitra, his eldest sister-in-law (Baroma) and Durga di were staying. In the evening Ma took us all for a walk on the sea beach. Huge waves came and hit the shore and carried back Ma's blessings by touching Her feet. I collected many shells. After the sunset we returned to the ashram. Outside in the courtyard, Ma sat on the cemented platform. We all sat below the platform and sang the evening kirtan. Ma after talking to the devotees present there came upstairs. There in the verandah, there was another cemented seat in front of Ma's room. Ma sat on that seat. Ma's hair was being blown by the gusty wind from the sea. Swamiji, Binu da, Girin da and Aurobindo dadu sat near Ma and discussed many things for long time.

Next morning Dadabhai went to the kitchen and asked me to sit near Ma's door. After a few minutes Ma came out of Her room and enquired whether I had my breakfast or not. I shyly replied in negative. Then Ma said, "You girls in Kanyapeeth are habituated to have breakfast." She opened the almirah and gave me few 'bananas', a bunch of lichis and a bowl of rabri (thickened sweet milk). Giving me these things She went back to Her bed. As soon as I had put one lichi into my mouth Ma called me "Vishuddha", but I could not respond properly as the lichi was inside my mouth. I felt ashamed. Ma told me to call Her at 9.30 a.m. Afterwards I enjoyed the delicious rabri with banana. Again Ma got up and said, "Here downstairs the bathroom is roofless, so whenever you bathe, stand near the wall so that nobody can see you from upstairs." Listening to this, I was overwhelmed to think that how much Ma was concerned for such a poor child like me.

One day Ma took us to have the darshan of Lord Jagannath. From the beginning till the end Ma caught hold of my hand. She took me straight to the temple and standing before Lord Jagannath said, "Look Vishuddha, have a vision of Jagannath." I saw the wonderful image of Lord Vishnu with four hands, bright complexion and gorgeous dresses and my eyes were over-flashed. I had the fortune of visiting Lord Jagannath several times afterwards but never had that vision again. At night Ma sat in Her room. Swami Paramananda ji, Girin da, Binu da, Aurobindo dadu, Gurupriya didi and myself were listening to Her. Relating to Jagannath's appearance Ma said, "Do you know what happened? Seeing Radha or a devotee as you think of it, Lord Jagannath is overwhelmed with love and His eyes are wide open in astonishment and His limbs melt in devotion." While relating this emotion Ma's eyes grew round shaped in wonder and Her hands bent down like Jagannath. We had the fortune of seeing Jagannath alive in Ma and did obeisance at Her feet.

Ma also took me to the other main temples of Puri. Every evening we had Mahaprasad with Ma in the courtyard. Following morning Ma used to make a special preparation called 'Panta' with the leftover rice of the previous night. After preparation I put some 'Panta' in Ma's mouth and then She would feed me, and in this way the feeding Leela of Mahaprasad went on almost every day. For Jagannath prasad no bar of caste and creed was followed. So anybody could feed Ma, that was the great pleasure. Binu da and Aurobindo dadu both arranged lavishly for different items of Mahaprasad every day.

One day Ma sent me to have a dip in the sea. The waves should not disturb the clothes, so She taught me how to tie the dhoti and put towel on top. She sent two-three persons with me, so that there would not be any problem. When we were going to the sea, I saw Ma was standing on the verandah looking at me. I had a good bath in the sea for the first time in my life. Ma remained standing till I returned. Those few days of joy passed away as if in a moment. Then we returned to Varanasi via Kolkata.

10

In 1952 Ma went for South India tour. A few brahmacharis and brahmacharinis along with many other devotees accompanied Ma. On Her way back She came to Varanasi. We heard the detailed description of the tour from Dadabhai and Kusum da. From the South, Ma brought sandalwood and ivory statues for us, Kanyapeeth girls. She asked Shree Manamohan Ghosh to make a temple like glass showcase and Herself placed the statues inside it before presenting the same to us. The showcase is still in our worship room. Ma also gave us sandalwood pen, incense stand, stainless steel lota (pot) individually. The same year a handicraft (Shilpa Pratisthan) institution was opened in Kanyapeeth. Ma brought different sized dry coconut leaf baskets to be used in the Shilpa Pratisthan. Whenever Ma went to some new place, She used to bring for us special gifts like a worldly mother.

Perhaps in the month of May or June in 1953, Ma's birthday celebrations were going on, suddenly in that intense heat Vimala di had an attack with severe cholera. Ma's devotee and the top most physician of Varanasi Dr. Gopal Das Gupta sent her to the hospital immediately. Kshama di, then in-charge of Kanyapeeth, went with her. Ashram's General Secretary Brahmachari Kamal da, Brahmachari Sadhan da and the doctors forbade Kshama di to attend to Vimala di since it was serious and highly infectious. Kshama di did not listen to anyone and remained with the patient.

Vimala di was in her last stage. All possible treatment failed. Vomiting and diarrhea stopped but the stomach swelled up. There was no sign of life. Whole body was bluish like a dead body. Those days cholera took an epidemic form in the city. There was no bed left for any patient in the hospital. Proclaiming Vimala di as dead, she was thrown out from the room to the courtyard. Her face and body were covered with flies. Kshama di was not a doctor but being the daughter of a renowned doctor she knew a lot about medicines, etc. and she had great love and affection for everyone. She thought that medicines given to the patient had controlled her vomiting and motions, but still there was infection in her stomach. Moreover, she thought that if the patient was given enema and the rubbish from the stomach could be removed, she should be O.K. The doctors and nurses were told about this idea but no one listened to her. They said that the patient showed signs of death from the feet to her bosom and within seconds she would be totally dead, so nothing can be done. Dr. Das Gupta told Kshama di, "Whatever happened has happened, now let us go to the ashram." Kshama di went to the bathroom and picked up one catheter used by another patient, cleaned it and inserted it in the anus of Vimala di and blew hard with her mouth. Blackish muck came out of the anus which had foul smell. After sometime the swelling in the stomach reduced and her body regained some colour.

Pulse beat could be felt. Doctors were dumbfounded at the sight of this improvement. Gradually Vimala di recovered her health. After a few days of medical treatment she got back to her normal life again. Kshama di along with Vimala di returned with much happiness to the ashram. She nursed her till she became completely fit. After she recovered Ma came to Varanasi. Dr. Gopal Das Gupta came to Ma and requested Her to call Kshama di. He said to Ma, "I want to do pranam to Kshama in front of you. In my whole life I have read many books about ideal nursing, etc., but never heard about such sacrificial nursing. Kshama is not a human being, she is a Goddess."

After a few years Ganga di had T.B. She was shifted to Anandamayee Karuna building. Kshama di used to nurse her. Ganga di was very upset with her ailment. One day when lunch was served to her, after taking two or three morsels, she began to vomit and started weeping. She said, "What is the use of eating? I am having T.B. They won't keep me in the ashram. I will not be able to do Ma's seva anymore. What is the benefit of my living long?" Kshama di pacified her saying, "Who told you that you have T.B.? You are sick, if you eat properly and take medicines you will be O.K." Ganga di thought since Kshama di was saying, might be she was not having T.B. In order to test Kshama di she said to her, "If I do not have T.B. then take some rice from my plate." She took a morsel from her plate. Seeing this Ganga di was sure that she does not have T.B., otherwise Kshama di would not have eaten from her plate. Since that day she started eating properly.

Later under Ma's arrangement Ganga di was admitted to a T.B. sanatorium and after prolonged treatment got cured and came back to the ashram. This is a noteworthy matter as those days, it was such a menacing disease that even hearing its name, no one dared to come in contact with the patient. But knowing well that Ganga di had T.B., Kshama di ate from the patient's vomitted plate only to please her. She didn't even bother about her own future. Her aim was to serve the patient whole-heartedly. Although she nursed cholera and T.B. patients in this way, she didn't succumb to these diseases. That was Kshama di's firm mental power, self-less seva and over-all Ma's divine grace alone protected her.

In March 1954, during Shivaratri, Ma came to Varanasi. Every year, we Kanyapeeth girls observed complete fast round the clock without even drinking water and do worship of Lord Shiva whole night for four times. Generally we sat in two circles to do worship in the hall on the bank of the Ganga. This time Ma instructed us to arrange our worship in the Chandi Mandap, where Durga (Basanti) puja takes place every spring time. As Ma was present many devotees from far and near came for Shivaratri. According to Ma's instructions, we elder ones arranged our seats in the Chandi Mandap, for the junior girls in the adjacent small room, for the ladies in the verandah and the gents in the courtyard and for the VIP gents in front of the Annapurna temple. In the centre of these different places big brass vessels with Shivalinga (phallic form) decorated with garlands and sandal paste were kept. Surrounding Lord Shiva were the seats of the worshippers. All required things for Shiva worship were kept in front of each participant. In the morning we had a good bath in the Ganga and went to do obeisance to Ma. She touched our head and said, "Look, this body has had bath in the Ganga." The whole day we made lots of sandal paste, arranged flowers, bel leaves, fruits, sweets, etc. in large quantity.

In the evening, we dressed in silk dhotis and namavali, put sandal paste and sacred ashes on our foreheads and did pranam to Ma. She blessed us with a sweet smile. Then we took our seats and started singing kirtan. Next started the first quarter (prahar) puja. Among us one girl led the mantra loudly and others followed. Outside in the verandah and courtyard brahmachari Jogesh da, Vishu da and Batu da guided other devotees to do their worship. There is a small Shiva temple in the courtyard. Brahmachari Kamal da (Later known as Swami Virajananda ji) did the special worship to Shiva for the whole night. The whole ashram was vibrating with sound of the conch, bell, recitation of scriptures and kirtan. Overall the divine presence of Ma moving from one corner to another, a celestial atmosphere prevailed all over the ashram.

Finishing the first quarter worship a main aarti took place. Whoever among the participants was unable to do whole night worship and the youngsters of Kanyapeeth, did the four times worship together at a time. The rest who were determined to do the whole night worship, did japa and kirtan, etc. and they didn't leave their asans. We kept the necessary things with us in such a way that we could pass over to others when they were needed.

After the second quarter puja and aarti Ma started singing–

Gangadhara Shiropara
Paridhane Baghambara
Deva Deva Mahadeva...

From downstair Chandi Mandap we could hear the sweet melodious voice of Ma but couldn't understand the wordings of the song, as it was a new one and sung by Ma just then.

Ma was singing in ecstasy and Bibhu da was following Her with a harmonium. It seemed as if the whole ashram was echoed by the divine celestial melody of Ma.

During the third quarter we were meditating when Ma silently entered the Chandi Mandap wearing a white Alkhalla, a rudraksha mala around Her neck, the hair tied like a coir on Her head. She put rudraksha mala around a few elderly girls' neck. I opened my eyes and witnessed Ma as Lord Shiva himself appearing before me. I was thrilled. Till date when I touch that rudraksha mala, I feel the touch of Ma.

Perhaps in 1955 Ma went to Vrindavan during holi festival. On the full moon day two statues of Mahaprabhu and Nityananda made of 'Ashtadhatu' were to be installed in the new temple. Then at Vriandavan there was only a two-storied building. On the first floor next to Ma's room was a small room where Didima and Dadabhai stayed. Downstairs there were satsang hall, two rooms, kitchen, courtyard, etc. The construction of the Mahaprabhu temple was going on in full swing. Mana da came from Varanasi for the construction and a local devotee, a staunch Vaishnav, Jogen da was helping him. From Kolkata Shree Nitai Paul, the renowned sculptor sent the statues. Ma was moving about supervising everything. One day while coming down from the staircase, Ma sprained Her ankle seriously. Later She said, "It was a kheyal that somebody may fall down from the top of the temple and die, so it happened on this body."

The Mahaprabhu temple was under construction. One day Ma asked me to bring one paper and pencil. I got it and Ma asked me to draw a parrot. Saying this She Herself started to draw a parrot with Her nails. I followed the line with pencil and it was a drawing of a complete parrot. It was Ma's kheyal to make four parrots at four corners of the temple-top of the Mahaprabhu temple. But later Ma must have instructed to make peacock's feathers instead.

When Ma stayed in Vrindavan She had to attend Haribaba's Satsang and kirtan twice every day. It was Baba's desire and Ma used to fulfil his wish like an obedient child. Frequently Haribaba would arrange for Rasleela and kirtan in the ashram. Since Ma could not go to his place due to leg sprain, he himself came to the ashram for daily satsang. For Ma's recovery he arranged for 'Ramarcha', continuous japa and 'Hanuman Chalisa'. Haribaba's devotion towards Ma was noteworthy. For some days Ma was in the Hari Kunja kutia. Only for Ma's service I was allowed to accompany Buni di and the rest was done by Kusum da. Ma did not take any medicine. She recovered by Her own kheyal and the heart felt prayers of all.

Swami Krishanandaji, Shree Shree Ma and Hari Baba

Gradually the temple was completed. Both the statues of Gaur and Nitai were to be installed at the new temple on the full moon day of Holi. Under Ma's guidance, all the arrangements were made to the minutest detail. After completion of all the rituals, Gaur-Nitai were dressed gorgeously, placed on a decorated chariot and with kirtan accompanied by music covered the city in an exclusive procession. Returning to the ashram they were installed ritually on the altar by Ma and the Mahatmas. Then full-fledged worship (Shodashopachar puja) was performed to Gaur and Nitai, proper offering (Bhog) and aarti took place. The full moon day of Holi was the birthday of Haribaba too. So he was offered clothes, garlands, fruits, sweets, etc. cordially. Offerings were made to the other Mahatmas also. Many devotees from Kolkata, Delhi, Dehradun, Varanasi and other places got together for the ceremony. In the end there was a round the clock Namyajna.

Swami Sitaramdasji, Didima and Shree Shree Ma

During this occasion the Raas party of Vrindavan performed Mahaprabhu Leela every day. After the installation of Gaur-Nitai we used to cook the offering under Ma's instructions in Ma's kitchen. Kusum da and myself used to prepare the bhog and carry it to the temple. There were lots of monkeys in Vrindavan, so it was quite difficult to pass through the monkeys and reach the temple with the bhog.

11

The Varanasi ashram was situated on the banks of the Ganga. In the rainy season when the river was in spate it seemed as if we were on a ship. On the eastern portion of the ashram at the edge of the Ganga, there was a large kitchen and dining hall at the basement, then on the next step was a large round satsang hall and Ma's room. On both sides of the hall towards the north and south were a few rooms for the brahmacharis and sadhus. On the top of these was a large round terrace. On both sides of this terrace there were two small temples. One on the northern end containing the sacrificial fire in a proper Kunda and at the other end in the south was a Viraja Homa temple. An expert engineer, Shree Manamohan Ghosh from Dhaka, an ardent devotee of Ma constructed these buildings. The scenic beauty of the ashram was quite inexplicable for me. People other than Ma's devotee used to come and take snapshots on the terrace.

The first sanyam week in 1952 and so many functions like Ma's birthday took place in that spacious hall. It was the night of the new moon (Amavasya) and a special bhog for the night was to be offered in Annapurna temple. Ma was sitting in

Her first floor room. When I was going to the temple to bring Ma's bhog prasad, Dadabhai came running to Ma with tears in her eyes and shouted, "Ma, just hear, there is a big crack in the hall's wall". Listening to this and with a tranquil smile Ma replied, "Didi, why do you mourn? The building has been standing for a long time and now it is time for it to be rejuvenated." Dadabhai said with a sigh, "Alas! To whom would I express my anxiety? The proverb says–A mad is glad in slaughtering a cow." Afterwards on the advice of many expert engineers that most attractive portion of the ashram was demolished. The building was so well built that it took about a year to demolish it.

Dadabhai fell ill. She was completely bed-ridden due to acute pain in her waist. She could not even turn from one side to other. Ma visited Mumbai at the cordial invitation of Mr. S.N. Sopory and a few ardent devotees of that side. It was decided that Dadabhai also would be taken there for medical treatment by specialist doctors and who would accompany Ma was also discussed. Finding her name not mentioned there, Didima whispered into Ma's ears "Nirmala, Hemant Pathak (a disciple of Didima) of Mumbai had written to go there once." Ma expressed a naughty smile and said, "Oh! I see, Paramananda, let her visit Mumbai before this body goes there." Didima burst into loud laughter finding herself exposed and all present there joined the laughter hearing this sweet joke between the mother and daughter. It is said that Didima took sanyas only to be with Her. After mamu's marriage Ma instructed her to stay with her son and daughter-in-law. But Didima didn't like to part with Ma's company. Ma said, "Then you will have to take sanyas." And she took sanyas to stay with Her (Ma).

Revered Swami Muktananda Giri Maharaja's (Didima) sanyas celebration took place for the first time on 13.4.1956 at Varanasi ashram. She was born on a Sunday in the month of April. She took sanyas on the thirteenth of April, the last day of Chaitra as per the Bengali calendar, i.e., middle of April. To this day, the day, as per the Bengali Calendar, figures in the list of days to be celebrated in the Anandamayee Sangha.

On one fine morning of the 13th April 1956, Ma came down to Didima's bed with our morning kirtan. She sat on the bed for a while and slowly lay down. Her head was on Didima's feet and Didima's head was touching her feet. Our kirtan was going on and Ma and Didima lay down for a long time in the same posture. In between Didima's first disciple Brahmachari Hiru da (Tanmayanandaji) did a short morning aarti to both of them.

Afterwards in the morning, mamu, maternal uncle to all Ma's devotees, did an elaborate (Shodashopachar) worship to Didima in the presence of Ma in the Chandi Mandap. Shree Naresh Chakraborty of Dehradun brought a beautiful big umbrella and held it on Didima's head. The humility of Didima and her affection to all were unparalleled. In spite of being the mother (human form) to Ma (universal mother) with so many ashrams and profuse wealth, Didima spent a life of a humble soul in a corner willingly. She had not even the least demand for any material comfort. Nobody came empty handed after meeting her. At least one puffed sugar candy she must give. That was the day of her worship. Plenty of fruits and sweets were offered to her. Still she did not touch them. Seeing this Dadabhai said to her, "Didima, these are for you only, distribute as you please." Listening to this, with

Standing Left to Right
Yogeshda, Hiruda (Tanmayananda), Kamalda (Virajanandaji), Atulda

Seated Left to Right
Mukti Baba, Shankaranandaji, Paramanandaji, Narain Swamiji, Shree Shree Ma, Gurupriyadi, Didima, Upen Maharaj, Nishikanta Mitra, Prabhuddhanandaji

a sweet smile, Didima distributed prasad to her heart's content. After she distributed in this way her joy and contentment overflowed her face. Then a group photo of Ma with Didima and others, was taken.

As a part and parcel of sanyas celebration, hundred and eight sadhus (monks) were offered clothes, money and good feast. In the afternoon Narayan Swamiji delivered a speech on Didima in the presence of Ma. Nobody ever witnessed any anger in Didima. Such a character in human form could be rarely seen. Once a girl did something wrong, Ma and Dadabhai were scolding her. Didima was present there. She couldn't stand this sight any longer and told Ma, "This girl is very simple and says everything to me." Hearing this Ma said to her," "Oh mother! Can't you find any fault with anyone, don't you have anger at all in you?" I was also there standing near Ma. Looking at me, She said, "Do you understand? This girl says everything to her means She asks for things and complains against her inmates to her. That is also a quality to the Mother of this Body."

Didima always used to do japa, i.e., repetition of God's name. One day I asked her, "Didima, you are the mother of the universal mother, then why are you doing so much japa?" She replied with a smile, "Those who take initiation from me are too busy to do Japa and if one is initiated and does not do Japa, it is a blunder. So I do Japa for them only." Blessed are those who are initiated by such a compassionate preceptor.

12

The following day was the Bengali New Year's Day according to the calendar. I planned to make a huge flower garland for Ma. Udasji used to help me on such occasions. She paid for the flowers. The whole day we were occupied with Didima's sanyas function. At night I was free and sat in Ma's second floor room with a good quantity of fragrant mogra flowers. I asked my friend Jyotidi to assist me. Starting at 10 p.m. we made a huge thick garland of three strings about six feet long in the whole night.

Next morning we brought Ma to the hall to celebrate New Year. As I put the garland around Her neck, she took us one by one inside it. We started singing *Jai Jai Ma* and danced around Ma clapping hands. After some time Ma made us come out of the garland. Seeing that after moving so long with so many heads the garland remained intact, Ma said to Dadabhai, "So it will last". I thought Ma meant we will stay in the ashram for lifelong. But afterwards many of the girls of that group left for their home. So I think Ma meant the Kanyapeeth institution will last long, as Ma's words cannot be otherwise.

Before Sanyam Saptah, Didima, Dadabhai, Swamiji and many of us went to Mumbai with Ma. There we stayed at Juhu beach. Above one bungalow a temporary abode for Ma was built. It was very large room, well-decorated with spacious verandah. It was like as seen in a cinema. On one side of the roof there was a small room and a bathroom. Dadabhai was to stay in this room as she could see Ma, who would be in the adjoining room. The scenery of the place was superb with rows of coconut trees at the seashore, the blue sea, sunrise and sunset.

In Dadabhai's room an iron cot was placed at one side for her use. But as that would not be convenient for her, she lay on a low plank and asked me to sleep on that cot. Since I had to look after Dadabhai in the morning and at Kanyapeeth we were in the habit of retiring for the night at 10 p.m., Dadabhai asked me to go to bed in proper time. At Juhu beach area there was a swarm of mosquitoes. I somehow fixed one corner of the mosquito curtain and lay down.

At night Ma, Swamiji, Yogi bhai and Kamal da (Virajanandaji) came to have a talk with Dadabhai. Coming near the door Ma said, "Paramananda, look at the girl, she should be helped immediately." It was found that the mosquito net had wrangled the cot and I being badly covered with it, was groaning. Swamiji took hold of the mosquito net and with a jerk freed me from it. Then he set it up properly tying the four corners. Surprisingly, I was in a deep sleep and did not know anything of the matter. Ma standing all through saw me sleeping properly and went away after talking with Dadabhai. Next night when I came to sleep, while setting up the mosquito net I found nails stuck on all the four corners. Then asking Renu di and Guni di I came to know what happened the night before.

'Sanyam week' passed away nicely. Ma sent some of us with Kamal da to visit Dwarka and Somnath. Dadabhai was very ill. There was a talk of her being put up at Mumbai for treatment. But where she would stay and who would arrange for her treatment–these issues were being discussed about. All this time B.K. Shah, a new devotee, came to see Ma and was also present during the discussions. Hearing everything he said that he could arrange for everything. It was extremely surprising seeing that he had come to see Ma for the first time, he did not even know didi. What else could it be but the infallible kheyal of Ma. He eagerly took upon himself the responsibility of arranging everything for Didi.

Later on I heard from Shrimati Leela ben, the wife of B.K. Shah, that after giving the word to Ma for arranging for the treatment of Didi, he went home and said to his wife, "Give me your word that you would do what I ask." When she gave the consent he said that the flat at Breach Candy house (where their children stayed for their studies) should be vacated as Didiji, the devotee of Anandamayee Mataji would come for treatment. They were Gujarati Jains and Didi was quite unknown to them–a Bengali Hindu. Language, food and in all ways they were totally different. The school and college of their children from the house in Ville Parle was at a great distance. They would be much inconvenienced if they vacated the Breach Candy flat. Yet she gave her word to her husband. So in spite of all inconveniences she vacated the flat and arranged it nicely for Didi.

Ma sent Renu di and Billo ji to look over the flat and finalise. In the meantime we came back from our pilgrimage. Dadabhai was shifted to the Breach Candy house with Kamal da, Renu di, Belu di, Parul di, Thakur ma and me. This large mansion adjoining Breach Candy swimming pool on the sea shore was magnificent. We stayed at a large flat on the fourth floor facing the sea. Ma dropped Dadabhai and us in the Breach Candy house on Her way to the station. Dadabhai was highly dejected.

Next day Mr. B.K. Shah came with an eminent doctor. After a thorough examination, Dadabhai's back and waist were fully plastered. Dr. Baliga, the best orthopedic of Mumbai at that time did everything himself. An experienced nurse was engaged for overall care and supervision of Dadabhai. In addition Renu di, Parul di and me were looking after her. The local devotees of Ma, frequently came to see Dadabhai and enquired after her well-being. Mr. B.K. Shah and his wife Leela ben came almost every day. They kept a watchful eye that nobody should have any difficulty. I noticed that difference of languages can make no hindrance where there is love and sincerity. Among the mahatmas who had come for sanyam week, revered Haribaba and Avdhut ji were in Mumbai for a few days. They had great affection for didi and used to visit her very often.

13

On the occasion of the completion of sixty years of Ma's birth on the next Baisakh, i.e., May 1956, the arrangements for celebrations of diamond jubilee were going on on a grand scale. But at that time Dadabhai was bed-ridden being in plaster and Kamal da, the General Secretary of the Sangha, was also held up at Mumbai to look after her. On one hand Dadabhai had to be away from Ma and on the other hand Ma's diamond jubilee was imminent and on account of her illness she would not be able to take part in the arrangements–for these reasons Dadabhai was highly disheartened. Whenever she was alone I found tears streaming down her eyes. At that time Kamal da, in order to cheer up Dadabhai, played on records of Rabindra sangeet and Najrul Geeti. I also sung for her at her request. At noon I used to tell her about my interactions and observations about Ma from my childhood. My relation with Dadabhai was mixed with a little fear though I had a liking towards her manly manners. Dadabhai said, "Write down these reminiscences of Ma." She also told me about her childhood and how she brought up her younger brothers and sisters. Her memory was very sharp. She could easily recite long poems like '*Devatar gras'*, '*Parasmoni*, '*Karnakunti Sambad*', etc. of Tagore read by her in her childhood.

Devotees came to her and discussed with her about Ma's birth celebration. She sent Kamal da to make copies of Ma's records. One day Avdhutji had come and hearing of Ma's birth celebrations said, "If you want to celebrate the festival of the Mother of the world make Ma sit on a lion." After listening to him Dadabhai made arrangements for making a silver throne on a huge lion by Shri Nitai Pal, the eminent artisan of Kolkata.

After Dadabhai recovered a little we started for Varanasi with her. Mr. B.K. Shah bought a trolley and made arrangements for travelling of Dadabhai and for us in a four berth first class compartment. Thus as she was emplastered, Dadabhai would not face any trouble to move with Ma. In the compartment he hung a poster with 'Om Ma' written on a cardboard thinking Dadabhai might like it. In due time we reached Varanasi. Ma was also there.

I was thinking that Ma's 60th birth celebration was drawing near, Ma would be in Varanasi after so many years for the occasion, and what I should offer to Her. For a long time I pondered over the matter and decided to make Kantha for Her. Because my grandmother had said that when a baby was born in a village the neighbours would stitch kanthas for the baby and presented it for the baby. On Her birthday Ma would be like a newly born baby, so I made up my mind to stitch a kantha, i.e., an embroidered cloth mattress for Ma and on that occasion I shall hoist a flag on the roof of the Kanyapeeth. But where shall I get the cloth for the kantha and the flag? I asked Bunidi and she took out a large sheet of white voile from Ma's almirah. It was like the use of Ganga water for the worship of Ganga. Before doing anything new, I don't like to make it known to anybody in advance. So, having obtained the cloth, first of all I went to the worship room and spread out the kantha length. Serving Dadabhai all day and going through the routine work of Kanyapeeth, the little time I could save in the noon, I spent in stitching the kantha sitting silently in our worship room. On the white sheet, I bordered all around lotus stalks of sky blue silk thread and the rest was filled up with usual kantha stitches with white thread.

In short time 19th Baisakh (2nd May, 1956) the great day of Ma's sixtieth birth anniversary came up. On that day the one month long diamond jubilee started with a shehnai performance by Ustad Bismillah Khan and morning kirtan by ashram Brahmacharis. I hoisted the new flag on the roof of Kanyapeeth. The flag was triangular shaped yellow silk stuff with a large white round shape in the middle enclosing a smaller red round shape and 'Om Ma' written over it in the centre. On Ma's direction we Kanyapeeth girls decorated our forehead with two marks, one red sandal paste mark and above that a white sandal paste mark. According to Ma the red mark is the emblem of power and white is for radiance.

All were immersed in joy of the festival. Ma herself was the central figure of everything, so it was very difficult to find Her by Herself. In the midst of all my work I was looking for Ma to be all alone. At last when after lunch Ma was resting and there was nobody else in the room, I entered the room cautiously with the kantha. I set it before Ma and bowed, at which She asked, "What is it?" I said diffidently, "A kantha." From Her lying state She sat upright, unfolded the kantha and handling it was very pleased and said, "Well done, a very nice workmanship. Who taught you?" I said, "My grandma." She also said, "When this body stitched a kantha..." She went over the same line and finished it. I was very happy seeing Ma so delighted with my ordinary gift–a kantha.

Dadabhai, Buni di and others were also pleased. Dadabhai said, "As Ma does not use quilt or mattresses, a kantha should be convenient for Her. Haribaba had given Ma a kantha sewn by a machine (The punjabis use a thick one like a bed-spread made of new cloth and it is machine sewn). Mine is hand-stitched, so this kantha would be soft for Ma." Since then by Ma's grace I had the good fortune of sewing quite a number of kanthas for Ma. Some for wrapping and some as bedspreads. At first I used new voile and then said to Ma, "Ma a kantha made of old cloth is more soft." After that She remembered it and provided me old cloth and said, "Here is the old cloth for you." Then I made kanthas of used cloth for Her and whenever I started making a kantha for Ma, I remembered my grandmother, as it was she who had taught me how to make a kantha when I was young and so I could offer these for Ma's service.

14

The huge metallic lion made by Nitai Pal of Kolkata and a throne with a large silver canopy were put in array at the Chandi Mandap. Ma's worship of the first day was to be performed at the Mandap. The Mandap and the throne were beautifully decorated with flower garlands. At 3 a.m., which was the time of Ma's birth, She was brought to the Mandap with the blowing of the conch shells and bells. She was prayed to ascend the throne. Ma was in half trance. She sat down on the step of the throne with folded hands. Songs, recitals and spell of silence went on. By the time the full-fledged worship of Ma was over it was dawn and light appeared on the eastern horizon of the Ganga. At the end of the worship and aarti, we offered flowers at Ma's feet.

A spacious pandal had been set up by the side of the main road. The pandal had been decorated by the artists from Shantiniketan arranged by Shrimati Leelavati Shah, wife of Mr. B.K. Shah. The main decoration consisted of fine paintings on earthen pitchers and plates. Such decoration was a novelty in this part of the country. The huge pavilion, the entrance to the pandal appeared to be an unprecedented sight.

At that time of Baisakh, the month of May, dreadful loo blows in Varanasi. It is very difficult to even stand outside. So, at the entrance of the pandal cold drinking water with wet gram and molasses were arranged for all.

Inside, khas-khas cooled by constant spray of water was hung on all sides and there were electric fans overhead. Despite the unbearable heat, people by thousands stayed at the pandal from morning to late night, attended different functions and were gratified at the sight of Ma and the saints.

Every morning the famous artist Ustad Bismillah Khan and his group played on the auspicious note of shehnai, which was followed by morning kirtan by Bibhu da, Bindu da, Hiru da, Moni da and the boys of the Vidyapeeth which echoed in the sky and air. The number of visitors increased day by day. From 8 a.m. the Raas party of Vrindavan performed 'Raasleela' and 'Mahaprabhu leela'. The numerous visitors eager to see the leela thronged the place which made it difficult for the other visitors and staff to even enter the pandal. Ma and the Mahatmas sat on one side of the dias, and the director of the Raasleela with his party of musicians took their place on the opposite side. Between them beautifully dressed Radhakrishna and their companions sat on decorated seats. Revered Haribaba stood behind Radhakrishna to fan them with a chowrie constantly. Each day a particular section of the play was staged. It was a unique leela, an experience to see how the small boys played such emotionally charged roles. The Raasleela produced a new devotion in the whole of Kashi. Raasleela was followed by the speeches of scholars and saints. After the recitals of Geeta and Chandi the morning session was over. Ma came back to Her room and the devotees started offering puja to Her. During this time we the girls of Kanyapeeth were busy sending the meals to the saints and eminent guests.

In the afternoon started religious discourses in the pandal. Learned scholars had arrived from different parts of India. They delivered speeches on different religious topics and about Ma.

After the evening kirtan fifteen minutes silence was observed. This was followed by many cultural programmes, which continued till late night. The famous 'Noder Nimai party' had come from Kolkata. They staged wonderful 'Mahaprabhu Leela'. Bibhu da and Bindu da had offered cordial invitations to the eminent musical talents of India for this festival. Ustad Ali Akbar Khan, Pandit Ravi Shankar, Ustad Alla Rakha, Ustad Bismillah Khan, Siddheshwari Bai, Girija Devi, Pandit Santa Prasad, Shri Sukhendu Goswami and many other singers, musicians, dancers in defiance of that intense heat, had presented themselves by the irresistible attraction of Ma and made their devotional offerings at Ma's feet by exhibiting their respective arts and enthralled the devotees present. We also, by Ma's grace, were charmed by seeing and listening to those rare talents.

I was told that Ustad Ali Akbar Khan and Ma belonged to the same village in East Bengal. Ustad Allaudin Khan's brother, uncle of Ustad Ali Akbar Khan, while in the country, used to sing together with Ma's father. Ustad Ali Akbar Khan conversed with Ma in their native dialect. Renowned dancer Uday Shankar, the elder brother of Pandit Ravi Shankar, was also a great devotee of Ma. Pandit Ravi Shankar was also devoted to Ma. Siddheshwari Bai sang a bhajan composed by her in praise of Ma. All greats were gratified performing for Ma and got blessings of Ma. Ustad Bismillah Khan stayed close to our ashram, almost every day the musical strain of the shehnai played by him spread out a message of solemnity in every direction. The rendition on the tabla by Pandit Shanta Prasad reminded the dance strokes of Nataraja Shiva.

On the occasion of Ma's birth anniversary there were different celebrations in the ashram. In the hall of our Kanyapeeth there were recitals of eleven Rudris, at the Chandi Mandap there were recitals of one hundred Chandi Patha, one hundred and eight Kumari worship, special offerings to the yajna kunda, etc. At the other temples of the ashram worship was offered and fruits and sweets were distributed among the patients of the hospital. One day Ma's Tuladan, i.e., weighing Ma with different articles took place. In the courtyard in front of the Kanyapeeth a huge balance was set up. Since morning the brahmins and pundits performed the allied rituals and recitals of the Vedas. Acharya Shri Agnishwatta Shastri (Batu da) conducted all the ceremonies. Ma was at that time in the basement (also referred to as 'cave') of the Kanyapeeth building. Batu da, Swami Paramanandaji, Haribaba and Avdhutji went to the cave to bring Ma to the venue. Ma was lying as if in a trance. After much prayer, Haribaba and Avdhutji were at last able to bring Her. Ma was made to sit on one pan of the huge balance. She sat with a copy of the

Shree Shree Ma during Tuladan

Bhagwat Geeta and a Shaligram in Her hands with eyes closed. On the other pan were placed rice, wheat, sesame and other crops, gold, silver, brass, copper and bronze, i.e., five metals, clothes and different kind of fruits to weigh and match Ma's body weight. All this was done in turns for different types of articles and materials. Dr. Pannalal, a staunch devotee of Ma, brought chunks of silver and weighed Her with silver alone. Strangely enough, Ma's weight differed on different times. As far as I remember it varied from a maund and a half to three maunds. At last during weighing Her against clothes we were tired of bringing out the clothes from the cave. Later on, these things were distributed among brahmins.

For one month, from the beginning of the festival to the end, there continued japa and kirtan in Ma's name. On the full moon day, 108 kumaris (virgin & maidens) and 11 batuks (little boys) with appropriate dress and make up, etc. were fed in the pandals. We the maidens of Kanyapeeth did aarti to Ma, the kumaris and batuks. Ma was moving about in the venue and placed (blessed) flowers on the heads of kumaris and batuks. By and by the last day of the festival approached up. The final offerings of Rudri, Chandi, etc., were done. People were arriving in unending lines not caring about the intense heat of Varanasi. From the afternoon onwards the pandal was packed to the full. The throne on the raised platform was decorated with flower garlands. On one side there were the seats for the sadhus. The recitals started from the evening. A little before 3 a.m. Ma was brought from the ashram to the pandal seated on a well decorated palanquin with the accompaniment of kirtan, blowing of the conch and striking of the bell metal. Ma was in a state of trance. On the insistence of the sadhus present, Ma sat on the throne, bowed to all around with folded hands and lay down.

Shree Shree Ma being carried back to the Ashram in a state of Samadhi after Janmotsav Puja

Among the chorus and shouts of 'Jai' the elaborate sixteen fold worship (shodashopachar) started. Songs, recitals and spells of silence continued. One bedecked kumari was worshipped and after the yajna the whole procedure came to an end. At that time the crimson glow of the sunrise in the sky seemed to spread out the joy of the festival in all directions. The worship was followed by aarti, flower offerings and obeisance by the devotees. A long line proceeded in a serpentine motion. Ma was lying in the same manner on the throne in a trance. First the sadhus then the ashramites and lastly the devotees made obeisance to Ma with flower garlands and received prasad and special silk handkerchiefs made for the diamond jubilee.

The obeisance went on till late in the day. After that Ma was taken back to the ashram. At noon in the hall of the Kanyapeeth, Ma was offered a royal feast (Bhog) consisting of 108 items. We offered food to Ma cooking various dishes. Generally when we cooked and fed Her, She commented about the cooking. But on that day somehow She was fed a little and She said nothing as She was in a trance.

After the festival Ma stayed in Varanasi for a few days and then went to Kolkata. It was October 1956. Durga puja was being celebrated at the house of Shri Binoy Kumar Banerjee, the father-in-law of Geeta, newly married daughter of Ma's brother Makhan (Shri Jadunath Bhattacharya). Many senior girls from Kanyapeeth accompanied Ma.

Kripalji and Bithu di stayed at Varanasi with some younger girls. During the few days of the puja, Bithu di and Kripalji arranged for amusing plays, eats and visits to see Durga puja. Bithu di asked the girls who wanted what kind of food the most. Those items and sweets were enjoyed during the puja. I recall that Guneeta (Kripalji's daughter) was at that time the youngest, only three and a half years old. When she was asked what she liked to eat, she said, "Fried neem (Indian lilac) with brinjal arum (water plantains) crushed." On hearing this we burst out laughing. She was a Punjabi girl and so young but she had the taste of a typical East Bengali. On the evening of Vijayadashmi, when we came from the worship room we found different kinds of presents on our desks. We heard that those were kept by Bithu di and Kripalji. We were delighted to receive the gifts.

15

After Durga puja Ma came back to Varanasi. She was seated on the marble seat in front of Kanyapeeth door and we were making obeisance, when She said to me, "Well you had a wish to go to Kolkata. If you had said this before you might go along with this body." I understood that Ma had been informed of my stomach ache. Ma said smilingly and I also smiled and thought as Ma said of my desire to go, then perhaps the matter may not be complicated one. I would be simply going to Kolkata and back. Ma left Jyoti di, a Kanyapeeth girl, at a hospital of Kolkata under the charge of Dr. Anil Maitra for her back pain. I was also sent there for treatment. After examination the surgeon diagnosed it was a case of appendicitis and it must be operated upon. The operation was done successfully. A few days later Jyoti di and I came back to Varanasi. As I knew nothing about the post-operation precautions, I continued to work as before like climbing steps, lifting heavy things and all, so the stomach pain relapsed. On hearing it, Ma sent me again to Kolkata. In spite of various investigations the pain continued. Then Ma took me to Dehradun for a change.

It was the winter of 1957. On Ma's directions Kripal ji was staying at Kishenpur ashram at Dehradun with five small girls namely Guneeta, Geeta, Sadhna, Bharati and Shakti. Yogesh da supervised the ashram at that time. Reaching Dehradun, Ma fixed all the details for me like in which room I should stay, what and when I should eat, when I would rest, where and who would give me an oil massage, when I should take a sunbath, etc., etc. She gave the charge of looking after me to Kripalji and Yogesh da. At that time Ma also stayed there for a pretty long time. It was the first time for me being at Dehradun. The place was very scenic, on top of it, being winters, the mountains were crowned with snow. The abundance of winter flowers was such a wonderful sight. Ma said to me, "Now you are in a cold place–take water, air and food regularly, walk along the hilly routes with nose and ears covered and do not expose yourself to plenty of cold."

One day the small girls were studying in the Sun, Ma put on a long loose fitting dress and sitting among the girls, said, "Look friends, this body has worn a frock like you." Ma was quiet in Her form. Pandit Agniswatta Shastri (Batu da) visited Dehradun for some time. Being well-versed in Sanskrit literature his pronunciation was perfect. Ma asked him to teach the girls to recite Mahimna Stotra of Shiva. So he started taking class every noon in the hall. It was not much crowded over there. Ma had a good rest and after sometime She went elsewhere.

We were quite happy in the charge of Yogesh da and Kripalji. Every afternoon we went for a walk along the hill tracts with Yogesh da. We visited a new place each day and sitting on a sheet heard the old tales of Ma from him while eating the afternoon tiffin.

When Ma was at Atpara (Bangladesh) in the house of the elder brother of Baba Bholanath, She had to do all the domestic work Herself. Just behind the room She stayed in, there was a shallow pond, in which She cleansed the utensils. The low caste women of the village came to Her and became acquainted. They helped Ma in Her work unasked. Since they were of low-caste they cleansed the utensils stealthily and Ma washed them anew with fresh water. In this way they formed a good relationship with Ma in a short time.

In the villages most people had mango and jackfruit trees in their gardens. It was the usual practice of the villagers to pick up mangoes under the trees during that particular season. One day those women picked up some good mangoes and gave them to Ma to eat. Ma could by no means refuse their heartful offering. She took a little and distributed the rest among them. She said, "You do so much for this body but this body can do nothing for you." Then the illiterate village women said, "You speak to us with a smile, this gives us a lot of pleasure."

I have heard from Yogesh da that once Ma was staying at the house of a Sub-Judge near Siddheshwari at Dhaka. Baba Bholanath was very ill then. The eminent doctors and surgeons of Dhaka diagnosed it as an abscess of the liver. It might burst if not operated at once. A homeopathic doctor was treating him from the beginning. His medicine was maintained. Ma arranged for some particular type of food—moong pulses, soup of green papaya and soup of Magur or Singhi fish (fresh water walking catfish). After making these arrangements Ma took Her seat on the cot of Baba Bholanath. Ma did not eat anything. About 17–18 days passed this way. Towards the end, the fruits brought by the devotees were kept in the shelf of an almirah. Ma took out from them a perfect stalked fruit and gave it to Brahmachari Kulada da to be offered to the yajna which was being performed at Siddheshwari Kali Bari. After the offering when the fruit burst open, a stick was put inside it and as Ma opened Her mouth it was touched to Her tongue at Her directions. She also directed to put into Her mouth a sip of water from what was offered to the deity in small brass glasses. This was Ma's food at that time.

From that time on started the custom of fruit offerings at yajna. At last while going to Siddheshwari, Ma called Yogesh da to accompany Her. After the offering, Ma took up a brass glass and began to rub Her hand on its edge and kept saying, "Will you be able? Will you be able? No, just see if there is a billhook." Kulada da said, "Yes, there is a billhook." And he looked for it which was there for splinting wood, but it couldn't be found. Ma again said, "Will you be able? Will you be able?" Saying so She went on rubbing Her hand on the glass-edge. Next She said, "No, seek out the billhook." Kulada da found it out. Due to constant cutting of wood, all its edge was crooked and it was not sharp anymore. Taking up the billhook in Her hand Ma pointed to a spot above Her elbow and said to Yogesh da, "See if you can cut it." Yogesh da pressed the spot with his left hand and began to slash with the billhook which was completely blunt. As Yogesh da tried to cut, the billhook pressed inside Ma's soft arm but did not cut. Ma said, "Can't you cut?" Hearing this when Yogesh da tried next, Ma said, "You will have to cut by one stroke only." Then Yogesh da used the billhook with full force and cut deep into Ma's arm, but there was no blood. Ma pressed and tried to get some blood. Seeing this Yogesh da pressed with full force and got one drop of blood. Then Ma asked him to put the drop of blood in a Bilva leaf and offer it to the yajna fire. In this way Ma took the operation crisis on Her own body and Baba Bholanath got well soon.

Once Ma was in Dhaka. Bhaiji was very ill. All of a sudden Ma asked Yogesh da to go on an Agyatvas for one year observing silence. She also said, "If you meet anybody on your way, even if you see this body, don't talk or introduce yourself to anybody." According to Ma's instructions he started towards Uttarakhand and reached Haridwar. He took abode in a small cave by the road side. At that time there was a Kumbh-mela at Haridwar. People used to pass in front of his cave. Suddenly he saw Baba Bholanath and Ma passing through that way. Yogesh da wanted to hint about his stay there. Since by Ma's instruction he could not face Ma, he went to his cave and tried to sing loudly, but alas! no sound came out of his throat. He used to sing well. At last giving up, he came out and sat lowering his head by the road side. As Ma passed by, he saw Her feet and bowed. Ma also saw him and this She disclosed when Yogesh da returned after one year. Ma said, "This body saw you and proceeding further showed to Bholanath also."

One day Ma asked Bhaiji to compose some prayers to sing everyday in the ashram. Bhaiji sat the whole night with paper and pen, tried his utmost. But nothing proper came up. He composed something and discarded it dissatisfied and then he fell asleep. Then suddenly the following verses were seen clearly and he took the pen and wrote down the whole prayer quickly. Next day he read these lines to Ma and She asked Yogesh da to set a tune for it. So it is very clear that this prayer song was composed by Ma's kheyal.

Jaya Hridayavasini Shuddha Sanatani Shree Anandamayee Ma,
Bhuvana Ujjala Janani Nirmala Punya Vistarini Ma,
Rajrajeshwari Swaha Swadha Gauri Pranbarupini Ma,
Soumya Soumyatara Satyamanohara Purnaparatpara Ma,
Ravishashi Kundala Maha Vyomakuntala Vishwarupini Ma,
Aishwaryabhatima Madhuryapratima Mahimamandita Ma,
Rama Manorama Shantishanta Kshama Sarvadevamayee Ma,
Sukhada Varada Bhakti Gyanada Kaivalyadayini Ma
Vishwaprasabini Vshwapalini Vishwasanharini Ma,
Bhaktapranarupa Murtimati Kripa Trilokatarini Ma,
Karyakaranabhuta Bhedabhedatita Paramadevata Ma,
Vidyavinodini Yogijanaranjini Bhavabhaybhanjini Ma,
Mantra Veejatmika Vedaprakashika Nikhile Vyapika Ma,
Saguna Swarupa Nirguna Nirupa Mahabhavamayee Ma,
Mugdha Charachara Gahenirantara Tavaguna Madhuri Ma,
(Mora) Mili Prane Prane Pranami Shree Charane jaya jaya jaya Ma.
Dako Ma Ma Ma Ma Ma Ma
Bolo Ma Ma Ma Ma Ma Ma!

16

Once Dadabhai was very ill. She had a plaster from the neck to her knees. She was suffering from loss of appetite too. She was staying in Mr. B.K. Shah's house of Vile Parle, Mumbai.

Renu di and myself were looking after her. All of a sudden Ma came there accompanied by Swami Paramanandaji and Buni di. At that time there was no room for Ma's use or stay. A tent was pitched up in the garden for Her. From the morning till night Ma instructed me to prepare different dishes made of suji and sometimes rice and pulses made with a different recipe. Everything was made with cereals, so Renu di and Buni di could not make or touch as they were not Shuddhacharis.

One day Ma ordered for a brass cooker. She asked me to prepare rice, pulses and different vegetables cut into small pieces. Then She put a little oil, turmeric powder, ginger and black pepper paste, water and the soft layer of a green coconut into a vegetable. After it was boiled Ma asked me to open the lid. But it was too hot to open. As Ma insisted, I asked Her to hold the legs of the oven so that I could open the lid. Since there was no piece of cloth around to hold the hot lid, I took Ma's silver spoon and inserted it into the ring of the lid and opened the same with both hands. Holding the oven, Ma's delicate fingers would have burnt, but nothing happened. She asked me to take out a piece of the vegetable and put it in Her mouth. I hesitated as it was boiling hot. But Ma was impatient and kept insisting, so I put one spoonful of vegetable into Her mouth. Keeping the vegetable on Her tongue She inhaled cool air to cool it and then swallowed the same. She said, "Go, go fast and feed didi this hot vegetable. Ah! fine taste, she will like it." Ma was in Her tent and Dadabhai was lying on her bed in the drawing room of Bhaiya's (Mr. B.K. Shah) house. I was feeding one spoon to Ma and rushing to the drawing room to feed Dadabhai next. It was a unique bhog of the Goddess and Her child indeed. I don't think such bhog occurred ever. Generally, we never fed Ma too hot lest it hurt Her. But that day She ate boiling vegetable and held the burning oven with Her delicate fingers, but nothing happened–everything was Her kheyal. Affection personified and love for Her child was displayed through this feeding leela. Later Ma asked me to have the prasad. It was marvelous!

The first batch of brahmacharis of Dhaka, Shahbag and Siddheshwari, consisted of Yogesh da, Kamalakanta da and Atul da. They underwent many hardships to do penance in the ashram, but were fortunate enough to have the affection of Ma, Baba Bholanath and Bhaiji. Yogesh da too was very affectionate. At Dehradun Yogesh da and Kripal ji took care of me. Pure milk was available there. Kripal ji used to buy lots of milk, churn to make butter and feed the girls. My appetite was poor due to illness. The doctor prescribed curd for me. But I did not like it at all. So Yogesh da prepared rasgulla every day for me. Giribala di cooked for us. Yogesh da instructed her to prepare various items. Truly there is no comparison to his affection. Kripal ji also tried utmost so that I had not to suffer a bit.

After some time a telegram arrived informing that Ma was to reach Kishenpur ashram within a short time. We had hardly done up Ma's room and the hall when Her taxi came to a halt at the portico. Ma was accompanied by Mrs. Rama Saxena who had just lost her husband; Kusum ji, a relative to Bhagwandas, Anasuya ji of Mumbai and a new Brahmachari from Gujarat. Ma got down from the car and came to the hall and said to me, "Buni and others have not come with this body, you have to look after everything. Those who have accompanied me are mentally very disturbed. So you should arrange for their food with care." The heavens seemed to come down on my head. I had never served Ma alone before. I did not know what should I do to take care of the grief stricken guests.

I entered into Ma's kitchen uttering *Jai Ma*. I understood that Ma had not taken even a glass of water all the way, as there was none to look after Her needs. I wanted to prepare candy water for Her. But when I tried to pour water from the pitcher the cover fell down with a sharp sound. Ma was standing in front. She said, "If you go on like this how will you manage? I said many words of praise about you on the way and is this how you should behave?" I said within myself–'What was the point of praising me or to descend on me without any of your assistants.' Well, I asked and She showed me how much candy and pepper I should add to the candy water. Ma also told me that for Her lunch I should make chapattis and vegetables. All kinds of vegetables should be sliced big, washed and should be boiled by adding salt. However food for the guests was cooked by Giribala di. I fed Ma chapatti, boiled vegetables and milk. After the meal Ma remained in the hall. She said to me, "Finish your meal quickly and then we should go upstairs." I ate, washed Ma's utensils, cleaned the kitchen and then went to Ma. She went to the upper room with me and lay down. After a while She asked me to bring a bottle of oil from the almirah. During those days a peculiar sound would be ringing in Her ears and head. As She didn't take any medicines, Haribaba had suggested that She should apply almond oil on Her head. She asked me to comb Her hair with my fingers and then to take oil on the tip of the fingers and rub it into the roots of the hair. She also said to take care that the hair did not turn oily. As I started applying oil slowly according to Ma's directions, Ma kept lying with Her eyes closed. She again said, "When you do something for this body you should utter the name of Shiva mentally." I applied oil in the same way on Her head.

In the afternoon Ma walked for a while on the roof of the portico and then came down. It was spring marking the end of winter. On all sides magnolia and various flowers peculiar to the hills were in full bloom. At intervals cuckoos were heard singing. A few devotees, who had learnt about Ma's arrival, came to the ashram. Those days there was no temple in the ashram except Ma's room and the satsang hall. We girls did our evening kirtans as usual and Ma was in Her own mood. Walking around for a while and then going upstairs She exchanged a few words with Yogesh da, had Her supper and went to bed.

Anasuya ji had come from Mumbai with Ma. She was a strict performer of austerities and took milk, fruits and boiled vegetables once a day. Ma told me to arrange for her meals. The problem was Anasuya ji did not care to have a proper meal. It was difficult to make her eat. I was at my wit's end, but it was Ma's order. She stayed for a pretty long time. Seva ji (Dr. Miss Sharda Sharma) came to Ma. It was strange that mere touch of Ma made Seva ji fall into a trance. Frequently at noon she and I used to massage Ma. I knew nothing about massage so I picked up the technique from Seva ji. Since she was a doctor her way of massaging was systematic and something special. Seva ji had a great affection for me.

One day while we were massaging Shree Ma, She said, “In Dhaka when this body used to lie on the mud floor for hours together, this body never suffered from any ailment or any kind of pain. Ants and insects used to go past this body without climbing on this body or biting it. Later since Jyotish and Khukuni felt that this body may feel cold or there will be pain in the body, they used to slip a mat or a sheet under this body. Since this thought came to them, this body also started feeling cold and pain.” Many times Ma had explained ‘this body’ to react to individual “thoughts” accordingly.

“In the village there was no custom of ladies wearing shoes so this body also never wore any. Jyotish was the first one who brought a pair of sandals and put it on my feet. They were leather chappals with lace. They remained on my feet. This body neither opened it nor tied it. After being bound like this for a considerable time the feet swelled up. On seeing this, Jyotish was greatly repentant. He quickly untied the sandals and started rubbing my feet.”

Another day Ma said, “Once at Siddeshwari this body had very high temperature. This body did not take any medicine. Seeing this Akhandananda baba (retired civil surgeon) as a doctor thought–Ma may not take any medicine but what is the harm in measuring the blood pressure? After taking Bholanath’s permission he wrapped the cuff of the blood pressure machine around my arm and took blood pressure. The side which he tied the cuff was swollen from head to toe after that.” This incident took place about 30–40 years ago and when Ma showed us in 1957, there was still swelling on that side. It was really unbelievable.

One day before bathing Ma, I was giving Her an oil massage. Ma showed me Her navel and said, "Are you seeing the navel of this body? It is in the shape of a conch shell." She pulled my right hand and placed my finger on the ridge of the nose between the eyebrows and said, "On Shree Krishna's nose they paint a 'Rasakali' (a sign of an inverted leaf of basil, etc. just below the 'U' shaped sign on the fore head) and here in the case of this body the bone of the nose is shaped naturally like that."

At that time there was no temple at Kishenpur ashram. One night Ma was walking in the courtyard near the mango tree. Kripalji, I and a couple of others were standing there. From the leaves of the mango tree, drops of honey were falling on the floor. The floor under the tree was sticky. Seeing this Ma said, "Once upon a time similarly honey used to drop from the hair of this body. As a result the hair had become matted."

One day I cut the nails on Ma's fingers. I spread a piece of paper on Ma's bed and was cutting Her nails. The nails of Ma's hands were semicircular in shape. So with a small scissor I was cutting them bit by bit. Ma was narrating some amusing tales and we were laughing profusely. In the meantime a gust of wind came through the window to blow away the paper with the pieces of nails on the bed. The pieces of nails got scattered on the bed. Ma said, "So you have scattered the nails on the bed, now prick this body with these nails." I did not loose my nerve and at once asked Her, "Ma, how many pieces of nails were there?" Ma replied sharply, "Thirty five." Well I picked up exactly 35 pieces on a piece of paper. Ma gave me an affectionate pat on the back. I felt to be on the top of the world.

This time Ma stayed at Kishenpur, a secluded place then, for quite some time. There were no festivities and no crowd. I was with Ma round the clock, and it was a real joy. One day She said that She would take a bath and asked to make arrangements for the same. A few buckets of boiled water were kept in the bathroom. According to Ma's directions, some powder (may be the seed of some flower) was soaked in a small pot. At noon I entered the bathroom with Ma. At first I massaged oil over the whole body. Then washed Her hands and feet with soap. At last She took the little pot with soaked powder and slowly put all of Her hair into it. Then She turned the pot upside down on Her head. Moving the pot round and round She soaked Her whole head neatly. Strangely enough the water of the pot didn't spill out on Her face or forehead. I went on seeing with astonishment the way She rubbed Her hair. Then She bathed with buckets full of water poured on Her head. After the long bath I wiped Her whole body with a towel. She wiped Her feet with a small towel and gave it to me saying, "Take it with you".

Ma's bathroom in Kishenpur ashram was rather small. Ma was seated on a small stool and I sat by Her side with both Her feet on my lap. The bath continued for two to three hours. After the bath Ma entered Her room and sat with Her hair disheveled. I was just feasting my eyes on Ma's exquisite beauty.

A devotee had started a new factory of making vests in Dehradun. He presented a number of vests of different sizes to Ma. Out of those Ma picked up one for me. I said, "I have all I need, what should I do with more?" Ma said, "I don't care, I give it to you and you wear it."

17

For a few days, we had a jolly good time with Ma. She left for Delhi and sent a word from there that I too should be taken to Delhi. As instructed by Ma I went with Yogesh da to Delhi by car. Dr. Santosh Sen (son of Dr J.K. Sen, an old devotee of Ma) the eminent surgeon of India was given a call. He examined me in Ma's presence and advised me to be admitted to his nursing home. Before my admission, one night Ma was lying in the hall. Dadabhai, Swamiji, Buni di and others were around Her. A talk was going on, I went to make obeisance to Ma. She softly said to Dadabhai and Buni di, "Can't you see the dark shadow of death always hovering around her?" I heard it later from Buni di.

The day of the operation was fixed. Before going to the nursing home, I bowed down to Ma. She put a garland around my neck and asked, "Are you not afraid?" With a smile I said, "Why should I be afraid? At the time of operation I would be put under anesthesia, I shall feel nothing."

Seeing Dadabhai in tears Ma said, "Didi, she smiles, then why do you weep?" On the day of the operation as I was being taken to the operation theatre, a few of Ma's devotees–Pankaj da, Bibi di (daughter of Shree Amal Sen), Kripal ji, my father and some other Guru brothers and sisters were present there. All were shedding tears. I wondered why they were weeping. I was an unattached ashramite, with no attachments back in the world, my death would be of no loss to anybody. I asked myself–do I find the idea of death peaceful? Then I felt there would be one loss, i.e., the life which brought me close to such a 'Ma', would be lost forever. That indeed would be a great loss.

At the time of my operation, Ma told Pushpa di to do kirtan and Billo ji to sit close to the phone. As soon as my operation starts, She should receive the call of Kripal ji from the nursing home and inform Ma immediately.

At that time Upadhyaya ji, the personal secretary of Pandit Jawaharlal Nehru had come to convey a message of Nehru ji to Ma. While talking to him Ma suddenly became silent.

Smt Indira Gandhi, Shree Shree Ma, Swami Paramananda and Pandit Jawaharlal Nehru

Seeing Ma's abnormal appearance with fixed eyes he was frightened. Waiting for a while Upadhyaya ji made a bow and went away. As per Ma's instruction Billo ji received Kripal ji's telephone call and went upstairs to inform Ma where she found Her silent and stiff. Billo ji also got scared to see Ma's lifeless expression. The operation lasted for about three hours during which Ma was silent.

The ward in which I stayed in Dr. Sen's nursing home had eight beds, each separated from the other by thick white curtain. After the major operation that night I could not sleep at all. Kripal ji who attended me the whole day was too tired and slept in an armchair near my bed. The nurse was not there either. Suddenly I saw near the white screen on my right side a dwarf, terrible to look at, with extraordinary big head and big roundish torch like eyes trying to reach me by stretching its short hand. I distinctly saw that it cast no shadow behind on the screen. I had heard that ghosts cast no shadows. Was it the messenger of death? I realised that as soon as it touched my bed, it would spell my death. I called Kripal ji several times but my feeble voice did not reach her. Then I remembered that Ma had given me a garland before I had left the ashram and I had kept it under my pillow. But it was not there. Before my operation, the nurse had kept it elsewhere and made the bed to suit post-operative care. Thinking that it might have been put in the locker, I touched the locker with great difficulty as it was pushed aside. The moment I touched the locker the dwarf like messenger of death vanished.

Ma came to see me in the nursing home the next day. Through the grace of Ma I recovered gradually. At Ma's direction Kripal ji and Buni di took great care of me. After one month I returned to the ashram. Those days Dadabhai was in the Delhi ashram. So Ma made all arrangements for me before moving somewhere else.

After that Ma used to come to Delhi ashram quite often. Many days had passed after the operation but I had not recovered fully. One night Ma called me aside and said, "After getting up from the bed tomorrow morning come to this body."

Next morning I went to Ma's room. Following Ma's instruction I raised Her mosquito net. She asked me to lie down on the carpet near Her bed and said, "Do just as this body does." Ma performed many asans and pranayams (breathing exercises) one by one in different postures. The expressions on Ma's face and eyes were beyond description (there were a great number of poses of Her hands). At least 30–40 types of yogic asanas She did along with harmonic pranayams. After about an hour's practice of asanas, Ma lay in Shavasana posture and I also followed the same.

After a long spell of training, one noon She said, "Bring one of your petticoats and scissors. As I brought them Ma instructed me to cut the petticoat in the shape of a salwar and asked me to sew it up. When it was done, She told me to try it. Finally She said, "Go to Dr. Santosh Sen, show him all the asanas and tell him that this body wants to know whether you can perform them or not. While displaying these asanas before the doctor, wear this salwar." Really, how much caring is Ma for such poor children like us! Santosh da was a very busy doctor, yet he saw me performing all the asans as Ma wished and said, "You must perform them as Ma said, I have nothing to say about it." As directed by Ma, I practiced the asanas for a long time, but gave them up when Ma asked me to discontinue them. It is sad to say that I forgot them later, being out of practice.

It was October 1959, when the queen of Mandi made arrangements for Durga puja celebrations at Varanasi ashram on a large scale in the presence of Ma. As usual the worship of Goddess Durga was started on a pitcher (a prevalent ritual) from the first day of the moon phase. Many devotees arrived from different places for the occasion. I observed Ma's unprecedented divine mood during all the days of Durga puja. The ceremony and celebrations were at a princely scale and it was a grand affair indeed. Starting right from the pratipada, Benarasi sarees and gold ornaments were offered everyday to the Goddess, Ma and the maidens (kumaris).

On Mahashtami day, when the worship at the mandap and the flower offerings (pushpanjali) to the Goddess by devotees were over, Ma took Her seat on the cot in the courtyard. Numerous devotees, men and women, were busy worshipping Ma. Sitting in front of Ma, I was distributing fruits, sweets, garlands and flowers hallowed by Ma's benediction. On Ma's cot, clothes etc. lay in heaps. After sitting in the same position for long, Ma moved about a little. I noticed that under Ma's knees there was a red lotus. Being concerned that it might cause ache in Ma's legs due to the liquid extract of the flower, I kept a watchful eye on when She would change Her leg's position, so that I could remove the lotus from her feet. Much later Ma raised Her knees a little. I quickly inserted my hand to take hold of the flower. I found that it was not a flower at all but the pink feet of Ma. One was forbidden to touch Ma's feet and I had just done it. I was afraid that Ma would give me a good scolding and order me to move away from Her. I looked into Her eyes in fear and was surprised to see that She was looking at me with a divine smile. This indulgence from Her, the look and touch of Her lotus feet filled my heart and soul with great delight.

The puja celebrations were over with great pomp and gaiety. After the worship on the tenth day (of the moon phase), we the girls of Kanyapeeth bade final goodbye to the Goddess.

Next the married women did the same to the Goddess and started applying vermillion on the Goddess. A few of us were playing bells and drums in the verandah. The bell plate was in my hand. Suddenly a lady from Marwar stood behind me closely with her body touching me. I felt uneasy and pushed her with my back. Strangely, I still found her sticking to me. I pushed her again and she moved again. The shoving went on till the lady was pushed back to the courtyard. Though she went down right to the yard, she did not retaliate even once. I wondered who she was. Looking behind I found a married woman with a long red gorgeous veil. In the meantime everyone started looking for Ma. She was not in Her room. Where was She? Suddenly in front of the mandap Ma cast aside Her veil and began to laugh loudly. Looking back I saw that the lady pushed by me was none but Ma Herself. I thought that in this way Ma made us understand that no matter how often we might push Her away, She never leaves us nor pushes us back. This is my Ma–kindness and affection personified.

Finding Ma in front, the married women, after performing the final ceremony for the Goddess, began to apply vermillion to the forehead of Ma. Generally Ma did not come to the bidding adieu ceremony of the Goddess. That day it was a special occasion when Ma presented Herself, so it was a great joy to see Her.

In the verandah of Ma's room stood some ladies such as Miss Lalita Pathak, Miss Nirmal Handu and others. Ma applied vermillion to their foreheads from Her own. Next, while entering Her room She called some of us (maidens) one by one and rubbed Her forehead against ours. The almirah in

Ma's first floor room was fitted with a large looking glass. She held my head with both Her hands, drew it to Her face, rubbed vermillion on my forehead, turned the face towards the looking glass and said, "Just see, how you look!" Seeing vermillion on my forehead in the looking glass, I blushed. Ma thus indulged in vermillion play with some maidens. Strangely enough Ma's constant companion Dadabhai, Belu di, Bimla di and some other married women were not present there at that time. They could not even know about this leela of Ma. All were Ma's infallible fancies.

18

Once at Varanasi Durga puja was being celebrated in the presence of Ma. On the Mahashtami day suddenly Ma went to Allahabad accompanied by Buni di. At Allahabad respected Gopal Thakur observed Durga puja every year. That year also the worship was going on. Since Ma was in Allahabad,

Gopal Thakur, Shree Shree Ma, Gurupriya di, Didima, Swami Krishnanandaji and Dr. Govind Gopal Mukhopadhyaya

Gopal Thakur cordially invited Her to the puja. Also he announced to his disciples that this year not only the earthen Mother but also the living Divine Mother would appear. When Ma reached there, Goddess Durga was being bathed in a ceremonial way. Gopal Thakur was loudly uttering mantras and pouring pitchers of different types of water on the Goddess. At that moment the Divine Mother (Ma) entered the pavilion and with great pleasure Gopal Thakur emptied the pitcher on Ma's head. The devotees started shouting '*Jai Guru, Jai Ma, Jai Durga*'. After the bath of Durga the worship began.

Ma would return to Varanasi. The devotees started doing obeisance to Ma. She distributed sweets to all. While coming from Varanasi, Ma had asked Buni di to bring some sweets with her. She had brought not more than 50 pieces in a small basket. During distribution, Ma told Buni di not to take off the cover of the basket and She distributed to innumerable people and at last, when the cover was taken off still there were two-three pieces of sweets left.

It was perhaps between 1960-61 when Ma, Dadabhai and a few of us were at Delhi ashram. I was not keeping well. After investigation the doctor diagnosed stones in the kidney. Hearing this Shree Jiten Dutta, a devotee of Ma said that he also had the same problem. On taking water of boiled kulattha kalai (horse gram) the stones got out. That evening a crowd of visitors assembled in the hall for Ma's darshan, a little later Ma entered the hall. Whoever approached Ma to do obeisance, Ma would ask him or her–"Do you know kulattha kalai?" Next day many brought different packets containing kulattha kalai for Ma. She told me to put them away and a full bag was collected. At night Ma called Hemi di and said, "Wash kulattha kalai at night and keep it soaked in water. Next morning boil it in a lot of water. When the water reduces to half take it down and sift it, then cook it with pieces of ginger in clarified butter. Otherwise it would not be palatable and she will not be able to take it." Listening to this Jitenda said, "I simply boiled it and drank the water. Ma is making special arrangements for Her dear daughter." Truly Ma's affection knew no bounds.

Two or three days later Raja ben (Smt. Raja Khaitan) came to visit Ma. She told her too about my illness. Hearing it she said, "Oh Ma, there is a very good homeopathic doctor in Kolkata. I shall take Vishuddha with me and get her treated by him. She will be alright." She was going to Kolkata next day by morning flight. Ma said that She would send me with somebody else by train. But Raja ben insisted on taking me with her by plane. So I had to be ready quickly. Since one was not allowed to carry heavy baggage in the plane, Ma managed to get one small suitcase from somewhere and decided Herself what should be carried in it. It was Ma Herself, who packed the suitcase for me. Seeing all these developments some ashramites teased me saying–"Ah, the Ma's pet! She is off in a plane simply because the kidney has developed stones. We too have many diseases, but none could avail a plane....."

Next day early morning I went to Ma's room to make obeisance to Her. It was a winter morning, so it was quite dark. But I found that expecting me, Ma was sitting on Her bed with the mosquito net raised up. As soon as I bowed She smiled sweetly, passed Her hand over my head and back, handed over Her wrapper to me and said, "While travelling in a plane one often vomits, if you feel uneasy vomit into this wrapper and put it into the pocket in front of the seat." As there was very little time, I set out in a hurry. Ma kept gazing at me as long as I could see Her. Later I came to know that shortly after I set out, Ma went up to the roof and stood there staring at the sky. A little later when a plane was passing overhead She asked Shakti da, who was there at that time, "Is Vishuddha in this plane?" After Shakti da confirmed Ma kept staring at the plane as long as it was visible. Later She went back to Her room. I am blessed with Ma's affection.

Once during summer Ma was in Varanasi. One day the afternoon snacks of the girls consisted of a drink of watermelon and mashed local sour mango. As usual first we offered it to Ma in our temple. I was distributing the snacks and as Ma was present there I thought I could serve Her some and She would like it. In such matters Buni di helped me a lot. At once I told Buni di. Ma was then lying in the ground floor room of Kanyapeeth. I took the snacks and fed Ma. While having the sour mangoes, Ma related in jest that in how many ways She had eaten mashed mangoes in Her childhood. Next day Ma ordered a lot of mangoes and asked us to sit in front of Her room and offered us as many mangoes as we could eat. While we served sour mangoes to Her, She gave sweet 'langra' mangoes to eat to our heart's content. We cannot give Her anything. If we give Her a mere trifle, She accepts it joyfully and returns a handful.

In the Kanyapeeth it is a strict rule with us to promote ourselves as shuddhachari after observing ashram rules for one year as per Ma's instructions (these days the duration is of three years). Afterwards we take bath in the Ganga, do japa for a particular number of times and feed Ma to become a shuddhachari. Since I had to be hospitalized and became a non-shuddhachari, I had to be sanctified again.

With Ma's consent there was arrangement for Ma's lunch (bhog) at the Kanyapeeth. It was a pity that Ma was not keeping well then. She went almost without food. Under these circumstances I asked Dadabhai that what should I cook for Ma. She asked me to ascertain Ma's wishes in this matter. When I asked Ma, She gave me a free hand to cook whatever I liked. I like light food without much spices. So I decided to prepare a number of such plain dishes. Kshama di, then in-charge of Kanyapeeth, however disagreed. She said each girl should cook for Ma–Brahmins and non-Brahmins. Younger, elder, all girls cooked different items according to their choice. All the ashramites and Kanyapeeth girls were invited. It was like a minor festival. Everybody was busy in cooking.

We made a place for Ma's bhog in our worship room and displayed many items of food there. Dressed in a silk dhoti given by Ma and with sandal paste on my forehead I went to call Ma to our puja room. Ma was delighted to see me and She said, "Yes, your dress is just for this body." I escorted Ma to our worship room and made Her sit at the place of bhog. The room was not spacious and there were so many items of food. After they were arranged in order, little space was left. First I helped Ma to sit on a wooden seat, offered Her a garland and sandal paste. Then I began to feed Her. On the verandah outside the puja room, along the three sides, Dadabhai and the girls of Kanyapeeth were having a sight of the bhog.

Ma was in a fine mood. She sat with one leg placed on the other, Her hair tucked up in a top knot. She looked wonderful. After having a few big morsels Ma asked me, "Who taught you to feed like this?" I smiled and said, "Dadabhai". Ma smiled mischievously and looked at Dadabhai. While I was feeding Her, She was telling us some amusing tales in a jolly mood. Beludi, Dadabhai's youngest sister came to put forward one item after another towards me. I continued to feed Her a bit of each dish. Generally after eating one item as much as She wanted She signalled not to give any more. But that day She was so absorbed in telling tales that She did not say anything to stop feeding. I was putting food into Her mouth one after another. I didn't realize that I should not feed Her so much. All the dishes in all would be about hundred. For a long time Ma had a problem in digesting anything. Some other time Dadabhai had warned me not to offer Her fried and spicy food in excess. But strangely enough, that day all were too absorbed in Ma's tales, nobody noticed anything. However, after Ma's meal was over, when I put the glass of water before Her, She took one sip of water and said, "I had a kheyal to be Damodar today. Did I restrict you to offer me more food?" Then I realised that Ma had not. I fed Her one item after another. I also thought that if Beludi had not removed the front plates and put forward those in the rear, I might have fed Her all absentmindedly. I noticed that in the pot of rice only small quantity was left and a number of pots were quite empty. There were many kinds of vegetables, pulses, fries, chutney, kheer, chops, samosa, etc. served in a large quantity in large bowls. Out of these the quantity that Ma had taken was not little. To have so much at a time was impossible, specially in view of Her poor health at that time. This was an expression of Her fancy and unending grace for us.

After this special bhog of Ma we had prasad. From the exuberance of happiness we forgot that Ma was unwell. However She was O.K. A few days later we were studying in the hall. Ma came and with folded hands said, "Friends, tomorrow you girls will have a feast on behalf of this body." Knowing this we were highly delighted. Generally, if it was an occasion of special bhog, we the shuddhachari girls of Kanyapeeth did the cooking. On that day we were special invitees of Ma, She didn't allow us to go to the kitchen. She ordered Bimla di, Belu di, Mami ma and Tulsi to cook for us. The other day we had prepared so many special dishes for Ma, so She also made an exclusive menu for us. The bhog was offered in the temple as usual. After the bhog Ma invited us to the hall. She Herself arranged the seats for us. When we were in the hall, Ma showed each of us where we should sit. Making me sit in the middle, She made others sit in order on two sides.

Ma's seat was laid opposite to mine. After we took our seats Ma offered flowers on each one's head and did our aarti with incense sticks and panchpradeep, i.e., five-wicks light. In the meantime Belu di and Tulsi started to serve us at the direction of Ma. On Ma's request we started eating. After the worship and aarti, first Ma folded Her hands and then made obeisance and then laying down on the floor with folded hands on Her head and tears in Her eyes, She exclaimed, "Oh! maiden Goddess forgive me, maiden Goddess forgive me." Saying these words She began to roll on the floor slowly as if in a trance and wept profusely. It was a strange sight. Obviously we could not eat anymore. We observed silence while eating, but listening to Ma we could not remain silent and prayed to Ma, "Please Ma, calm down." After a long time Ma got up slowly, still in trance, went to Her room and laid down on Her bed. Dadabhai sat in front of Ma's room. Ma was in such a sad mood that none of us had a word to say. The whole day passed like that. In the evening Ma moved about a little. Dadabhai then put in a word or two. As Ma ate nothing the whole day She was persuaded to drink a little candy water. Dadabhai said slowly, "Ma, why do you ask for forgiveness? It is we who commit offences at every step." Ma said, "Didi, if those who have come at the call of this body are guilty of any offence, those become the doings of this body only."

Dadabhai got the Kanyapeeth established on Ma's kheyal. She used to love the girls of Kanyapeeth like her own children. Thus it was obvious that if any one commented adversely about any girl of the Kanyapeeth, she used to be hurt.

Today when Ma said, "Kumari Bhagwati forgive me" and was weeping profusely–Dadabhai repeatedly said to her– "We keep doing things wrong (worth punishing) repeatedly at every step, please do forgive us, why should You ask for forgiveness?"

Till about dusk Ma kept lying in the same mood. After that when Dadabhai noticed Ma moving around a bit, she asked me to enquire from Ma–if some candy water could be offered to Her. Ma consented and I made some candy water and fed Her. Gradually Ma started speaking in Her normal self.

Ma mentioned the names of four senior ashramites and said, "Didi, someone said to this body, 'my mother never said such words', another one said 'we never saw such things in our house', someone wants to leave the ashram and go back, etc. etc. For those who have left their home and hearth and have come to this body–their faults are also the faults of this body–that is why this asking of forgiveness from the 'Kumari Shakti'."

About that day's incident or leela of Ma weeping and asking for forgiveness–many thought that I may have done something wrong and that's why Ma was in such a state. But on being repeatedly asked by Dadabhai "Why should You ask for forgiveness?", Ma explained the reason by way of such a leela.

This reminds me of something I heard from Yogesh da. Ma was then in Dhaka. Bhaiji used to visit Ma every day. Ma was strolling in the ground of Ramana. Bhaiji used to keep an eye on Ma from a distance. In due course Bhaiji used to leave for his office. One day while Ma was strolling on the ground, Bhaiji was due at home for some work. He asked Brahmachari Kamlakanta da to stay on and keep an eye on Ma. Kamlakanta da kept standing there even when Ma asked him to go somewhere else on an errand. He told Ma politely that Bhaiji had ordered him to look after Ma and so he might be excused from going somewhere else. To protect Ma's body was his foremost duty. Ma made no comment. Just a few days later Ma fell seriously ill. Then Ma said, "That day I said something to Kamalakanta, but he didn't listen to me. That accounts for this present state of this body. When something is said, some energy is associated with the word, when that word is not listened to, the energy comes back and hurts the body of the speaker. I told something to Kamalakanta, because it was for his good, even then he did not listen to me. Remember that this body can never be instrumental in harming anybody."

19

Ma was in Varanasi. One day I went to Her room for some work and I found Ma sitting alone with nobody around Her. She peered at me with a questioning look. I never went to Ma for any personal business. If She in Her own fancy called me, that was a different matter. That day Ma seemed to say, "Tell me what you want to say." I had nothing to tell Her, but I thought Ma hinted that I should say something. For a long time a question was hovering over my mind, so I opened my mind. The matter was that my elder sister Shraddha had lived in Kanyapeeth for a short time. Since there was no arrangement for studies, my parents took her back home. Meanwhile, my mother died. We children were quite young, so didi had to do all household work and also look after us. She was only 10–11 years old. She was good in studies and so even after doing all the work she always stood first in her class. She was skilful in everything–drawing, sewing, sports and what not? Her nature was exceptional. Everyone was fond of her and praised her. As compared to her I was a good for nothing. Both at home and ashram many people said, "Who would say that you are a sister of Shraddha? You are useless except giggling. Your stay at the ashram did you no good, while Shraddha staying at home is so good." I told all this to Ma and asked, "Ma, is it true that while didi excelled in everything staying at home, my stay at the ashram has left no mark on me?"

Ma smiled sweetly, took my hands in Hers, pressed them and said, "No friend, that is not true. Remember, staying in the ashram, either sitting or lying down, willingly or unwillingly, if one hears even the softest sound of the holy discourses or recitation, it leaves a positive effect on him. Then She also spoke of didi, "Shraddha is really a good girl." At the assurance of Ma I smiled broadly, making my obeisance and after being cuddled by Her I left.

Speaking about Shraddha, I remember that Ma in the course of her sojourn stayed mostly at Varanasi ashram. Ma's presence meant regular festivities, worship, recitals, feeding people, etc. For us the maidens of Kanyapeeth, festivals claimed a lot of our time and hence studies suffered. Once our senior teacher Gangadi took the girls to task for unsatisfactory results in the examinations. One girl said, "What can I do as the work of the festivals claim so much time and I am left with no time to study properly." As the words reached Ma, She said, "What! doing a bit of service prevents you from study. How can Shraddha stand first every time after attending to all domestic work and bringing up her brothers and sisters? Can't you learn by example?" Truly, I don't speak of her as she is my sister. Such qualified, talented, gentle, graceful, void of temptation, disciplined and obedient to the rules of the ashram girl can rarely be seen. Ma, Didima, Dadabhai, Swami Paramanandaji, Yogeshda, Atulda, Udasji, Kshamadi, all had special love for Shraddha.

When the occasion demanded Ma also rebuked us. Once Ma called us all and chided us. A few girls began to weep. Then Ma said, "Friends, you have left your hearth and home and come to this place, if this body keeps silent when you are at fault, how will you mend yourselves? Don't you think we should live an ideal life? If harsh words bring tears into your eyes, what this body can instruct you. I cannot speak to others the same way as I talk to you. And if I don't say anything then you will say, "Ma didn't care to point out our faults."

Dadabhai at once said, "Instead of shedding tears, ask for forgiveness of Ma, say Ma, pray ensure that I may not offend You again. You girls are most privileged ones as Ma's 'kheyal' is on you."

In this connection I remember that perhaps in the month of April, 1959, we were performing a sanyam saptaha in Rishikesh. Revered Daya Mata–a disciple of Swami Yogananda and the chief of Yogada Math then, came to Rishikesh to visit Ma. She had given the responsibility of Daya Mata's food and care to me. One day I served her food. She said she would not be able to eat so many items and asked me to take some away. I said, "I have served them at the direction of Ma, if you don't accept then Ma would rebuke me and say I did not serve you properly." At this Daya Mata was surprised and asked, "Really! Does Ma rebuke you?" I replied, "Of course She does if She finds anything wrong." Then Daya Mata said with tearful eyes, "How lucky you are! You know the preceptor sheds grace upon the disciple even through discipline and makes the disciple fit for the path of austerity. Such an event happened in my life as described in a verse of Shree Chandi:

Chitte Kripa Samara Nishthurata Cha Drishta
Twayeva Devi! Varade! Bhuvana Trayepi.

With kindness at heart and cruelty on the exterior–
O Goddess! You are sublime in the three worlds."

Ma was particular about all things concerning our visits to holy places and meeting saints. So under Ma's arrangements we went to visit Yamunotri, Gangotri, Kedarnath and Badrinath. The Maharaja of Tehri Garhwal, Raja Manavendra Shah, an ardent devotee of Ma, sent his jeep for us. At that time Shailesh da was in-charge of the 'Shree Ma Anandamayee Vidyapeeth, Haridwar'. Accompanied by him we visited some temples of Haridwar and bought a few necessary things for visiting temples.

Royal Families of Tehri Garhwal and Mysore taking Blessings from Ma Anandamayee

Standing: (2nd from left) Raja of Amb, Naraindasji, Dr. Pannalalji, Narain Swamiji, Maharaja Manabendra Shah of Tehri Garhwal, Gurupriya Didi

Middle Row Sitting: Swami Paramanandaji, Ma Anandamayee and Her Mother Swami Muktananda Girijee (Didima)

Sitting: Princess Swarupa Kumari and Anupama Kumari, unknown, Maharani Suraj Kumari of Tehri Garhwal, Maharani Satyaprem Kumari of Mysore

At an auspicious moment, uttering, "*Glory to Ma*" six of us, namely Panu da, Belu di, Padmaji, Chandan di, Geeta and myself left for Uttarkashi. We arrived at the ashram there before evening. Located on the bank of Ganga, there stood a fine ashram and a Kali temple. Image of Mother Kali besides a Shiva temple was set up by Baba Bholanath. Uttarkashi is an important centre of pilgrimage in Uttarakhand. So it was well populated, boasting of schools, colleges, hospitals and government offices. As the Ganga gets northbound there, the place is called Uttarkashi.

Next day we visited the local temples and promptly got ready to travel by jeep to other places. The jeep took us as far as car service was allowed. The rest was covered on foot. These centers of pilgrimage were a part of Tehri Garhwal. So everywhere the ruler of Tehri was held in high esteem. The Maharaja of Tehri is regarded as the living Badrinath. We heard from the Queen Mother of Tehri, that the special oil and perfumes needed for the daily worship are prepared by the King's consorts with great devotion. As we were sent by Ma and were under the arrangements of Maharaja of Tehri, we got a special treatment everywhere. At every step, we were aware of the special concern of Ma. The old caretaker of Kedarnath opened his register and showed the names of Baba Bholanath and my grandmother Virajmohini Devi. The caretakers (Pandas) have an uncanny ability to trace out the names of any visitor's ancestors who had gone there as pilgrims earlier. The caretaker requested Panu da to start an ashram for Ma at Kedarnath. We had brought all articles required for worship from Varanasi, such as flowers, basil, bel leaves smeared with sandal paste and dried under pressure in a book. Over and above we worshipped in each temple with the local things available there. We went everywhere on foot except Badrinath. Walking on foot has a pleasure of its own. The beauty of the Himalayan Hills and the flora make one forget the strain of the journey. I have a special fondness for hills. I usually reached the destination before others trudging along the spiral route leading to the top. This led the pandas to ask me if I belonged to a hill tribe. I collected some flowers and leaves along the route and sketched a few landscapes. The secluded, solemn and awe-inspiring surroundings of the Himalayas, the unprecedented beauty of the mountain ranges, varieties of plants, wealth of flowers accompanied by the musical notes and chirping of various birds collectively made me forget myself and seemed to carry me to a celestial spiritual region. Creations of the almighty are wonderful indeed!

In this connection I remember that during my surgery, Ma called my father to Delhi. The ashram was a long way off from the nursing home. So father was lodged at the house of Kripalji. He used to come with Kripalji after breakfast and went back after evening. At noon he relaxed at the lounge. 'The India 1958 exhibition' was going on at that time. The exhibition ground was at a stone's throw distance. So Kripalji suggested my father that instead of being bored sitting alone in the hospital it would be better for him to visit the exhibition. In reply father said, "Not at all. What can I see in the exhibition? In God's universe there are so many wonderful sights that catch our eyes. They are too marvellous for our eyes to explore. What do I stand to gain by seeing man-made works of art? As soon as we create something we are busy exhibiting it, while endless objects of art are constantly appearing in the caves, caverns, at the bottom of the ocean, in deserts and everywhere coming into existence, only to disappear."

Ma sent me to Shree Gangacharan Das Gupta's house at Kolkata for treatment. I had rarely seen a devout family as theirs. Gangacharan babu used to pluck flowers every morning from the trees and arrange them before the pictures of revered Bholagiri–his Preceptor and Shree Shree Ma. One day he was plucking flowers and I was sitting in the verandah. He said, "People ask where is God? We cannot see Him. I say here is God, visible before my eyes. He is apparent in the form of delicate flowers of many colours and scents coming out strangely from the hard trunk of the trees. What is the need of going elsewhere to see Him?"

20

Ma was in Naimisharanya and Geeta Jayanti started. As per Ma's instructions, for three days we did a short worship and read six chapters of Bhagwad Geeta each day. On the fourth day, the whole 18 chapters were read and then a grand worship of Geeta took place. Generally, we offered eighteen plates with eighteen varieties of fruits, sweets, lamps and garlands for the eighteen chapters of Geeta. But at Naimisharanya there was no such arrangement. Even there was no time to arrange. So Ma called me and said, "Do with whatever you get and decorate." I collected a few things from Ma's stock and was decorating. It was late night and it was a calm and quiet place. All of a sudden, a car blew its horn at the gate. It was found that a royal family had come from a distance with baskets full of fruits, sweets, flowers, etc., the articles of worship. They had started in the morning to do worship to Ma. But the car got stuck on the way, so they reached late. At the midnight no worship was possible, so Rajmata handed over the baskets to Ma and after dinner went to rest.

Ma was very pleased to see the things and said, "Look, God sent everything. Now decorate to your heart's content. Since it was a royal arrangement for worship, there were plenty of things, fruits, sweets, dry fruits, flowers, basil, garlands, handmade wicks and beautiful leaf plates. While giving those to me Ma said, "Look here, the right offering for the right function, how alert the Omnipresent is! If they would reach in time, they would have offered these to this body, then it could not be offered to the Bhagwad Geeta." It was worth seeing how nicely they arranged for their offerings. Gladly I took the things and decorated accordingly. The Geeta Jayanti got over and was up to the mark. Rajmata was highly pleased to see their offerings were utilized in Geeta worship by Ma Herself.

I had heard a nice anecdote about the affection of Ma from Smt. Indulekha Devi, the wife of Shree Gangacharan Das Gupta. Bhaiji had sometime told Ma that Ramanand's mother (Smt. Monikuntala Devi–the wife of Bhaiji) could make delicious sweet (sandesh) from milk curdled by 'Kagaji' lemon (key lime). When Ma went to Dhaka from Kolkata for the last time before the death of Bhaiji, with the consent of Gangacharan Babu, She took his wife and said, "Ma, you will have to make Jyotish eat lemon sandesh by having it made by his wife." On the other hand since Bhaiji stayed with Ma so his wife out of anger, petulance and sorrow kept no connection with her husband. Reaching Dhaka, Ma sent Indulekha Devi directly to Monikuntala Devi's house.

Monikuntala Devi couldn't even bear to hear Ma's name. Indulekha Devi went to Dhaka but couldn't stay with Ma. She didn't like to stay with her niece either, though she had to make Bhaiji eat as ordered by Ma. One day she lay down without taking her dinner, feeling disturbed by the thought of how to carryout Ma's bidding. The niece came and called her repeatedly. Then the aunt said, "I have come to you after a long time, but Jyotish does not stay here and you are not in a good mood. All these make me uncomfortable, so I have no appetite for food. But I can eat if you fulfil one of my wishes." At the insistence of the niece, she said, "I wish one day you invite Jyotish and make him eat what he likes, in my presence." The niece was compelled to agree and making all arrangements, invited Bhaiji. On the appointed day Bhaiji arrived. The aunt fed him sitting in front. That was the last time Bhaiji had food cooked by his wife. After that Ma accompanied the aunt to Kolkata and dropping her at home said to Gangacharan babu, "Here I return back your wife. It was a work which none but she could have done." Blessed is Ma's affection for Her child.

Before going to Kailash, Bhaiji gave the manuscript of his book 'Mother–as revealed to me' to his uncle Shree Gangacharan Das Gupta and asked him to get it printed as a book. He also told him to whom the books should be given after it was printed. Among those few fortunate persons were included the name of my father. I learnt this from Gangacharan Babu. Before the book could be published Bhaiji breathed his last.

Brahmachari Yogesh da told me that once Ma was in Her sojourn among the hilly tracts of Uttarakhand with Baba Bholanath, Bhaiji and Yogesh da. They went to Uttarkashi from Mussoorie on foot. They all lay down at night in a small temple which had no door. Ma said, "Be alert." Bhaiji said, "Ma, why should we fear when you are with us?" Hearing this Ma smiled and said, "The thief also is directed by this body."

On another occasion Ma and Bhaiji were travelling along a hilly region. They had nothing to eat since morning and on top of it the way was up and down. Bhaiji was afflicted with hunger and sat down on the roadside. Ma was watching all this. She understood the reason of the affliction of Her child. Some food was needed, but where could it be found? Strangely enough, after a short while a boy appeared with white dried milk in a semi-circular leaf and said, "Babuji, will you buy it?" To Bhaiji it was heaven itself coming down on his hand. He at once bought it with a small amount of money, made Ma take some of it, ate the rest himself and recovered his energy. Initially he did not notice due to extreme hunger, but after eating he thought that where did the boy go? It was not possible to walk so fast on that difficult path, then? Seeing a smile on Ma's lips he had no difficulty in understanding that finding Her child hungry, Ma Herself brought for him the food in the form of a boy by Her kheyal. In the divine play of Ma, this boy appeared a number of times.

In the Bhagwad Geeta God says:

Ananyash chintayanto Maam
Ye Janah Paryopasate
Tesham Nityabhiyuktanam
Yogakshemam Vahamyaham

—Geeta, 9th Chapter, Sloka 22

I remember in Varanasi ashram the first Sanyam week started in the hall on the banks of Ganga (Now immersed in the river). The collective morning meditation was on from 8–9 a.m. in the presence of Ma. After an hour, the following ditty was pouring out in a wonderful tone from the mouth of Ma in a trance:

Hey Pitah, Hey Hitah, Hey Brahma Bhutam.
Hey Pitah, Hey Hitah, Hey Brahma Tattwam.
Hey Pitah, Hey Hitah, Hey Brahma Swarupam!

Later Ma said that after completion of the maun, She saw that a boy was singing it whole heartedly. "You too may sing it after the completion of the meditation." At first at the direction of Ma only Bibhu da used to sing these couplets. When Bibhu da fell ill, Ma allowed Pushpa di, Chhabi di, Kanti ji and me to sing them. Now the maidens of Kanyapeeth also sing the same. Ma forbade its singing except on Sanyam Saptah and by all.

The first Sanyam Saptah (Sanyam–restraint, Saptah–week) took place at Varanasi. Restrictions for the meals for the first degree of restraint and the second degree were directed by Ma. Dadabhai asked Ma that what would the Kanyapeeth girls follow regarding the meal of sanyam. Ma said, "Didi, the maidens of Kanyapeeth observe sanyam all through the year. They need not observe the rules of food during this week." So for those seven days the excess offerings (prasad) would go to Kanyapeeth and for that period it was a regular feast for us. We only took part in the meditation twice a day, attended the religious discourses, kirtan and Matri Satsang. Elder girls observed the rules of meals on their own accord.

On the occasion of the swing (Jhulan) ceremony Ma had come to Varanasi. We duly fitted a swing in the hall, made Ma sit on it and were busy everyday in the delight of the festival. In the mean time we heard that an idol of Gopal (the baby form of Lord Krishna) had come to Ma and She was seeking us. We ran to the Chandi Mandap area towards Ma and saw that on Ma's cot a rolly-polly large Gopal was seated on a brass vessel. Gopal was made of black touch-stone and had a silver ball and a flute in hands and a silver crown on his head. His

Gopal made of black touchstone in 'Smriti Mandir'

Gopal being brought down from the Throne for the Ceremonial Abhishek

big eyes were very lovely and beautiful to look at. After we made obeisance, Ma said to me, "Take Gopal upstairs in the 'Smriti Mandir' and offer some bhog and make him sleep." He was very heavy and seated on a wooden seat brought with him. Though Gopal was in the 'Smriti Mandir', we girls used to clean and decorate him. A few sets of dresses were made.

On the night of 'Janmashtami' (i.e., birth day of Lord Krishna) following 'abhishek' (full-fledged worship of installation) grand bhog was offered to Gopal. Before this Gopal came, on the occasion of Janmashtami at the time of Lord Krishna's birth, previously we used to make Ma sit on the silver throne in our worship room and performed worship, etc. Since the coming of Gopal, all other idols of Krishna of the ashram were bathed and worshipped together with this Gopal in presence of Ma.

Gopal had no gold ornaments when he came. Kanta ben, the wife of Nandu bhai, both devotees of Ma, had come from

Mumbai. One morning Kanta ben came to Ma weeping and offered Her a thin gold chain taken out of her neck and said, "Mataji take this necklace. Gopalji was trying to snatch this chain repeatedly from my neck the whole night which troubled my neck very much. I told him that I am poor, have kept only this chain to bless my daughter-in-law when my only son gets married, but he did not loosen his grip and kept it in his tight grip." Ma took the chain and put it on Gopal. On the bright black colour of touch-stone the gold chain glittered.

Sandhya di, a young widow of a landlord stayed near the ashram. Looking at Gopal she thought that the idol had necklace on its neck, but hands were bare, it looked odd. She gave Ma two broad gold bracelets from her jewellery box for Gopal. They were of a rare design. They could be made smaller and larger. When worn, enlarged, two beautiful stone-studded bright butterflies could be seen. Now Gopal had gold ornaments on his neck and hands but on his head was a silver crown, not a gold one. Now it was to be seen that how 'clever Gopal' got the gold crown.

The maidens of Kanyapeeth go every morning to Annapurna and Gopal temple to make their obeisance. They were accompanied by an elder. At that time Kalon di (Urmila Das), an old devotee of Ma from Dhaka, was in-charge of Kanyapeeth on Ma's direction. She attended to the girls while making obeisance. After the girls left, when Kalon di was making obeisance to Gopal, she heard, "Does one feel happy to wear the silver crown everyday?" When she got up she thought that someone had said it. Next day, when she made her obeisance, she heard the same words but could not find the speaker. She felt restless in her mind. On the third day having carefully watched all around that nobody was there, just as she bent her head, a distinct sound came from Gopal, "Everyday silver crown does not look well." Having heard this, Kalon di made her bow and prayed, "O God, I am not able to make a gold crown for you. If Tarun (her son, who had gone to Bombay in search of a job) gets an employment, I shall make you a gold crown." After she promised, Gopal did not say any more. A few days later she came to know that her son had got a job and had sent the full amount of his first month's salary to his mother. Having got the money Kalon di said to Kshama di that she must go to the goldsmith to order a gold crown for Gopal. But it was delayed and the rains started. There was a heavy downpour for some days. So they could not go out.

Kalon di stayed in a room attached to the hall of the Kanyapeeth and the room was always under lock and key. That day in the afternoon when she entered her room, she saw on her spotless clean bedcover there were two imprints of small dust-laden feet. Kalon di was very angry with this. She called the small girls and asked them who came to her room and had done the deed. But none of them admitted. Kalon di and Kshama di began to chide the girls for not having confessed the guilt. What nobody thought was, how anyone could enter into the locked room and how the dry dusty imprint was possible amidst so much rain. The rebuking was going on for a long time and yet there was no solution. At last Tara, the Kanyapeeth girl said, "All right, let us measure the feet of the little children to find whose imprint it is." Shukla was the youngest at that time. By measuring her feet it was found that the dusty imprints on the pillow cover were much smaller than hers, then who had come? Then Kshama di said, "Kalon di, is it not the doing of your Gopal? You promised him the crown and you are not keeping your promise, so he might have come." Then Kalon di burst into tears and said, "That is it Kshama, putting it off from one day to another, I have made much delay. How kind of Gopal that he has reminded of it by coming into my room himself. Bowing to the bed cover, she put it away and even in the midst of rain she went out with Kshama di to order a crown for Gopal. What was more astonishing is that it cost exactly, i.e., as much money as Tarun da had sent.

Ma was then at Kishenpur. A letter was sent to Her including the demand of Gopal. It was mentioned that on Janmashtami Ma must come and put the gold crown on Gopal. Ma came in due time. With great celebrations Janmashtami and Nandotsava were performed. Gopal looked splendid with the gold crown with pendants of small pearls. One devotee of Varanasi arranged for a ladoo of condensed milk to be offered to Gopal daily. Smt. Rani Mazumdar, a rich devotee from Kolkata offered a set of silver utensils for bhog of Gopal. Next, Yogibhai, the King of Solan, also offered a gold crown, chain, bangles, flute and small golden bell anklets to Gopal. In this way, one by one, Gopal collected lots of gold ornaments.

Looking at the ornaments of Gopal, Ma one day said, "Gopal, it is for this reason, you didn't go to Vrindavan, and on some pretext stayed in Kashi." Vrindavan is infested with thieves. It is not safe to wear gold ornaments always. But Gopal has a fancy for wearing gold ornaments always. So he played a trick to remain in Varanasi. It is heard that this idol of Gopal was established in a temple of Kashi long ago by a landlord of East Bengal. For the service of Gopal, there was a large amount of property in His name and people were employed to serve Him according to royal arrangements. But gradually all the property and ornaments were sold out and even the daily service became difficult. Then the worshipper expressed his desire to transfer this idol somewhere else. On knowing about it Batu da informed Ma. It was settled that it would be placed in Vrindavan ashram. But the worshipper demanded a lot of money for the idol. Hearing this, Paramananda Swami ji said, "If we have to pay money we may as well make a new idol". So Gopal did not have to go to Vrindavan. Next there was the Jhulan Purnima (swing festival) in the ashram. Ma was at Varanasi. The swing festival was going on in Kanyapeeth. In the meantime Batu da said to Ma, "Ma, they are not able to continue the service of Gopal. So they have decided to immerse Him into the Ganga." At once Ma said, "Bring Gopal here." Gopal came, but by that time another idol of Gopal got installed in Vrindavan temple. Hence this Gopal stayed at Varanasi ashram. Now He is staying in the first floor room at Ananda Jyoti temple on a sandalwood throne as a Maharaja.

When Gopal stayed at the Smriti Mandir, Ma's younger brother Shree Jadunath Bhattacharya worshipped Him every day. Ma's direction was that on two occasions of the year, i.e., Janmashtami and Holi, Gopal should be brought down from his throne and installed again.

Once Ma was staying at Dehradun. She had severe pain in Her hand. She saw that Gopal was showing his hand as there was pain in his hand too. Seeing this for two or three days, Ma said to Gopal, "Wait I will find out." Getting this assurance from Ma, Gopal stopped showing his hand. Ma sent a letter to Varanasi enquiring whether the Jhulan Celebrations are being conducted properly or not. The reply came saying that everything was followed according to established customs. Again Gopal showed his hand. Then Ma said to him, "Well this body is going to Varanasi and will find out." Gopal stopped disturbing Ma anymore. Ma went to Varanasi. Over there She enquired about Gopal's swing ceremony. She asked Narain Swamiji, Atul da and Mamu (Ma's younger brother) separately about Gopal's swing festival and learnt that during Jhulan once he was left on the floor while decorating the swing. So he got hurt and had pain in the hand. He was not supposed to be put down, but by mistake it was done. But the wonder was that when during Holi festival he came down and we played with him, he never complained. In one winter I knitted one baby set for Gopal and asked Mamu to put on the dress on Gopal. He said, "Let Ma come and dress him, if I do, it may hurt Him and He will complain."

It was in 1979, after the opening ceremony of the Ananda Jyoti Mandir that Gopal was installed on a sandalwood seat. Ma was staying in the room adjacent to the Gopal temple. One day an old lady of Varanasi came to Ma with some money. She told Ma that she was very poor and had no relatives. She was a widow and cooked in people's houses to earn a living. A few days ago she was seriously ill and was lying down unconscious. Then she saw a rolly-polly black Gopal come and said, "Open your eyes, look Ma has sent me, open your eyes." She saw Ma standing there in quite hazy appearance. Again Gopal said, "Shall I touch your eyes with my feet or hand? The lady said, "Will you touch my eyes with such big feet?" Then Gopal said, "I shall make my feet small." Then she said, "I can't open my eyes, I am dying." Gopal said, "You will not go just now, the boat is sailing, it has not touched the shore. You will now survive, look, look." Then the old lady opened her eyes with great difficulty and saw one small Gopal was moving around her room. It was beyond description. Again Gopal spread his small hands and said, "Give, what shall you give." She had saved Rs. 200 from what she earned by cooking at other's place for her funeral expenditure. But where to find out this Gopal? She heard that there is a Gopal of this kind in Ma Anandamayee Ashram. She came to the ashram and luckily Ma was in the Gopal Mandir. She gave the money to Ma and narrated the whole story to Ma. Then Ma asked to buy ten ser (1.25 kg) of yellow (Kesari) perha sweets, fruits, etc. with that money. It was offered to Gopal and Ma distributed the prasad Herself saying, "Have a special prasad".

Gopal exacted gold ornaments, silver utensils, sweets, butter and many other things from so many people. I thought that he had not demanded anything from me. At that time Gopal was in Smriti Mandir and the sandalwood seat was not made yet. I was suffering from stomach pain and couldn't sleep well. One night I dreamt that I went to Smriti Mandir and found Gopal shivering with cold since he had no dress on his body. In a hurry I took him in my arms. Due to cold, Gopal had hung his two legs on the two sides and clinched to my belly and waist. I wrapped him with my cloth and somehow bore that heavy Gopal from Smriti Mandir to our worship room on the second floor and asked the girls to bring a throne. I saw that in the worship room there were many thrones of different sizes lying vacant. The girls got out one and said, "Put Him on this." I said, "No, no, don't you see that Gopal is too big to fit in, take off Ma's picture from the large throne and he would sit there."

On waking up I thought what a blunder! I cannot give Gopal Ma's large throne. We make Ma sit occasionally on it. I didn't say anything of the dream even in whispers. I was afraid that if it reached Ma's ears She might give it to Gopal undoubtedly. I also thought that I used to think that Gopal did not ask anything from me. Now for once he has asked for something, but I could not give it. So mentally I was defeated and asked forgiveness for it. A good many years later an exclusive sandalwood throne was made for Gopal and He was seated on the auspicious day of Janmashtami. My dream pricked me, so after Gopal was seated in a new throne, I told Dadabhai about the dream. Even she was scared and said, "There is no need to tell Ma, this sandalwood throne is more expensive than Ma's throne."

21

Shree Shree Ma Anandamayee Kanyapeeth was founded by Dadabhai in Ma's kheyal. The initiation, education and character building, everything of the girls were under Ma's direct instruction and supervision. Miss Swarn Kumari Jaspal (Billo ji) used to remain with us day and night. She maintained a register of our presence and absence. It was her routine duty. When Ma visited Varanasi, Billo ji showed that register to Dadabhai and she took the girls in front of Ma. Sometimes Ma would say a few words to us, sometimes rebuked softly.

If needed, She punished the small girls by making them touch their ears and doing squats counting Ram one, Ram two and so on up to 50 or 100 times. Ma used to say that along with the punishment if they uttered God's name it would help them spiritually.

Ma had Her kheyal for our education also. At first our senior Gangadevi Panchatirtha taught us Sanskrit and Billo ji, Renu di and Kshama di took other classes. For the primary classes the syllabus of Viswa Bharati, Santiniketan was followed under the guidance of Kshama di. Later, when Ganga di left, Kshama di managed to engage Pandit Triyambakam Atmaram Bhandarkar, a triple Acharya and M.A. in Sanskrit, for Kanyapeeth. He was an excellent teacher and very simple. Sati di, Chandan di, Jaya, Geeta, Guneeta, Gauri and myself were proud of being his students. He inspired the girls to deliver speeches in Sanskrit and to take part in the Sanskrit speech competition organized by the Ramakrishna mission. He also taught us to recite Vedic hymns. A devoted teacher like him was difficult to find. For a pretty good time, he was associated with Kanyapeeth and breathed his last in our hospital. By the efforts of Dr. Padma Mishra and Dr. Bithika Mukherji, both lecturers of Benaras Hindu University, modern course of education was introduced in Kanyapeeth. Next, Kanyapeeth was affiliated under the Sampurnanand Sanskrit University. The girls of the Kanyapeeth appeared at the Prathama, Madhyama, Shastri and Acharya examinations. On Ma's special instructions I did Matric, Intermediate, B.A. and M.A. instead of oriental studies. Due to poor health I could not study well but passed my exams by Ma's grace.

I was bed ridden with serious illness before my B.A. exams. Padmaji and Bithudi asked me not to appear but I wanted to finish my studies otherwise I had to linger for another year. Then Bithudi took me to her quarters of B.H.U. with Ma's permission. At that time of the examination, my condition of health was so critical that in-between the exams I had to drink orange juice with coramine frequently. Bithudi, Padmaji, teachers and staff of the women's college were very affectionate and helpful to me, which I couldn't ever forget.

Everything is possible by Ma's grace. When the results were declared it was found that my name was among the first twenty candidates in order of merit. Then Ma was in Varanasi. As I was the first girl of Kanyapeeth to pass B.A., Dadabhai was so glad that she brought a big can of Rasogolla and after feeding Ma, distributed handful to everybody. Bithudi presented me a 'Waterman's' pen from abroad. Patal da gave different varieties of best mangoes to eat. Dr. Radharani Choudhury and Dr. Manorama Verma, who tutioned me for the exam, praised me a lot in Ma's presence and suggested that Vishuddha should study further. Ma ordered Dadabhai and she arranged for my M.A. exams. I did M.A. in Ancient Indian History, Culture and Archeology under Bhandarkarjee and Dr. Manorama Verma's guidance.

Before our exams when we did obeisance to Ma and touched our pens to Her hands, She used to say, "Prepare well, pass well". As we passed well She said, "Passing well in this worldly exam is a bondage." That means if we are successful we feel proud and that is also harmful for brahmacharinis.

A devotee sent a four track Akai tape recorder from abroad. Panuda asked me to operate it. I had never operated such a machine before, but somehow managed to operate after going through the manual of that machine. Dadabhai recommended to keep the machine with me. It was very heavy, but still I used to carry it in a bag on my shoulder and moved around Ma recording Her sayings and songs off and on. One day in Varanasi ashram we gathered in Ma's room on the first floor. Ma was talking about Her Sadhana Leela in Her own kheyal. I kept the machine under Ma's cot and sat near Her while the machine was recording. The mike was hidden in my hand so no one could make out that I was recording. I was scared that if Ma saw the machine, She might stop talking. After a long time Ma bent down to ask me whether I was recording or not. At once I switched off the mike with a smile. Some people forbade me to record lest Ma's mood of talking would vanish. Ma said, "When this body talks, how much enters in your ears, how much goes in the machine and how much floats away in the air, everything is clear in my kheyal."

I remember another incident regarding the tape recorder. Once there was a fortnight of Bhagwat recital arranged at Nimsar. The most renowned and learned speaker of Bhagwat, Swami Akhandanandaji would explain the Bhagwat Puran. Ma asked me to tape record all the explanations of the Puran. On the dias there was a main seat for Swami Akhandanandaji and asanas for many other Mahatmas were placed in row. Ma took me on the dias and made me sit behind Akhandanandaji's seat with the tape recorder. Ma asked Dadabhai to sit near me. Akhandanandaji was also told about it. I recorded during both morning and afternoon sessions. One day, when the discourse ended, I did obeisance to Bhagwat and as I stood up, Ma came forward and said to Akhandanandaji, "Pitaji,

Vishuddha is a girl of Kanyapeeth and has passed M.A." Swamiji asked me whether I did M.A. in Sanskrit. I replied that I had done in Ancient Indian History, Culture and Archeology. Ma said again, "No Pitaji, she has not done in Sanskrit, that is the sad thing." Then She praised me too.

Hearing this Pushpa di discussed what Ma said, "It is the sad thing......" Now the question was who was sad. As Ma was beyond sorrow and happiness and Vishuddha did not like to study at all, then who was sad? I was fearing that I would have to study again. Dadabhai told Dr. Padma Mishra and Pandit T.A. Bhandarkarji to get me prepared for M.A. in Sanskrit. So again studies started. The Rigveda was my desired subject. The vedic language and its grammar were totally different from the classical Sanskrit and the required books were not available, except in the University library. Being a private student I could not even avail myself of the library facility. Due to these problems Padmaji didn't agree at first but seeing my insistence she allowed and praised my confidence. Bhandarkarji helped me most in this matter. He said, "Veda means knowledge, it will reveal itself to you. Let us go through it." In my class some times he used to explain one hymn, while some times I would explain on my own the other. It was a peculiar class indeed. After doing my daily duties and taking seven periods for the girls, I had very little time to study and due to my ill health I couldn't even study at night. At that time I also used to maintain the accounts of Kanyapeeth. In this way with so many difficulties I studied and got a first class in M.A. I mention these here not to boast, but to express my gratitude to Ma, as I believe that I passed satisfactorily only because of Ma.

In the month of December in 1961 a few girls fell ill with serious typhoid. There was a cold wave sweeping the whole of North India at that time. Kshama di's eldest niece died in spite of her exclusive nursing. Kshama di came to Ma in her teens and settled here as an ashramite. Her selfless service to all was a rare example. She brought her four nieces to Kanyapeeth to provide them education along with an ashram life. Her three younger brothers were well settled as a professor, an advocate and a doctor respectively. She not only brought her nieces to Kanyapeeth but she asked her brothers to arrange for electric fans, clothings, sheets, blankets, desks and seats, etc., for all the girls of Kanyapeeth. But after the premature demise of her eldest niece, the rest three were taken back home. Chua (her niece) died on 5th January, 1962 and I got the shocking news of my elder sister's death the next day, i.e., on 6th January, 1962. When the other girls recovered from typhoid Ma sent us to Vindhyachal for a change.

In May, 1962 Ma's birthday celebrations took place at Kishenpur ashram, Dehradun. Under Ma's instructions, we the girls of Kanyapeeth went to Dehradun. The small ashram of Kishenpur was full of Sadhus and devotees. Rasleela, religious discourses, kirtans, etc. took place from early morning till night.

Ma's devotee Mr. Kania Bhai sent a parcel containing satin of different colours to be used in the festival. Ma asked Ms. Mahalakshmi Tankha and Rama Saxena to sew nice dresses for the Raas party with that satin. One night when I was cutting papers to decorate the ashram, Ma sent for me. Reaching Ma's room upstairs, I found that Ma was sitting on the cot and the senior girls, Sati di, Pushpa di, Chitra di,

Chhabi di, Shovana di and others were standing around Her and everybody was carrying a satin piece in her hand. As I entered and bowed before Ma, She showed me two satin pieces, one yellow and one blue, and asked which one I should take. I picked up the yellow one. Seeing me serious, Chhabi di thought I didn't like the yellow one. She had a pink one and offering that to me she asked, "Will you take this?" I said, "No". Then Ma said, "Take it, she is giving you." So I took it giving her my yellow one. Ma said, "You should sew the edges of the pieces."

The queen of Mandi came to Dehradun for the function. She wanted to worship Ma after decorating Her with floral ornaments. Since it was not available in Dehradun, she asked me to make some ornaments with flowers. I couldn't find flowers, so I made the same with leaves and 'Salma Chumki'. The queen dressed Ma in a beautiful Benarasi saree and put the ornaments made of leaves on Ma. During aarti and worship Ma closed Her eyes. But when the queen of Mandi was doing aarti, I noticed that instead of closing Her eyes, Ma was looking at those leaf ornaments minutely. I understood that Ma liked them.

The night before the full moon, Ma said to me, "Can you make a few leaf ornaments tomorrow? Make it in such a way that one can understand this is for Shiva, this is for Radha-Krishna and this is for Rama-Sita. Nobody should know that this body has ordered you." I thought that Ma would offer these ornaments to the Raas party along with the dress. During Ma's birthday celebrations ladies do the whole night kirtan on the full moon night. Chhabi di asked me to make set of leaf ornaments for Ma. Next morning I collected a good quantity of leaves and sat in a small cave to make the ornaments. Whoever saw me doing several sets asked if I was doing this for some VIPs. Anyhow, I finished my job and when I found Ma alone in Her room, I entered and gave the ornaments to Her. Ma asked me to keep the same under Her cot. She also enquired whether anybody had questioned me about it or not. I replied that whoever saw it asked, but I answered that one who ordered had forbidden to expose the name. Ma was pleased to hear this.

At 10 p.m. after offering garland and sandal paste to Ma, Chhabi di started singing kirtan. Local ladies and we Kanyapeeth girls were accompanying Chhabi di. After some time Ganga di went away. Then Mala left. Kirtan sounded well when all joined in playing drums and cymbals. But one by one the girls were going away, what was the matter? Next Chhabi di got up. Seeing all this, I was perturbed and after a few minutes someone told me that Ma was calling me. Ma was in the adjacent room of the hall. Entering that room I saw Ma, Buni di and Mahalakshmi ji taking out exclusive Benarasi sarees from a big box. Next to the wall, Ganga di and Mala were standing as Shiva-Parvati, Basanti and Swapna as Ram-Sita and Chhabi di dressed as Krishna. As I entered, Ma asked me if Chhabi di was looking OK or not. Chhabi di's long hair was turned up with a knot on the head and it looked like the curly hair of Shri Krishna and she was dressed in a skirt made of multi-coloured satin frills. Seeing the scene I burst into laughter.

Then Ma made me wear a beautiful golden Benarasi saree. She put scented 'Bhasma', i.e., sacred ash of yajna in Her dhoti and puffed on my face to make the effect of powder.

Next She decorated my forehead with white and red sandal paste, put garland around my neck. Then Ma set the leaf crowns made by me on our heads one by one. I laughed and said, "Oh! you ordered me to make these crowns for us only?" Ma also laughed. While dressing Gangadi as Shiva, Ma told her to stand in meditation with her eyes closed. So she was standing there with closed eyes and saw nothing whatever Ma was doing with us in the room.

After dressing us Ma went to the hall and sat there for some time in the kirtan. Then She said, "Look, Haribaba puts off the light during kirtan. You also switch off the light." In this way she made the hall dark and came to take us. First she took Shiva-Parvati to the hall and made them sit on the seat of the Mahatmas. Ma asked Mahalakshmiji to dress herself as mother Kaushalya and take Rama and Sita to the hall. Then She took Krishna and Radha, i.e., Chhabidi and me to the hall and placed us in the centre. After that She asked to switch on the lights. The kirtan was going on. As soon as the lights went on, everyone exclaimed, "Jai Ma, Jai Ma". Ma called Chitradi and made her dress like Mahaprabhu and asked her to stand behind Radha and Krishna with her hands stretched upwards. Then Ma started doing aarti, first with incense, then with panchpradeep and then lastly with the chamar. The way of aarti was also peculiar. She asked the elder girls to bring their pieces of satin cloth. Ma made them hold the pieces with both hands and then She caught hold of each girl by hand and moved swiftly to and fro in front of us. That day a South Indian devotee of Ma, Mrs Kalpakam was present there. Seeing Ma's aarti she said, in South India there was a very old temple where they did aarti in this way.

As the aarti ended, Ma made Shiva stand and danced in the posture of 'Nataraj' with Shiva, embraced Parvati and indicated both to go. She asked Kaushalya to take away Rama and Sita with her. Then She started dancing Raas with Krishna. What a dance it was! She caught hold of Chhabi di's hands crosswise and in great ecstasy danced in the rhythm of kirtan. At the divine touch of Ma Chhabi di was also overwhelmed with emotion. Next she embraced me and danced with me and signalled us to go inside.

After changing our dress we came and joined the kirtan. At midnight Ma came and sat in the hall. Chhabi di and I started dressing Ma as Krishna. We dressed Her with necklace, bracelets, earrings and crown made of leaves and when Chhabi di gave the flute in Her hands, Ma looked at me like a child and She grumbled and said in a low voice, "You didn't give me flute..." She meant why I didn't give the flute when I decorated Chhabi di as Krishna. Saying this She touched Chhabi di's lips with the flute. Then we did a good kirtan moving around Ma dressed as Lord Krishna. After some time Ma went back to Her room. The whole night we did wonderful kirtan. In the morning we went to Ma's room to finish the night long kirtan. Ma gave us sweets. Then She disclosed, "That day when Chhabi and Vishuddha exchanged their pieces of satin, then the kheyal came to this body to do this leela."

Shree Shree Ma dressed as Lord Krishna

The final day of Ma's birthday celebrations drew near. We decorated the whole ashram. On the courtyard of the two temples the place for worship was settled. The main worship occurs at 3 a.m. Since flower garlands were not available in Dehradun market, I planned to decorate Ma's cot with paper garlands. I made jasmine strings with paper and made it like a mosquito net on Ma's cot. When Renu di and myself were decorating the cot, Renu di's brother Bindu da commented, "Why are you using delicate Jasmine flowers? They will wither by late night when the worship will take place." This made us laugh a lot. Then he touched the flowers to see what the matter was. After making the mosquito net with paper jasmine I sprayed the perfume of jasmine on it. The final worship to Ma was performed elaborately. Recitals, songs, kumari puja, flower offerings and aarti, etc. were completed and prasad was distributed as usual. After the celebrations, the Mahatmas and devotees went back to their places.

22

Ma stayed at Dehradun for some time. I was in Ma's service. Daily there were lots of letters received in Ma's name. When Dadabhai was in Ma's service she did everything herself– cooking, looking after Ma's each and every requirement, ashram management, etc. Along with so many duties she used to go through Ma's letters regularly and after reading the same to Ma, replied them accordingly. Since Dadabhai fell ill, Ma's letters gathered in a heap. Whenever Ma stayed in an undisclosed location, i.e., 'Agyatvas' the letters used to be read out to Her. During functions it was impossible for Ma to get the leisure to listen. Now the function was over so Ma asked me to take the responsibility of Ma's letters. She said, "Take out some time to read the letters to this body." I found out it was not an ordinary bag but a very large bag full of letters. At noon I used to go through the letters and underlined the main points to be read to Ma. Every evening after the daily kirtan, I used to go to Ma with the letters. Elder girls also came to Ma's room to enjoy Ma's company. Ma told Pushpa di and Chitra di to read the letters too. She also instructed that we should reply the letters from the ladies in the name of Gurupriya didi and the letters from the gents in the name of Swami Paramanandaji.

One evening Ma was lying on Her bed and I was reading letters to Her. There were four lengthy letters of one lady who wrote that her husband was bed ridden due to serious illness, the son was unemployed, the grown up daughter was still unmarried and she herself could not sleep at all due to wind and acidity, etc. So she prayed to Ma that Ma should bless her to get rid of all these problems immediately. Listening to this Ma said, "As if this body is an orderly." Thinking this was Ma's reply to the letter I wrote it down at once. Noticing this Ma laughed a lot and said, "Do you know what had happened?" A small boy lost his father. He had to observe the last rituals for his deceased father. The priest instructed the mother of that boy to clean and wipe some portions of the courtyard with cow dung and to keep the things required for the rites. When the priest started the ceremony he told the boy to utter whatever he said. The priest said, 'Take water in your hand.' The boy repeated, 'Take water in your hand.' Whatever the priest said, the boy also repeated the same. The priest thought that the boy was deliberately irritating him. He got furious and slapped the boy, he too slapped the priest. In this way they crossed the wiped area. The mother of the boy was sitting there to see the rites. She thought whatever was going on between the priest and the boy, was a part of the Shradh ceremony. In that case she could have kept more space sanctified for the ritual had she known that it would require more space. Hearing Ma's anecdote we and Ma laughed a lot. Listening to the letters Ma said, "As if this body is an orderly". This statement of Ma was not a reply to the letter. It was of course a saying of Ma alone.

The place for letter-reading sessions in Ma's room was accepted by Ma and others. So I used to enter Her room without any barrier. We assembled in Ma's room regularly and had a fine time with Ma. After a few days, when I had read the last letter, Ma was very glad and touching my head said, "So you have saved me". Then I used to read letters to Ma regularly. Swamiji also made me write his letters. There was no limit how many letters I wrote in a day. Due to the letters I got Ma's company for a long time, that was my great fortune.

Once I was travelling with Ma. She asked me to write some letters. I put the paper on Ma's seat and was following Her dictation. Since the train was running fast, my handwriting got untidy and being ashamed I looked at Her. She understood and said, "Have you seen the handwriting of Tripurari baba (Prof. Tripurari Chakraborty, the renowned speaker and elucidator of the epic Mahabharat)? His normal writing was like that, so you need not be ashamed." Once She also said, "Your handwriting is so clear this body can read."

Once we were at Dehradun. Ma sent an exercise book and asked all elder girls to write something in it. Chitra di said, "Maybe Ma would study our nature by seeing our handwriting." After seeing our handwriting Ma made me write a letter to Pandit Jawaharlal Nehru, the honourable Prime Minister of India, at that time.

Ma's disciple Maharaja of Gwalior ordered the renowned sculptor Shree Nitai Pal of Kolkata to make an idol of Lord Krishna with 'ashtadhatu' (eight metals). The Maharaja wished to install Shree Krishna's statue in his kingdom. But before the completion of the statue, Maharaja breathed his last. Then Maharani Vijayaraje Scindia offered the statue to Ma and said, "Ma, Chhaliya gave such an end to Maharaja, so this statue cannot be installed at Gwalior." She made Ma sit next to Krishna as Radha and did an exclusive worship to both of them. On hearing the word 'chhaliya', Dadabhai asked the Maharani wherefrom did she hear this word? This word was uttered by Ma long ago.

Once Ma was in Solan, a small town near Shimla. One day while taking rest, a beautiful song was sung by Ma. In extremely sweet melody Ma was singing–

"Aao mere salona Chhalia re Banwari re..."

Hearing this Dadabhai called Bibhu da to memorise the words and the tune. For a long time Ma was singing in great bhav. Bibhu da followed the song and got it. Afterwards Ma said to Bibhu da, "Sing this song in your daily prayer you won't otherwise try unless this body says to sing." But whenever Ma asked him to sing he played on the harmonium, uttered one or two words of the song and started to start crying profusely. He felt the divine touch of Radharani in these words and tune. He could never complete the song due to the great bhav.

In Vrindavan ashram 'Chhalia temple' was to be constructed in between Mahaprabhu and Shiva temples. The Rajmata of Gwalior and the King of Solan were financing the expenditure. The grandmother of the Maharaja of Solan wished to install a pair of Radha and Krishna statues at Vrindavan. As the digging process started, solid ground could not be found as there was sand everywhere. The construction could not be done on sand alone and hence an extended portion was dug. Naturally the expenditure exceeded the estimate. Then Ma fulfilled the rest of the requirement. It was heard that erstwhile Yamuna river of Vrindavan flowed through our ashram complex during the Dwapar Yuga, i.e., at the time of Lord Krishna, as per the historical and geographical data. At last a huge temple and satsang hall, etc. were completed. There ought to be a pair, i.e., Radha and Krishna, to be installed. So Mr. Ranjit Kumar Banerji of Kolkata ordered for an ashtadhatu metal idol of Radha as the representative of Ma Herself. These statues were to be installed during the forthcoming Janmashtami, i.e., the birth anniversary of Lord Krishna. The preparations were going on.

Ma was at Kishanpur ashram, Dehradun. One day revered Prabhudutt Brahmachariji of Jhunsi (near Prayagraj) came to meet Her. Ma told him about the installation of Radha Krishna statues at Vrindavan. The pair of idols given by Yogibhai, the Raja of Solan was named 'Anandalal'. The Rajmata of Gwalior named her Krishna as Chhalia. What should be the name of his Radha? Prabhuduttji instantly said, 'This Radha is Chhalia Anandamayee Radha.'

23

I was in Ma's service at Dehradun. One day Ma said to me, "Observe 'kashtha maun' (silence as a wood)." All of a sudden I became totally silent. Kashtha maun means no signal by expression, no sound, no signalling, not even expressing anything by looks, no writing, nothing. It's not so difficult if one stays at one place alone. But it was quite difficult to serve Ma and to travel with Her. Nobody knew anything about my silence and they discussed what had happened to me.

After a few days Ma started for Vrindavan via Delhi. As Delhi station arrived everybody in my compartment went to visit Ma. I was sitting near the window. Many devotees of Delhi came to have a darshan of Ma. When they went past my window and on seeing me said, "Jai Ma Vishuddha di", but getting no response some frowned at me and some grumbled and proceeded towards Ma's compartment. Some asked me, "Don't you recognize me?" In those days a music conference was held at Delhi and a few artists came to Delhi from Kolkata. Among them were Ma's devotees Smt. Utpala Sen and Kumari Chhabi Banerjee, etc. They also came to visit Ma at the station. Chhabi di was very happy to see me and talked a lot. But as she noticed me sitting with a void expression she got frightened and thought something wrong had happened to me. She came inside the compartment and with both her hands, shook me and shouted, "Vishuddha, what has happened to you? Why don't you talk?" But got no response and went to Ma's compartment. There she learnt about my observance of silence.

At Vrindavan ashram, Prabhuduttji came to meet Ma. Since I was on Ma's duty, I sat on the staircase. Brahmachariji came out of Ma's room and seeing me, caught hold of my hair as he used to do, and jerking my head said, "Hey Nath Narayan." As he was silent for years together, he used to laugh like a child and uttered, "*Hey Nath Narayan...*" Swami Bhaskarananda ji was with him. He told Prabhuduttji that she was observing 'kashtha maun'. I did obeisance to him but did not laugh. Seeing me stiff he said, "Kashtha, but not a stone?"

Ma and everybody else were busy arranging for the forth-coming installation ceremony in the ashram. One afternoon Ma opened a bundle and gave me small pieces of velvet and told me, "Make four sets of small pillows, side pillows and asanas for bhog, etc. Whatever you have learnt, make the best use of it." It was quite astonishing that the cloth was neither less nor more. I put frills on the borders of the pillow which Ma appreciated.

The swing festival of Lord Krishna started. Every day there were kirtans, Raasleela, spiritual discourses. In the evening placing Radha Krishna on the swing and Haribaba's kirtan, etc., so many programmes took place. On the full moon night eleven swings were decorated in the hall and eleven pairs of boys dressed as Radha and Krishna were seated and swung. After kirtan, aarti, etc. the eleven pairs staged wonderful Maharasleela in the courtyard of the temple. Under the full moon light the small boys dressed in bright white dresses, their performance made the audience spellbound. In the audience were seated Ma and revered Mahatmas of Vrindavan. Since I was silent Ma made me sit just behind Her and was talking and laughing with me.

After the swing festival the rituals for installation of the idols started. Four tanks were made to bathe the four idols in the water of Yamuna River. Offerings of rice, fruits and cloth, etc. were made. The whole ashram was decorated nicely. I painted designs on the floor and staircase of the temple. Next I thought to paint the whole entrance road from the main gate to the temple. Then the road was not paved yet, so painting was not possible on the sand. I took a pot with a hole (a kamandalu) and put flour mixed in water and poured that white colour on the road making a floral design. Since I was silent, I couldn't ask anybody to buy me white paint, so I used flour instead. Ma was moving all over to inspect and stood to see my painting on the road. The smell of flour drew some dogs to lick it. Somebody mentioned that to me, but I was not bothered at all as my purpose was served, i.e., Ma had seen. Everything we did was centered around Ma. She had seen my painting with appreciation, so I was satisfied.

On the Janmashtami day the idols of Radha-Krishna in royal dresses were seated on well decorated chariots and accompanied by a band and singing kirtan we went around Vrindavan in a procession. Coming back to the ashram two pairs of Radha-Krishna were installed on the marble altar at the auspicious moment by Ma and the Mahatmas. The size of the idols were of teenaged boys and girls. There was a wall of mirror made behind the idols, so that one could see multiple reflections of Radha-Krishna. Swami Nirmalanandaji performed the whole worship as the main priest. At midnight during the auspicious moment of Lord Krishna's advent on this earth–abhishek, shodashopachar pujan, etc. took place. Next day was the Nandotsava. Ramaji, Kamalaji and Laxmiji came with pitchers on their heads and dressed as milk-women danced around Ma. Kanu da and Dasu da dressed themselves as cow boys and sang, "*Brahma dances, Shiva dances...*" with great joy. Ma also raised Her hands with the rhythm of the kirtan.

After the inauguration of the Chhalia Temple, Ma used to rest in the surroundings of the temple at night. One early morning we went to do kirtan and saw through the window, as the temple was bolted from inside. Ma was singing something loudly and moving around the temple swiftly. Nobody knew since how long She was doing this. After some time She retired to Her bed in great bhav. Later when She was asked about it, She said, "Whole night Radha-Krishna, Chhalia, Shiv-Parvati, Nitai-Gaur, all danced in Raas and this body was also with them." Then She sang, "*Krishna Chhalia Anandalal, Braj Ramana Pran Gopal.*" Very often Ma gave dresses, sarees, ornaments to me and Chhabi di to decorate Radha-Krishna. We used to dress them in new styles and Ma appreciated.

When the installation of Radha-Krishna was over successfully, one morning Ma took me to the door of the temple. First She made me do obeisance to God, then She said, "Your maun (kashtha maun) is completed. This body had the kheyal to keep you silent so that the installation of God would be done flawlessly." Then I did pranam to Ma and She patted on my head and back. Coming back to Her room She said to Paramananda swamiji and Buaji (Ms. Lalita Pathak), "Vishuddha has done her P.hD. in kashtha maun. She has observed silence nicely along with her other responsibilities." I believe that everything was possible by Ma's grace only. Otherwise it was impossible to do Ma's seva, decoration, etc. while keeping silent as a wood.

This reminds me of an incident. Before the inauguration of the Chhalia temple, one day Ma was in the hall attending to some Mahatmas. I was busy in Ma's kitchen. Suddenly I burnt two fingers badly on the right hand while taking out a hot pot from the oven. Since I was observing silence I could not ask anybody for some remedy. One old lady was cutting vegetables there at that time. Seeing my condition she suggested to put my burnt fingers in cold water at once. I took cold water from the pitcher and dipped the fingers and just then someone told me that Ma was calling me in the hall. I rushed to the hall leaving behind the water. Ma signalled me to sit near Her. The fingers were burning like anything, so I pressed them on the marble floor to cool them. I was worried to think that how should I clean Ma's teeth next morning with these fingers and was praying to Ma that there should be no hindrance in Ma's service.

One Mahatma with his disciples came to have Ma's darshan. He was relating his own experience about sadhna. He said, "Ma, I also go through the stages of penance as you had and I attained trance." It was clear that he must have gone through Ma's life story. So long Ma was listening to him. When he mentioned his own stage of trance Ma said with a smile, "Pitaji, where there is 'I' there it can't be and when it is there, there can be no 'I'." In the literature of Vaishnavism it is said, "The lane of love is very narrow, if there is Shyam (God) there is no room for 'I' and if there is 'I', there 'He' can't be." When the Mahatma went away I got busy arranging for Ma's lunch and totally forgot about the burn. Ma said, "Prayer has got endless power." I prayed wholeheartedly and really Ma listened to it.

24

Once in Vrindavan ashram a Nam yajna, i.e., continuous recital of God's name was held. In the presence of Ma, it was started by Viren da, Noni da, etc. The gentlemen sang for some time, then the ladies continued. First Saroma di and then Chhabi di led the kirtan. Ma was also moving around the mancha with us. She also joined the kirtan in great bhav. Naturally the emotions ran high during the kirtan. After a long time Ma caught hold of both Chhabi di's and my hands with both Her hands and walked straight to Her room. Ma entered Her room and ordered both of us to lie down in Didima's room adjacent to Her room. We could not disobey Her but did not like to sleep at all. For some time we took rest but were restless as well. Ma understood and said, "Now you go to the kirtan." Whenever there was a Nam yajna, we both used to continue the whole night. But that year we both were sick, so Ma did this. Ma said, "What does the word 'Ma' mean? Ma means–one, who provides everything to her child according to the needs, she is the mother."

One summer we went to Patna with Ma. There we stayed in Mr. Shambhunath and Mrs. Maya Choudhury's house. They behaved with Ma as parents behave with their daughter. Maya di's attitude towards Ma was very affectionate. She prepared many things for Ma and was always keen to give Ma some rest. After staying there for a few days Ma left for Rajgir. Ma left behind Didima and Vimala di for 'Ambubachi' (a ritual observed by the widows only). Swami Paramananda ji, Sati di, Jaya and myself accompanied Ma in a taxi. On the road there was a damaged railing on a bridge towards Rajgir. So it was controlled by the traffic police and the vehicles were made to run in one way at the speed of 10 miles per hour. The journey was delayed. Since I was in Ma's service, I sat at Ma's feet in the car. As the taxi proceeded on the bridge, I wanted to see the damaged railings but Ma caught hold of us three girls in Her arms till the taxi reached the other end of that long bridge. She held us in such a way against Her chest as if we would fall down from the taxi.

We reached Rajgir quite late in the evening. Since no information of Ma's visit was sent before, no arrangements were made there. Only one Brahmachari was there. As Ma instructed me, I took out curd and sattu (powder of puffed rice) from Ma's basket, mixed and added candy powder and fed Ma. We also had that prasad that night.

Next day Swamiji made a make-shift oven and I cooked 'Khichri' for Ma and all of us. One day in the afternoon Ma ordered a taxi. She Herself sat near the driver and Sati di, Jaya and myself at the rear seat. Ma was the guide for us. She showed us Venuvan, where Lord Buddha used to walk, Sonebhandar, supposed to be the store of the Mahabharata era, Jarasandh ki baithak, the seat of the renowned king Jarasandha of the Mahabharata, the mark of Lord Krishna's chariot, etc. etc. At night Ma went to have a dip in the hot spring with us. General public takes bath the whole day, when they close the door the spring gets cleared and by special arrangements Ma bathed only at night.

Dr. P.R. Ghosh came from Ranchi to meet Ma. In the evening he was reading some important letters to Ma. Since there were lots of insects around the electric light he switched off the light and lit a torch. An insect entered into Ma's eye. Immediately Ma raised the upper lid of the eye and sent for me. I was cooking in the kitchen and rushed to Ma's room. The room was dark, only one torch was throwing light upwards. Dr. Ghosh was standing with a long face. If the torch was focused on Ma's eyes, insects would hover on Ma's face. Ma said to keep the torch focused upwards and try to take out the insect. I made a thin string with the corner of Ma's dhoti, turned the eyelid upwards and removed a tiny green insect. Ma said, "See whether the insect is alive or not." I saw the insect moving under the torch. Ma was very glad and patted my back sweetly. We enjoyed our Rajgir trip for a few days. Then we packed up to return to Patna.

One morning we took our luggage and sat in a taxi with Ma and started for Patna. Ma's lunch would take place at the destination. After going a little distance the taxi stopped near a crowded shopping area. The driver opened the bonnet of the car and left. Swamiji and Panu da sitting in the taxi thought the driver was repairing something. Ma was narrating something and we were listening to the same. After some time Ma asked Swamiji, "Paramananda, what has happened?" Swamiji got down to see that the driver had vanished. Panu da also got down. Ma said, "You two were there, still the driver vanished, you didn't even ask where he was going?" Then Swamiji on one side and Panu da on the other end stood in vain. Swamiji was moving his hand on his head and Panu da was seeing his pocket watch frequently. Ma laughed a lot seeing this and said, "Look, two of them are standing on two ends." We also laughed hearing Ma's words. The driver returned after one hour with a horn in his hand and chewing betel leaf as if nothing had happened. He tied the horn on the carrier and started. Later it was exposed that his in-law's house was there and he went there only to relish his lunch. He brought the horn only to show. After Bihar Sharif on the highway the road was not crowded at all, still the driver blew the horn off and on. Ma said, "He is blowing the horn only to show that it was needed."

In this way we reached Patna after an amusing journey. Vimala di was waiting for Ma with Her lunch. After Her bhog we had our prasad. Shambhu da and Maya di made nice arrangements for Ma and us. One afternoon a high-profile businessman, Ma's devotee, Mr. Jalan came to Ma accompanied by one Brahmakumari. He had a palatial building on the bank of Ganga. He wanted to take Ma there. Next day we went to Jalan kothi with Ma. It was situated on the outskirts of Patna, a huge and spacious palace on the banks of the river. It was probably a fortress of the Mauryan Emperor, later purchased by the ancestors of Mr. Jalan. It included an exclusive museum with many rare things of India and abroad collected by the Jalans. It was a palace worth seeing. Ma's room was also beautiful with carved doors and windows and mural paintings. We girls were accommodated in an annexe building just over the Ganga. It seemed as if we were on a ship.

Two main Brahmakumaris were staying there. They had many centres all over the world. Well educated ladies from well to do families had joined this institution. They learnt that Sati di and me were holding the degrees of Master of Arts, so they met us and talked for a long time. We heard that they hypnotise people. But nothing happened to us. One of them went out with Ma in a car. I was with Ma. The Brahmakumari sat beside Ma and I was sitting near Ma's feet. My hand was in Ma's grip. The kumari was looking straight into my eyes. I also stared at her thinking nothing would affect me since Ma was holding me.

Once I went to Patna with Ma. Respected Haribabaji was also there. He wished to visit the sacred places of that area with Ma. We visited the local Temples, Gurudwaras, and Buddhist Stupas, etc. Patna is the birth place of Sikh Preceptor Guru Govind Singhji. One day Ma and Haribaba went to visit the Gurudwara at Guru Govind Singhji's birth place. As per the Sikh traditions there were two small water tanks on both sides of the steps for the visitors to wash their feet. Haribaba and his disciple washed their feet in one of the tanks and went up the steps. I was with Ma, She dipped Her feet in one of the tanks. How could I put my feet into that? I touched the water of the tank to my head and went to the other tank to wash my feet. Ma was holding my hand since we got down from the car and throughout She held me. When I went to the other end, She also covered the distance with me and nodded Her head in appreciation. We went up and visited the place of birth, a well (water body) used by the Guru and other things of Guru Govind Singhji.

After visiting Patna and Rajgir we went to Ranchi. A few days before, the new Kali temple was inaugurated at Ranchi. A satsang hall was built in front of the temple. Haribaba did kirtan in that hall regularly. Ma ordered me to decorate the temple of Kali. I made Kali's favorite flower Jaba (Hibiscus),

Aparajita (Blue pea) and Shefali (Jasmine) with paper. At noon I was decorating the temple when Paramananda Swamiji came to see. He stood there staring at the flowers for a long time. Then he commented, "Why are you decorating with these flowers? They will dry up in a few hours." In the temple we don't talk, so I kept silent but smiled. When in the afternoon Ma came to see the temple I told about Swamiji's comment. With a naughty look Ma said, "Paramananda is also deceived?" Seeing Ma's joy and expression I was overwhelmed.

25

The Durga Puja on a grand scale took place in the Delhi ashram organized by Swami Swarupanandaji and the devotees of Delhi. To the north of the Nam Brahma Mandir, i.e., the round shaped hall for the recital of God's name, in the premises of the Panchvati a round shaped new Mandap was built for Durga Puja. Renowned artists from Kolkata came to make a beautiful idol of the Goddess Durga.

Ma asked somebody to call Varanasi ashram to tell Vishuddha that she should cut and dry coconut cheera and jeera (coconut grated in the shape of flattened rice puff and cumin–a favourite of Ma which she would give to the Mahatmas and VIPs explaining the speciality of it) and bring it to Delhi. In due time we reached Delhi and went to do obeisance to Ma. Seeing us Ma was so glad that she said, "Well you have come, now take the responsibility of the worship. Special pitcher for Devi would be installed on the first day of the New Moon. From that day the full-fledged puja would start." Shantaji (later Swami Purnanandaji) and I had the responsibility of the mandap. There were Benarasi sarees, gold ornaments for everyday worship. Swami Swarupanandaji bought a lot of brass vessels for the occasion. Big brass drums were filled with water from the Jamuna river. Every article for the puja was washed in that water only. An exclusive pandal was made on the courtyard in front of Panchvati. Many renowned music artists from Kolkata and locals were invited to this function.

On the auspicious moment of the first day of the New Moon the special pitchers were installed in the mandap. Brahmachari Nirvananandaji did the worship according to the scriptures. After the early morning aarti Ma taught Shantaji and me to do obeisance to Devi Durga. She told us the prayer should be like this–*"Ma you are my resort, I am yours and bless me all the time."* Ma also instructed both of us to do this prayer and pranam by prostration on the ground early in the morning and nobody should see us doing this.

Many devotees from Kolkata, Varanasi and Dehradun assembled at Delhi ashram on this occasion. Ma was moving about all over the ashram in great 'bhav'. We were doing paper-cuttings for the decoration of the Ashram. Quite often Ma visited and addressed us, "Where are my beauties?" Buli di, Chhabi di, Taru di, Sati di and I were overwhelmed with joy hearing Ma's address and in between Chhabi di and I used to sit in the mandap to sing devotional songs. Ma is Ananadamayee, always She is full of 'ananda' no doubt, but during Durga puja I noticed a special ananda and brightness overflowed Her complexion. We witnessed Durga Herself moving in human flesh.

During Durga puja we made a bed for Devi to sleep, at noon and at night. One early morning while awakening Devi I found 'Kajal' (collyrium) on the pillow. Seeing that Ma said, "It proves that Durga is accepting the worship." As the function occurred in Delhi, many VIPs including the Prime Minister Mrs. Indira Gandhi visited the ashram very often. During the 'sandhipuja', i.e., the main worship to Durga, Mrs. Gandhi came and attended the whole function, received prasad and Ma's blessings.

Ma was in Vrindavan and I was in Her service. A 'Bhagwat Saptah' (week) was going to be held at Baghat House, Haridwar, for Dadamahashay (Ma's father). I was cutting papers for decoration of the Baghat House. Ma asked me to bring the paper and the scissors to Her. She told me to show how to fold and cut the paper and then She cut the same nicely. Since the Bhagwat week was done for Her father's well-being, as a daughter She should do something Herself. I preserved that piece of paper cut by Ma in a basket with an instruction of giving it to Dadabhai. She would have been very glad to add it to her collection of Ma's used articles. But alas! It was lost as I was in Ma's compartment and my luggage was with others in their place. Till date I cannot forget it.

In Varanasi one day Ma had a vision that God had fed Her a special sweet made of thickened milk and flour. Dadabhai prepared the same under Ma's instructions and fed Her. Then Ma served us and said, "Take Amrita". She named that sweet 'Amrita' (nectar).

In July, 1966 Ma was going to Dehradun from Haridwar by car. On the rear seat, Ma, Udasji, Manada's two daughters Gouridi, Rama and I sat. In the front seat was Swamiji and a devotee was driving the car. Ma was talking about something and the devotee also joined the conversation. The car reached the Parade Ground crossing when a school bus all of a sudden crossed the road and our car stopped with a jerk. Nothing did collide but we found Ma's left palm had a long cut and the same was bleeding profusely. A serious accident could have taken place but nothing serious happened. Ma's wrappers and dhoti were soaked in blood. People were waiting at Kishenpur ashram to visit Ma, but Ma directed the driver to go straight to Kalyanvan, a two furlong distance garden of our ashram. Reaching there Ma went to the half completed cottage of Amritananda (a foreign lady devotee of Ma).

Mr. P.N. Deogan, a retired forest officer and a staunch devotee of Ma was present in Kalyanvan at that time. Seeing the cut in Ma's hand he said if Ma permitted him, he could apply a herb found in the garden. With Ma's consent, he gathered some leaves from small plants and asked me to take out the juice of those leaves. Since there was no grinder, I washed two pieces of stones and crushed those leaves, used Ma's dhoti's corner to squeeze out the juice and with Ma's permission put a few drops on the cut. But before I could finish Ma forbade to apply more. Where the juice was applied the cut healed up within a short time, but where it was not applied it took months for healing.

We felt very sad due to this accident. Then it struck me that once Ma told me to utter the name of Shiva whenever I do anything to Her body. So for Her early recovery we started doing kirtan of Shiva's name with Ma's permission.

Afterwards from third July to eighth August we did continuous kirtans round the clock. Every evening I used to ask Ma which name and in which tune should the kirtan be sung.

They were:

1. Om Namo, Bhagwate Vasudevaya.
2. Jai Ram, Shree Ram, Jai Jai Ram.
3. Bhaja Nitai Gaur Radhe Shyam, Japo Hare Krishna, Hare Ram.
4. Jai Shiva Shankar, Bam Bam Hara Hara.
5. Shree Ma, Jai Ma, Jai Jai Ma.
6. Shree Hanuman Chalisa.
7. Haribol, Haribol, Haribol, Haribol.
8. Naraina, Naraina, Om Om.
9. Hari Narayana Om.
10. Ma Durga, Ma Kali, Ma Saraswati, Ma Mahalakshmi.
11. Hare Krishna, Hare Krishna, Krishna Krishna, Hare Hare.
    Hare Rama, Hare Rama, Rama Rama, Hare Hare.
12. Satyam Gnanam, Anantam Brahma.
    Shantam Shivam, Advaitam Brahma.
    Anandrupam Amritam Brahma.
    Ekamevadwiteeyam Brahma.
13. Jai Guru Jai Ma, Jai Guru Jai Ma, Jai Gurudev.
14. Gauri Shankar Shiva Shambhu.
15. Bhaja Govindam, Bhaja Govindam,
    Govindam Bhaja Gopalam.
16. Shree Guru Sharanam, Shree Guru Sharanam
    Na Guroradhikam, Na Guroradhikam, Jai Guru.
17. Hey Gananayaka, Hey Gananayaka, Bhavabhaya Taraka Palayamam,
    Siddhivinayaka, Siddhivinayaka, Varabhaya dayaka Palayamam,
    Namo Ganeshaya Namo Ganeshaya Namo Ganeshaya Namo Namah.
18. Jyoti se Jyoti Jalao Ram, Jyoti se Jyoti Jalao Ram.

26

In my earlier days when I visited Ma for the first time I saw Dadabhai with Her. I have seen a good many persons who regarded her with fear. But I know not why I was attracted by her intellectual appearance from the very beginning. I think she was also affectionate to me, a bit more than others. Her father Swami Akhandanandaji was also very affectionate towards me. In his former life when he was a civil surgeon at Naogaon, my father was acquainted with him.

We have seen Dadabhai performing tremendous work in the ashram neatly and perfectly–service to Ma, management of the ashrams, collection of donations for the Kanyapeeth and Vidyapeeth, reading out to Ma the letters of innumerable devotees and replying to them, recording the facts and figures of Ma's life, Her sayings and conversation, cooking for Ma and bhandaras, reception and entertainment of endless devotees and so on. All along she did this selflessly.

Only when she came to Varanasi the girls of Kanyapeeth gave her a helping hand if necessary. Once Ma was in Varanasi. Late in the night after getting Ma to lay down and hanging Her mosquito net properly Dadabhai went to her bed. Gangadi, an elder girl of Kanyapeeth spread her bed in the narrow space in front of Ma's door and Dadabhai fell asleep as soon as she took to her bed due to her day long tiredness and Gangadi was caressing her feet lightly with her hands. In the meantime Ma came out with a torch in Her hand to go to the bathroom. Suddenly She turned Her torch towards Dadabhai's bed and saw Gangadi. At once she said, "I see you have opened Kanyapeeth to have service from the girls and not to serve them?" Dadabhai got up startled and sat up immediately. Hearing Ma she said with tearful eyes, "Pardon me, pardon me Ma–to serve kumaris of course..." Next day we heard this from Ganga di.

After a few days I was admitted to Kanyapeeth. One day Dadabhai was cooking bhog for Ma, I too was doing something. Pushpa di came hurriedly and said to Dadabhai, "Didi, Ma is saying to sing from the 'Prempukar', but I have not got the book, what to do?" Dadabhai said, "Quite so, what to do? How can I give it?" Then I told, "Dadabhai, there is a book in your trunk." Dadabhai was astonished and asked, "In my trunk? How do you know?" I said, "One day I went into the cave to call you, there your trunk was open. I saw inside the book titled 'Prempukar'." Dadabhai instantly went there and brought the book, gave it to Pushpa di. She was very glad, otherwise she couldn't have given the book to Pushpa di. She fondled me affectionately again and again.

In the worship room of Kanyapeeth there was a reading session in the afternoon where Ma's life and lives of the Mahatmas were read out for half an hour at the instruction of Dadabhai. Mauni ma and Ganga di used to sit there. Dadabhai also came and took her seat there at times when she could find time in the midst of so many occupations. She would move about to see whether everybody had attended the evening aarti of Ma or not. If she found any girl still cooking in the kitchen, she would say, "Take off the pan and put coal in the oven, attend aarti, some ten-fifteen minutes will cause no harm, it is a must, or it will be a disregard for Ma."

When Varanasi ashram was established, Kanyapeeth was shifted to Varanasi from Dehradun and Ma stayed there very often. In the morning Ma supervised the whole building and instructed Mana da every detail for convenience of the girls. Sometimes She said to make one thing, next day She ordered something different. Whatever Ma said Dadabhai would say– "Yes Ma, it is OK." Afterwards as Ma changed the whole thing Dadabhai would say, "Yes Ma, this is perfect." So one day Mana da said to Dadabhai, "Didi, Please don't say anything. You have got no sense of your own. If Ma says, "Didi, the sun rises in the West", you will say, "Yes Ma". Hearing this Dadabhai said with tears in her eyes–"Brother, bless me that I can be like that forever."

When Dadabhai was seriously ill Ma sent Renu di and me for her service and nursing. Renu di wilfully took the charge and Dadabhai being my preceptor, it was my duty to serve her. So I think I was blessed as Ma gave me the chance to serve her.

There was an old photo of Dadabhai in our office. Her date of birth was mentioned in it. Since she was seriously ill, Sati di suggested to Kshama di that we should celebrate Didi's birthday. It is said that if one observes birthdays, the longevity of life prolongs. When Ma was told of this, She said, "Didi's life is of a disciplined one, so you should observe Sanyam to celebrate her birthday."

First year Dadabhai's birthday was celebrated in the presence of Ma. We offered her new cloth, garland and sandal paste. Her favourite dishes were prepared and after Ma's bhog she took prasad. In front of Ma we meditated for an hour and after maun Narain Swami ji and Dadabhai's elder cousin Mr. J.C. Mukherji gave a talk about her. Then on Ma's orders Kshama di, Sati di, Buba di, Chandan di and I delivered short speeches about Dadabhai. While talking about her I mentioned that Dadabhai used to scold us for our good. Dadabhai was sitting next to Ma. Hearing this at once Ma said to her–"Scold more, as she has mentioned it in the gathering."

Once we were celebrating Dadabhai's birthday as usual. Since Ma was not present, her mood was off. Narain Swami ji offered a basket of fruits and sweets on our behalf. One little girl put a garland around her neck and offered sandal paste. But Dadabhai was sitting in a state of indifference. I thought under the circumstance, what I could give her. I had a piece of cotton soaked in perfume touched at Ma's feet. As I handed over that piece of cotton to her, tears flowed from her eyes and she blessed me touching my head with both her hands.

The ring finger tip of my right hand was hurting me badly. In winters the pain was severe. A Homeopath doctor treated it for a long time but in vain. Ma sent me to Dr. Santosh Sen, the topmost surgeon of Delhi. He operated suspecting a foreign particle inside. After the operation and dressing the finger bled profusely. At that time Ma was in Delhi. Due to bandage in the right hand I could not eat properly. Vimala di cooked and fed Ma. After Ma's bhog Vimala di used to mix rice, pulse and vegetables, make balls of it and put inside my mouth. Days together I ate in this way. Ma's endless love reflected on my seniors such as Vimala di, Kshama di, Buni di, Renu di, etc.

The finger was alright after some time but the pain remained. Then Ma sent me to Mumbai for further treatment. I stayed at Bhaiya's place for one and a half months. Bhaiya engaged Dr. S.B. Seth to investigate the case. He contacted the topmost neurologist of Mumbai. The finger was operated upon again.

Lots of blood oozed out but of no avail. Experienced surgeons diagnosed that it was a very rare case of fluid tumour known as glomus tumour on the nerve on the flesh below the nail. It was extremely painful and in the long run it might be a case of gangrene. I was called back to Varanasi by Ma. Then Ma started my treatment by doing hot and cold fomentation etc. She asked me to make a double lined cap in the measurement of the finger, put heated mountain salt and put on the same on the finger at bed time. Still the finger was not painless. But I believe that by Ma's treatment, the fear of gangrene would be no more.

My elder brother Dr. Satyananda Chakraborty is a homeopathy practitioner. He and my father were scared listening to the expert's opinion. He wanted to see the case and wrote to me to come home with Ma's permission. Since I was in the ashram, Ma was doing whatever was good for me. Secondly if I asked Ma, She would think that I wanted to go home. Hence I kept quiet. Then my brother wrote directly to Dadabhai. Ma was in Varanasi. She was in the adjacent room of Annapurna Temple. One morning I went to do obeisance to Her. Dadabhai was also there. She said to me, "Have you heard that your brother wants to treat your finger?" Ma said, "Yes, your brother wants to take you home with affection, go and get cured from all your ailments." Dadabhai didn't like that I should go home for a long time and said, "Ma, for homeopathic treatment she will go once, consult the doctor, get the prescription and come back. Afterwards she can continue the treatment through mail." Ma said, "No Didi, she has got so many complications associated with headache and pain in the abdomen, let her go and come back being completely cured." At that time I was preparing myself to appear at the M.A. final examination in Sanskrit by Ma's order. Also then I maintained the whole accounts of Kanyapeeth. Ma asked me to go home just after my examination, which was scheduled shortly. So I got more occupied with the accounts than my studies.

A Bhagwat fortnight by the renowned speaker Swami Akhandanandaji was taking place shortly at Varanasi. A huge pandal was erected on the grounds of Shree Shree Mata Anandamayee Hospital. I received the timetable of my examination which indicated that my exam would start a day after the Bhagwat was over. The final examination of the Kanyapeeth girls also was scheduled a little later. The principal restricted the girls from attending the Bhagwat. The girls were disheartened. I decided to listen to the Bhagwat as I could appear at the examination again even if I failed. But the chance of listening to Bhagwat at Varanasi from the lips of Swami Akhandanandaji in Ma's presence, would not come again. I completed the accounts sitting up the whole night.

The Bhagwat started on a grand scale. The girls of Kanyapeeth sat to study in contrary moods. I was going to the pandal and they said, "Vishuddhadi, we want to go with you." I replied, "Chandandi forbade you to go, what can I do? I am going, if you can come in your own responsibility. I have no objection." The girls were very pleased and followed me. While going every time they used to pray, "Oh! Vishwanath, let Vishuddhadi pass her M.A. in first class." They didn't bother about their own results. This made me laugh.

One day I was listening to Bhagwat in the pandal. Bithudi was shocked to see me and said, "Vishuddha, day after tomorrow your exam starts and you are sitting here?" I replied,

"Bithu di, if I don't attend the Bhagwat people will think that I am studying hard and after that if I fail they will blame me saying that after trying so much she has failed. But if I attend Bhagwat and fail everybody will understand that I couldn't study well. Moreover if I pass after listening to Bhagwat it would be appreciated much." Bithu di said with a smile, "Naughty one". The Bhagwat ended with a grand success.

My exams started. Since Ma was present there, every morning I used to do obeisance to Her. As I was appearing at the exams in Sanskrit, Ma looked very pleased. After the exam Saraswati worship took place. Ma presented me a marble idol of Saraswati with four hands. Then She went elsewhere and I started for Kolkata with my father.

27

From Kolkata I went to Durgapur to my brother's house. He started my treatment immediately. He also wanted me to join the Burdwan University for research course. But I disobeyed him as I had no interest in studies. Since I stayed in the ashram from my childhood I didn't like to stay at home. Hence after a few days I went to Kolkata with my father. There also I didn't fit in well. With my father's consent I used to go and stay with Chhabi di (Geetashree Chhabi Banerji). In between I had to visit Durgapur for treatment. On Ma's instructions, Chhabi di implemented strict rules. Like an ashramite she served the idol of Radha Krishna given by Ma.

Dadabhai wrote letters with Ma's sayings and enquired about my health regularly. After a few months she informed me the King of Trivandrum had invited Ma and her entourage to go there to attend the special 'lakh-lamp' festival of Padmanabh temple, which occurred every sixth year only. I heard from the girls who went there that when they were there for the festival, Ma uttered thrice slowly 'Vishuddha, Vishuddha, Vishuddha'. What a divine kheyal of Ma for such an ordinary child like me. It was just beyond my imagination.

I was in Chhabi di's house. After a few days I had acute pain in the abdomen and one midnight blood vomiting started. At once I was hospitalized at the Ramakrishna Mission Seva Pratishthan. Ma was at Vindhyachal ashram. Udas ji was with Her. At night Ma was in Her bed and Udas ji slept near Her door. At midnight she awoke by some sound. It was a winter night and getting up from sound sleep she could not trace wherefrom the sound came. After listening for some time she found that the sound was coming from Ma's bed. She stood before Ma's cot to see that Ma was lying on Her chest and rubbing Her nose on the pillow uttering, 'Vishuddha, Vishuddha'. For how long She was doing this Udas ji could not guess. Hearing 'Vishuddha' she said, "Ma, Vishuddha is not here, she is in Kolkata." She repeatedly said this but there was no response. She understood that Ma was in a trance. The whole night Ma was in the same state. Next morning Dr. Gopal Das Gupta called to inform Ma that Vishuddha's ulcer had burst, she was on death bed. Later Udas ji told me, "I am in Ma's service since many years, but never had I seen Ma lying on Her chest and rubbing Her nose against the pillow in this way."

After transfusion of nine bottles of blood and long treatment, I was fit to be operated upon. Ma's devotee Dr. Gunendra Narain Roy's friend Dr. H. Paul, M.R.C.P., F.R.C.P., Head,

Dept. of Medicine of that hospital, treated me. Another devotee of Ma, Mr. Ranjit Kumar Banerji's nephew Dr. Subir Chatterji, the renowned surgeon of Kolkata operated my ulcer. I was recovering gradually when one day the Matron said to me, "You are a little better now. So I am accommodating one old lady in your cabin for a short while. She will be shifted to another cabin as soon as it is available." After enquiry I learnt that she could not sleep since long. Seeing my dress she asked which ashram I belonged to. On knowing that I was from Ma Anandamayee ashram, she said, "I have heard Ma's name but had not the fortune of visiting Her." While talking she turned towards the wall and slept.

All of a sudden I saw Ma entering my cabin. Sister Kalyani guided Ma to my cabin and left. Ma came and stood in front of me. I tried to bend down but Ma prohibited and signalled that I shouldn't bend as I had an operation in abdomen. Those days Ma was observing maun. So She took my hand and wrote on it whatever she had to say and I replied in the same way. Ma wrote that She intended to take me with Her. I asked what was preventing Her? Ma wrote, "Your father and brothers have arranged so many things, treatment is going on..."

For about one hour Ma and I communicated. Then Ma enquired about that lady. I said she could not sleep, but at that moment she was in sound sleep. I tried to call her but Ma prevented me from doing so. Then Biren da brought my lunch from Chhabi di's house. He was surprised to see Ma. She hinted at him to call Chhabi di. She came and Ma wrote many things on her hand about me. Ma stayed for one and half hour or two and then left. Chhabi di followed Her and I was looking at Her standing by the door. Ma passed the long corridor towards the lift and came back again to my cabin door, signalled Chhabi di to stay with me and left alone.

I was surprised to see that the old lady was sitting on her bed. Ma was there for such a long time but the lady slept and couldn't see Ma. Knowing this she wept and repented. I understood that it happened only by Ma's kheyal. As Ma had some private talk with me she didn't wake up. Poor lady, she missed Ma's darshan. At that time my sister-in-law came and had Ma's darshan in the car. Ma enquired about my father and brother in sign language. Later I learnt Ma had come to Kolkata with Paramananda Swami ji and one or two girls. Only Dr. Gopal Das Gupta was informed and She stayed for a short while at Mr. Ranjit Kumar Banerji's house.

After my recovery I went to Varanasi for Ma's darshan with Biren da and Chhabi di. Ma was very pleased to see us. Then She was not in maun. She talked a lot and at the end asked Chhabi di, "Chhabi do you remember, when this body went to see Vishuddha at the hospital, while coming back you were with me, but after some time it was my kheyal that with whom I was leaving Vishuddha. So it was in you I stayed with her and took you to Vishuddha and instructed you to stay near her." While saying this Ma's eyes were full of tears.

According to the rules of the Kanyapeeth, whenever we come back from home or hospital we should not eat with the girls. We should sit separately in some other place for some time. So I sat in the verandah when somebody came running and said, "Ma said, Vishuddha should sit where she used to sit before going home." We stayed for a short time in the ashram. While coming back we did obeisance to Ma, She asked Chhabi di to take out a green plastic bucket kept under Her cot filled with chosen fruits and handed over to me saying, "Somebody gave me few plastic buckets to distribute. This body gave the elder girls and as you were not here, I reserved this bucket for you under my cot, so that nobody should take it away." This made me overwhelmed. Her kheyal was always with me.

28

In 1967 the Durga Puja took place at Haridwar, Baghat House and Chhabi di's brother Dulal da and my brother Nityananda with their families accompanied us to Haridwar. We faced some difficulties in the beginning regarding reservation in the train. Then at midnight we got down at Burdwan station and found our reservations in a puja special train. Next day being Monday, Chhabi di and Shyama both observed maun. Shyama got down to fetch water at Mughalsarai station without informing anybody and the train started. Since the bathroom of the train was closed we thought she was there. But after a long time it was found Shyama was nowhere in the train. She was travelling for the first time and knew nothing. Very scared, we just prayed to Ma that She should protect the girl. Next morning reaching Haridwar we informed Ma about Shyama that she was missing. The way She reacted I understood that Shyama was alright. Ma expressed pleasure to see us. Since I was sick, at once Ma asked for the storekeeper Ganga di and ordered her to arrange milk, etc. for me according to my requirements.

That was the sixth day of Durga puja. A maiden was to be worshipped on that day. But the maiden had not arrived yet and Nirvan da, the priest was waiting for the maiden. That very moment my niece Rai did obeisance to Ma and She asked my sister-in-law pointing towards the girl, "How old is she?" My sister-in-law replied, "Today is her birthday and she is only six years old." Very gladly Ma said to Nirvan da, "Look, your maiden has come". She also said to my sister-in-law, "Go fast, bathe her and take her to the worship pavilion. In the presence of Ma, Rai was worshipped as a special maiden of Durga puja. Nirvan da took a snap of Ma with Rai.

Next morning Shyama, the chosen girl arrived with Dr. Padma Mitra, the President of Kanyapeeth from Varanasi. We heard from her that when the girl saw the movement of the train, she started crying loudly. Then one sadhu came forward and asked, "Mother, where will you go?" Shyama said that she wanted to go to Ananadamayee Ashram at Varanasi. Since the sadhu was also going to Varanasi, he brought her to the proper destination.

My sister-in-law was eager to be initiated by Ma, but my brother was not prepared at all. Ma was too busy to spare time, still She did a long private talk with my brother and said, "It is more effective if husband and wife are initiated together." At last he agreed. On the Mahanavami morning they were initiated by Ma in front of the Goddess Durga. Ma also explained the deep meaning of the mantra to them. A big crowd assembled to be initiated by Ma. The worship completed with great satisfaction. We went back to Kolkata with Ma's blessings.

A big gathering for Bhagwat week was organised by the renowned businessman Mr. Singhania of Kanpur. Their preceptor Swami Akhandanandaji delivered the speech on Bhagwat. The Singhanias had palatial buildings, temples, parks, factories, offices, etc. in Kanpur. A separate building was erected for Ma, Akhandananda ji and the devotees. Nearly every year they used to arrange for religious programmes, discourses, etc. There were exclusive arrangements for all the prasad prepared cautiously under proper supervision. Those were wonderful and we relished.

I was fortunate to listen to Swami Akhandanandaji's speech on the Bhagwat quite a number of times. Every time he gave a new dimension to the Bhagwat. On the fifth day Lord Krishna's birth ceremony was celebrated on a grand scale.

The pandal was decorated and offerings of curd, butter, sweets, fruits, cloth, jewellery, etc. were made. Flower garlands were placed before the Bhagwat. At the end of the evening discourse Lord Krishna's birth celebrations started. After the aarti, offerings were made on behalf of Ma, Singhanias and the public. Ma's seat was next to Swami Akhandanandaji. We were looking at Ma and the Bhagwat. All of a sudden Akhandanandaji spread his cloth in front of Ma and said, "Ma give, you give". Bhaskar da and Nirvan da were looking at each other and thinking that the offerings on Ma's behalf were already offered, so what could Ma give now? In a moment Ma bent down on his cloth with folded hands and sweetly said like a little girl, "Pitaji, this body has offered itself." Akhandanandaji's eyes were filled with tears as he didn't expect such a present from Ma, the embodiment of selflessness. I was sitting just behind Ma, so I could witness the spectacle and was overwhelmed.

This reminds me of another occasion when the president of the Divine Life Society, revered Swami Chidanandaji spoke about Ma while paying homage to Her. He said, "Ma's way of giving is unique and no one can think of it."

Ma and Swami Chidanandaji, The President of the Divine Life Society, Rishikesh at Gondal Palace.

Sitting from left to right
Kantanada, Swami Chidanandaji, Shree Shree Ma, Jaya Bhattacharya, Puspa Sen, Vishuddha Chakraborty.

Standing from left to right, 1st row
Mala Bhattacharya, Renuka Mukherji, Kanti Gurtu, Indu Singh, Geeta Dey, Maitreyji, Pramilaji (Swami Pragnananda), Udasji, Ansuya Dave, Swarna Kumari Jaspal (Billojee), Vasumati Mehta.

Standing from left to right, 2nd row
Parul Banerjee, Sunita, Ganga Chakraborty, Aruna Pandya, Gopalpriya Sen, Kripal Kaur, Chitra Ghosh, Nilima Chatterjee (Swami Nilam Giri), Jaba Chakraborty, Hansa Mehta.

It was the month of February, 1974 when the devotees had arranged a Bhagwat week in the ground adjacent to Shree Prativa Kumar Kundu's house and invited Ma. Mr. Kundu built a new accommodation for Ma in his own house. A beautiful spacious pandal was made for the Bhagwat week function. Professor Narain Goswami, a learned Vaishnav Pandit of Kolkata explained the whole Bhagwat in a lucid, but scholarly language. Apart from that Vaishnavacharya, Dr. Mahanamvrata Brahmachari ji also enthralled the audience with his unique art of describing the leela of Lord Krishna. Ma had come to Kolkata after a long time. So there was a huge crowd of visitors round the clock. A lot of people had initiation from Ma. The great wonder was that those prominent Naxals for whom Ma was not brought to Kolkata for a few years came to Ma and took Her blessings.

Ma came to our house at Tollygunge on Sunday the 24th February, 1974. Since it was not planned before, an ordinary arrangement was done within a few minutes. But Ma was in a good mood. While my sister-in-law did aarti to Ma, She Herself sang the kirtan and then distributed the prasad to all present. She stood in front of our worship room and said, "Beautiful Shivalinga in honey colour is very rare. This body gave word to Virajmohini to come to her house, so it is fulfilled."

In this reference I must mention that Mauni ma, a Sanyasi of the ashram was very friendly with my grandmother Virajmohini Devi. When the Kolkata ashram was at Ekdalia, Mauni ma stayed there for a long time. Then she used to visit our house very often and sometimes she liked to stay with my grand ma. She was a sanyasini so she was not supposed to stay with the householders. Hence it was criticized and reported to Ma. She mentioned the same to Mauni ma and she replied, "Ma, Viraj di's house is the abode of Shiva, I get peace over there."

Hearing this Ma said, "Oh! This is the matter, then this body can also stay there." Then my grandma made a new room for Ma and invited Her to come. But at that moment the political situation of Kolkata was not peaceful so Ma did not come. She asked grandma to get in the new room in an auspicious moment and it was done accordingly. And after a few days, grandma breathed her last.

The Bhagwat week was over. Dr. Gunendra Narain Roy took Ma to his polyclinic 'Niramay' which was under construction. Ma had come to Kolkata after a long gap, so wherever She went heavy crowd gathered, visitors stood hours together in a queue to have Ma's darshan. On the other hand the chief minister of West Bengal Mr. Siddhartha Shankar Ray along with his family and many other celebrities came to Ma and had private discussion with Her. In between Ma had gone somewhere else. Nobody informed Ma about the waiting crowd. As Ma stepped out the public saw Ma going, they became crazy and threw the offerings towards Ma. Anyhow Ma managed to accept their offerings and rushed to the car. Sitting in the car Ma said, "Paramananda, what a scene! In future it is to be pondered over whether this body should come here or not."

Swami ji and those who were in the car said, "No, no, no question arises to come here again." I was sitting at Ma's feet in the car. I said, "Ma, the visitors were from respectable and educated families, they came earnestly to see and get your blessings only. They stood for hours together in the line since early morning and suddenly found Ma going away, so they couldn't control themselves and threw the offerings towards you. They were very sad naturally." While saying this, my eyes were filled with tears. That very moment I noticed Ma's appearance changed totally and She said, "Yes it is true. They came with great difficulties from far and near. They came to give darshan to this body but I could not spare some time for them. Paramananda, remember, in future make proper arrangements for the public and then only bring this body to Kolkata." This is called 'God accepts the emotion', 'Bhavagrahi Janardana'. Ma used to say, "This body is a doll made of emotions, as you play so you listen."

29

In 1977, November, Swami Brahmanandaji, the head of the Sanyas ashram, Mumbai, arranged the Sanyam week at Badarik ashram on the banks of the river Narmada. We girls went there with Ma. The region around the river was an appropriate place for sanyam and penance. The sanyam week was very successfully organised under the efficient arrangements of Swami Brahmanandaji from the 18th to 24th November. After the sanyam week we stayed at our Bhimpura ashram with Ma for a pretty long time.

There were many old temples on the holy banks of Narmada. Hence under Ma's arrangements one early morning we the ashram girls, sadhus, brahmacharis, householder devotees all were doing obeisance to Ma and uttering 'Jai Ma' while boarding two big boats. The gents took place in one boat and we ladies were in another boat. Chhabi di was in our boat, she sang for long hours and we enjoyed the journey. The river was very deep and with frequent turns and as there were no motor-boats, the boats moved only by sail. So it took a lot of time. But the scenic beauty entertained us. We visited Anusuya, Shukdev, etc. and at noon reached Vyasdeva where all over on the banks were only 'Shiva and Shiva'. We walked on Shiva to take a dip in the river and all of us collected many 'Shivas' (stone resembling Linga) as we could. On our way back we had some snacks brought with us. We reached the ashram in the evening and went straight to Ma's room.

We heard that since we left in the morning Ma was in Her bed and just as we returned She got up. The whole day she took nothing. Seeing us She said, "You left and this body lay down in a different bhav. It was seen that a white hand with bangles caught hold of Chhabi's hand." Hearing this we thought that Chhabi di must have had the fear of drowning in the river. But it was not so. Next Ma said, "There was a chance of somebody drowning in the river, but since Mother Narmada caught hold of Chhabi's hand it was saved."

We placed the Shivalingas collected from Vyasdeva in two baskets in front of Ma. She took each Shivalinga in Her hand and after examining them minutely She put 50% out and asked to immerse them back in the river. The rest of the Shivalingas were kept in a basket and Ma asked Chhabi di to offer Narmada water and bel leaves on them daily. In the cave under Ma's room we kept the basket. Chhabi di said to me, "Look, we brought such Shivalingas that Ma had to discard half of it, it is shameful indeed." In reply I said, "What are you saying? At least 50% Ma kept from our collection.

But whatever Ma collected touring all over India, out of those none of us would be saved after scrutiny."

After two days Ma asked to bring the basket of Shivalingas (a weighing balance and rice to Her room). Each Shivalinga was weighed with rice and kept covered in the same quantity of rice varying from one or three days. It should be covered well so that no rat or insects reached it or could eat the rice. Again after the stipulated time the Shivalingas were weighed with the same rice only. Sometimes the rice became heavier than the Shivalinga as it was supposed to give you more and such a Shivalinga might be worshipped in a household. If the rice becomes less, that means it is a Shivalinga suitable for the Sanyasis and not fit for householders people. It will eat, but does not give. If the rice remains of the same weight as the linga, neither more nor less, that means it should be of no use. They should be immersed in Narmada or Ganga again.

During Shivratri we accompanied Ma to Pune. Since Ma was there on the occasion, lots of people gathered there from all over India. Ma asked me to arrange the worship in the hall as we do in Kanyapeeth. Ma Herself came to the hall to instruct the placing of everything. In the evening the worship started as usual and Ma was moving around to see everybody. In the late night Ma went to Her room.

After finishing the whole night worship Chhabi di and I went to do obeisance to Ma. It was still dark. Udasji was waiting for us at the door of Ma's room. As we entered She said, "Ma asked me to make grape juice and hot candy water separately and said mix both when Chhabi and Vishuddha would come and make them drink it." Moreover she said Ma gave me this responsibility and went to rest. Listening to this my whole day's fatigue vanished in a moment and eyes were filled with tears. How affectionate is indeed Ma!

When the Pune ashram was established, once I went with Ma from Mumbai for an 'Agyatvas' (undisclosed stay). I was in Ma's service. There was a beautiful garden in front of the ashram building and on the backside beyond the boundary wall there were only cultivated fields. In the morning Ma used to sit here on a small stool under the Sun and I used to massage oil on Her. One day while I was massaging suddenly Ma said, "Look, somebody is passing through the field." I got worried that Ma would not allow to massage Her anymore. I brought one bedsheet and tried to hang it. One side was tied but the other end was quite far to reach the bamboo and neither there was any string to add. I was holding the sheet in hand and touching the bamboo with the other. Suddenly I touched a nail on the bamboo and gladly exclaimed, "Ma I have got a nail here" and pushed the other hemming loop of the sheet into the nail. Ma smiled and said, "God provides everywhere whatever is required and people think they have found it and done it."

After staying alone with Ma for quite some time we started for Mumbai by the 'Deccan Queen' train. The train was beautiful as its name indicated. Ma and I were in a first class coupe. While leaving, someone had gave a small longish shaped papaya for Ma from the ashram garden. As the train moved Ma asked me to take out the papaya and a knife. I washed the same and Ma took both from my hands. She cut the upper portion of it and neatly took out the inner layer of the papaya with a silver spoon. Then She scraped the papaya by spoon and handed over the spoon in my hand to feed

Her. Ma said it was very sweet. I fed Ma many times in the same manner. Then She gave me some inside my mouth. Ma scraped very neatly and at last handed over the skin to me and said, "Take this glass of papaya, you can drink water in it if you like."

Ma was in Kankhal, a full kumbh mela was drawing near and on the 13th of April Didima's statue would be installed in her Samadhi temple. Many devotees from all over India came to Haridwar. Chhabi di and I also went there. On the auspicious moment of the last day of Chaitra month, i.e., 13th April, revered Swami Muktananda Giriji's beautiful marble statue was installed in her Samadhi temple. Same day there was a big procession of the sadhus with Ma seated on the snake-designed (Ananta Nag) silver throne placed on an elephant and thousands of devotees and ashramites followed with band parties, kirtans, etc. proceeded towards Brahmakunda to bathe in the Ganga. After the bath we came back.

Procession towards Brahmakunda to Bathe in the Ganga

At first the Kankhal ashram was limited to a two storied small building named 'Shantiniketan' and a Shiva temple donated by Shree Nitai Basu Mallick of Kolkata. Afterwards Mahant Shree Giridhar Narain Puriji, the head of Nirvani Akhara donated a big piece of land to expand the ashram. A three storied guest house, a three storied Sadhu kutia, Satsang hall, Matri nivas, Yajnashala, etc. were constructed over the ground.

Ma was staying in room no. 18, on the first floor of the new guest house. I was sleeping upstairs in Guneeta's room. At 3 or 4 a.m. Ma called me and made me stay in room no. 14. Later I learnt that it belonged to Chhabi di. She had not taken possession yet. I stayed first under Ma's instructions. Afterwards the ceremonial entrance took place when Ma asked me to enter first with a pot full of water on my head, then Chhabi di with her idol of Radha Govinda and at the end Ma came inside the room.

Swamiji (Paramanandaji) told me that Ma had reserved two rooms in the new guest house in the names of Ranjana and Bhanjana. 'Ranjana' is the name of Tulsi, consort of Narain and as Chandan di worshipped her ancestral deity Narain, 'Ranjana' was her room and 'Bhanjana' was for me. After his retirement, Dr. Triguna Sen, the education minister of India expressed his desire to stay at Kankhal. Ma accommodated him in room no. 2 named 'Bhanjana' and made me enter into Chandan di's room. Since then I have been staying in that room. There was no suitable place for Radha-Govinda, so I made one small temple under the window. Ma was glad to see it and said, "Chhabi, your Thakur had no temple yet, here it has taken place."

One evening Ma was going to Dehradun for a short while. We 8–10 senior girls were in Ma's room. Ma was ready to start. Suddenly She asked us to mention a colour. Everybody said but were incorrect. I said 'Yellow'. Ma nodded in affirmative. Again She asked for another colour, all turned to be incorrect. I said, 'Black' and it was correct. In this way Ma asked four times and I was correct every time. In the end Ma stood up and said, "Victory to Vishuddha", and with a sweet smile, She left.

Ma's car was off. Everybody especially Chitra di questioned me, "What is the matter sister, only you answered correctly all the four times, did Ma hint anything to you in advance?" I replied, "No, Ma said nothing before. But as Ma asked for the first time I noticed Ma's hand was touching the yellow towel on Her head and I answered 'Yellow'. Next Ma touched Her hair and I said 'black', then She put Her finger on Her cloth, I mentioned 'white' and at last Ma was holding the border of Her dhoti which was 'brown', so I repeated 'brown'. Ma meant 'red' but I could not see 'red'. Still Ma said my answer was correct as there was red in brown colour. Everybody praised me a lot. But the truth was that if we concentrate on God in every aspect, He makes us win in every field of life. As Lord Krishna said in the Gita:

Yatra Yogeshwarah Krishno
Yatra Partho Dhanurdharah
Tatra Shrir Vijayobhutir
Dhruvaneetir matirmama

—Shrimad Bhagwad Gita,
Chapter 18, Shloka 78

30

Ma was in Varanasi. She was not keeping well. She had temperature and acute headache. She was in the first floor room. In the morning I went to have a glimpse of Her. I peeped through the door. The room was dark, so it took me one minute to set the eye. I found Ma lying with eyes closed and straight on Her back. I felt bad seeing Ma suffering so much and prayed, "Ma, you suffer not for yourself as you have no pending karma, i.e., 'Prarabdha', you suffer due to our sins. Please forgive us and get well soon." I was surprised to see that Ma turned left and looking at me, said slowly, "When a child clings to her mother's bosom, she kicks and hurts her but does the mother take that as an offence?" I thought that means whatever offence I do, Ma won't take it as offensive. It was not so as Ma was very strict with us. Then why did She say so? In the course of time it was clear to me, that Ma won't take an offence if only I cling to Her as a solely dependent, egoless and fearless baby.

There was Kumbh mela in Allahabad. We went to attend it with Ma. She was welcomed to enter Kumbha Nagar by the Mahatmas and devotees. There was a spacious ground allotted for Ma's camp. Swamiji went there in advance to set up kutias (cottages), pandal, kitchen, etc. Our hut was adjacent to Ma's kutia. For some time the fair-ground turned into a crowded city. Huge crowds came to have Ma's darshan. The Mahatmas of different ashrams and Political dignitaries came to Ma's pandal. Two main bathing dates during the Kumbha were over and the final auspicious days were on. The new moon day was drawing near. Every night after the whole day programme we used to sit near Ma's kutia. That night I was with

Ma till 11 p.m. and afterwards we went to sleep. Next day early morning while awakening for the Usha kirtan I found myself seriously sick to get up. Due to severe chest pain breathing was difficult. Ma was informed, immediately I had to be shifted to the city for treatment. The main bathing day for Kumbh was due on the next day so the roads were closed for the traffic. At that moment the Governor of Uttar Pradesh Dr. Chenna Reddy arrived for Ma's darshan. Ma Herself asked him to arrange for me to go to the city and reserve first class tickets for Kolkata. Before starting I went to Ma. She enquired about my pain. It was very difficult to speak. Ma touched my chest, back and head and was staring at me for as long as She could see. Renu di took me to her house first and looked after me with a lot of care. She was an expert in nursing. Under the arrangements of the Governor, as instructed by Ma, I went to Kolkata. The doctor diagnosed it as a spontaneous Pneumothorax. By Ma's kheyal and proper treatment I was OK soon.

So many times I fell ill seriously with peculiar symptoms which disturbed Ma. Once I went to Vrindavan. All of a sudden my ulcer burst and I was on the verge of death. Ma asked Patun (Shri S.K. Dutta, son of Shri Jiten Dutta) to shift me to Delhi in an ambulance. At that time Ma Herself was not keeping well. As She was staying upstairs She was not able to come down and I was lying invalid in the ambulance. Ma asked Patun to park the ambulance in such a position so that She was able to see me and I too was able to see Her. Ma sent me ginger honey drops, candy water, etc. I prayed to Her mentally, "Ma, pass on the ailments of your body to me, let me die with those and you stay for long in this world." Later I heard that Ma said to Dadabhai that my subtle body came to Ma and said, "Ma sanction me leave, I am going."

But Ma said in reply, "No, not now, there is some duty for you." With Ma's permission my brother took me to Kolkata and there after a long treatment I recovered. But to this date I don't know for which duty Ma has kept me alive.

Sutapa di (Mrs. Sutapa Roy) was then in Vrindavan. Sometime before she had expressed her desire to her uncle Dr. Gunen Roy that she wished to be initiated by Ma. Dr. Roy had told her to ask Ma. She didn't do so and made a resolve that if Ma initiates her of Her own will she would accept it, but she wouldn't ask Ma and neither be initiated in her life otherwise. During this incident Ma called her and gave her a mantra and asked her to accompany me in the ambulance and do Japa of the mantra touching me with her hands. Ma also gave her some potion and asked her to feed me with it in drops during the journey to Delhi.

Dr. Chenna Reddy invited Ma and party for the celebrations of Ma's birthday at Bangalore Governor House in the month of May 1978. The Reddy family cordially welcomed Ma with a dance aarti by their grand-daughter. Many saints from North and South India were invited to join the function. A good and compact programme of music and discourses took place. Bharat Ratna Mrs. Subhalaxmi offered her homage to Ma by singing beautiful songs. Ma's devotee Mrs. Sadashivam and her husband invited Ma to their place. There in her worship room Subhalaxmiji sang bhajans and offered at Ma's lotus feet a few gold coins soaked in tears.

Three days before Ma's final worship of the birthday celebrations a telegram was received that my father had breathed his last after doing obeisance to Shri Ramakrishna Paramhansa, Shri Ma Sarada Devi, Shree Shree Ma Ananadamayee and his preceptor Swami Shivananda on their photographs. He asked himself for Ganga Water and passed away in a calm and quiet state while bowing on his knees.

As my father's last rites were completed I went to Puri. Over there a very good satsang was going on in the presence of Ma. Learned Vaishnav Dr. Mahanambrata Brahmacharijee was delivering lucid speeches on Bhagwat. He said, "It is said that Lord Krishna used to steal butter. You welcome God uttering–come, come, sit, sit and make him sit at your altar. When you invite someone to your place, he is your guest. A guest is not supposed to enter your house on his own. We do worship him but keep our sins hiding inside ourselves, so that nobody finds it out. Hence kind Krishna steals our sins breaking the hundi when we sleep soundly in 'ignorance'.

We visited Rath yatra of Jagannath under Ma's arrangements and came back to Kolkata with Her. Lots of people were initiated by Ma at Agarpara Ashram. A Nam yajna took place.

Ma was in Smt. Raja Khaitan's house at Dehradun. Udasji, Chhabi di and I were there with Ma. In the afternoon Swami Virajanandaji used to come to read out some of his writings to Ma and discussed the same with Her. We also attended the sittings. Ma was in full rest and was in a good mood. One day after lunch Ma was resting while Chhabi di was fanning Her. Cuckoo was heard from a distance. Chhabi di said, "Ma, do you listen how sweetly the cuckoo is singing?" At once Ma asked Chhabi di to bring a paper and pen. She dictated, "*Radha sits near the river Jamuna and cries for Krishna...*" Ma told Chhabi di to sing it in the afternoon sitting when Virajanandaji attended.

31

Regarding music I remember that once the King of Gondal, Gujarat arranged a Durga puja on a grand scale and invited Ma and her entourage there. The puja pandal was wonderfully decorated and the idol of Durga was made by the artists from Kolkata. On the previous night of sashthi I was doing something in the mandap when Ma called me and sang in a beautiful morning tune:

Awake, awake, awake, pranam to Ganesh
Durga awakes, Laxmi awakes, awakes Saraswati
Kartik awakes, Ganesh awakes, awakes Bhagawati
Yaksha awakes, Kinnar awakes, awakes Devi Devi
Universe awakes, awake men women.

Ma taught me this song and asked me to sing in the early morning of Durga puja. Since then every year we do this.

The worship was arranged by the royal family. The king and queen were religious in nature and were eager to know about this puja. Ma explained to them every detail of Bengali Durga puja. She sent the plates of prasad decorated by us to the palace. They were blessed by attending the worship of the earthen Goddess sitting at the feet of divine Mother. After Durga puja Ma sent us to visit the temples of that area.

Next, Ma went to Panchmarhi via Bhopal. It is a hill station of Madhya Pradesh. The motor journey towards the higher altitude of Panchmarhi, was marvellous with its high peaks, dense forests, different types of flowers and springs. We went up and up amidst clouds and at the end reached our destination. A Gujarati family being the followers of Lord

Buddha, stayed there. They arranged everything nicely for Ma and us. The atmosphere was quite suitable for meditation. They did regular meditation three times a day. They continued the same in front of Ma. We also joined the meditation on Ma's instructions. Ma's mood was serene. Mostly we observed silence as they did. Ma said that long ago when She was in Sarnath She had the bhav of Buddha. Panchmarhi was named after the five Pandavas, five caves or abode of the five Pandavas. There we visited a few more temples. We came back to Bhopal after 8–10 days. From Bhopal Ma sent us for pilgrimage to Mahakaleshwar, Ujjain, etc.

Ma's ardent devotee Shri Surendra Nath Dutta and other devotees of Assam took Ma and Her party to Dibrugarh. On Surendra's special invitation Chhabidi and I went there by plane. Northeast (area) of India was the ancestral land of Mahaprabhu Shri Chaitanya. Really the devotion and love for kirtan of that region was worth seeing. Those people get mad while singing kirtan. They arranged a day and night Mahanam Yajna to celebrate Ma's visit. The loud melodious voice of their kirtan filled the air round the clock. They sang kirtan in a sweet and touchy folk tune. Ma was in great bhav and we all bathed in it. Renowned kirtan artist Chhabi Banerji also added a special mark to it.

Next day at noon the special bhog was offered to Mahaprabhu, Krishna and Ma. Usually we decorate the place of bhog with flowers and garlands. But since flowers were not available according to the requirements, I decorated the place with colourful peels of the fruits cut for Mahabhog. It was looking nice and unique. When Ma sat for Her bhog She saw the decoration and looked at me with an appreciating smile. Ma

Herself is the beauty itself, so whenever She sees something beautiful, She is glad.

Ma's devotee Shri Sitaram Jaipuriya arranged a hundred long drums (Mridanga) function and a Nam Yajna at Ghaziabad in the presence of Ma. The Vaishnavas of Navadweep who were experts of Mahanam Sankirtan conducted the whole programme successfully. Hundred drum players along with their drums from Bengal's different corners were invited by Mr. Jaipuriya. The procedure of kirtan of the Navadweep Vaishnavas was different. First of all drums were covered with new cloth and then a short worship was offered to them. All hundred players were beating their drums together in unison. It sounded like the deep sound of the cloud. The beginning of the Nam Yajna took place in the morning by the typical Vaishnava singers of kirtan. We were waiting near the dias to receive the kirtan party. Till this date the scene flashes before my eyes. I could see Ma standing in great bhav at the onset of dawn and the kirtan singers also in ecstasy dancing and singing the Mahanam beautifully. After the kirtan, Ma and her entourage went back to Kankhal.

Ma's birthday celebrations of 1982 drew near. We went to Kankhal to join in. Everything was going on as usual. Preparation for the Janmotsava was done but there was no enthusiasm in anybody as Ma was not well at all. Ma didn't take any medicine, only the prayers of the devotees and Her kheyal made Her alright. But that time She had no kheyal to keep Herself fit. Revered Shankaracharya came to visit Ma and prayed to Her to get well soon. In reply Ma said, "Pitaji, the 'Avyakta' (unmanifested) is drawing." The visitors were allowed to see Ma shortly from a distance. We were doing continuous recital of the Ramayana, Hanuman Chalisa, Jap, kirtan, etc.

The Janmotsava was over. Chhabidi and I went to do obeisance to Ma before we left for Kolkata. When we bowed, She touched our heads and backs with Her frail hands. We didn't know that was Her last touch. As we proceeded towards the door She was looking at us as long as She could see. We also turned our face to see Her till the end. Miss Aruna Pandya was fanning Ma at that time. When we left, Ma said to Aruna, "Go, and see them off on behalf of this body." Aruna came and waited till our car moved and then informed Ma.

As the birthday celebrations ended Ma went to Dehradun, at the cordial invitation of Mrs. Raja Khaitan for Gurupurnima. After that celebration She came to Kishenpur ashram. Swami Krishnanandaji of the Divine life Society, Rishikesh, came to worship Ma on the auspicious day of Radhashtami, i.e., the birthday of Radha. That was the last worship of Her body. Gradually the last moment was not far behind. On 27th August, 1982, Friday evening Ma moved Her head to look at every corner and said, "Engage yourself towards your goal." Saying these words, She closed Her eyes forever. From the state of 'Vyakta' (manifested) Ma entered the state of 'Avyakta'.

Though we can't see Ma anymore, She is with us and helping us in every way. On every occasion, Ma's presence is felt. Whoever saw Her physically, had touched Her, listened to Her, received prasad from Her hand–it was easy for them to concentrate on Her no doubt. But those who missed such fortune, might feel Her blessings through the 'Satyam Shivam Sundaram' aspect of Ma. She used to say, "This body was there in the past, it is same at present and would be there in future."

Now before I conclude my worship to Ganga with the water of Ganga, I must mention a few incidents which prove that after Her 'Maha Samadhi', the unmanifest state, Ma has been still showering blessings on us.

In 1993 September, during Janmashtami I suffered from acute headache and when it was unbearable I was admitted to the hospital. I was unconscious and on the threshold of death. Later I heard that Chhabi di, Anu di and my sister-in-law were sitting in front of me repeating the name of Ma. I was not in my senses but my eyes were wide open and I uttered–"Here is Ma". It was a lost case, even the oxygen cylinder was kept aside as the body failed to inhale it. At last Dr. H. Paul, who was treating me, tried a lumbar puncture and my body responded. I recalled even in my unconscious condition I was seeing Ma constantly in a hallow of bright light floating in the space over my chest and was looking straight into me.

I went to Kankhal during Ma's birthday celebrations in 1998. On my way back to Kolkata I dropped in at Varanasi for a break journey. At the railway station while stepping down the staircase, I fell down and fractured my right ankle. The bags slipped off from my hands. An old rickshaw-puller in rags was walking with me enquiring whether I needed the rickshaw. As I sat down on the steps with a broken ankle the rickshaw-puller came and set the ankle, stretching it straight, massaged a little and said, "Mataji, stand up". I said, "Brother, I can't stand." Then a thin and short auto-driver came forward and took me in his hands and the old rickshaw-puller gathered my bags and chappals and followed. That day was the bathing ceremony of Lord Jagannath, i.e., Snan-yatra. So the station was overcrowded with numerous yatris from the nearby towns and villages. There was hardly any space to step in. The auto-driver seated me in his auto rickshaw and the old rickshaw-puller put my bags near me. The very moment I opened my bag to offer tip to that old man and looked up, he had vanished. I asked the auto-driver where the rickshaw puller had gone. He looked for him in vain. I thought how could an old man disappear through that heavy crowded street.

Anyway, I reached our ashram and the auto-driver carried me to the Kanyapeeth. Seeing me in that condition all were stunned. Since I reached in the evening the X-ray department of our hospital was closed. Next morning the ankle was X-rayed and it was found that both sides of the right ankle had compound fracture. The doctor plastered the same and with his consent I went to Kolkata. In Kolkata three topmost orthopaedic surgeons advised to set the bone after operation lest I would be crippled for my whole life. But my physician Dr. H. Paul said that the patient was highly sensitive to anaesthesia and hence the bone operation was not possible. Then Dr. Paul brought his friend Dr. Sukhendu Banerji, a highly qualified orthopaedic of world fame to my house. He also suggested operation but after knowing the details dropped the idea and replastered my leg. When the plaster was removed after one month, Dr. Banerji said, "Very good, 99.5% is healed up miraculously." I told him, "Doctor, the actual setting was done by that old rickshaw-puller. No doctor set it later." More wonders were awaiting when shortly after removing the plaster I went to Vrindavan and easily surmounted the length of twenty-one kilometer path around the mountain Govardhan on foot in a day. Ma's grace in reality, is endless.

Udasji came to Kolkata and stayed there for some time. One day she came to my place and talked about Ma and my grandmother for a long time. While leaving she said, "Just try to hold Ma." I replied, "Ma is beyond my hold. But I feel that Ma has been always holding me." Udasji said, "That would do."

Brahmacharini Atmanandaji (Ms. Blance, an Austrian lady) the ex-editor of 'Ananda Varta' (The quarterly journal in English of Anandamayee Sangha) published one beautiful anecdote of Ma–The Varanasi ashram had just been established. It was in 1945. India was then under the British rule. A responsible dignitary of the British Empire came from the Buckingham Palace for a short visit to India for some important job. From London he had enquired at the Indian Embassy "while visiting India, where shall I get the essence of India?" Pandit Jawaharlal Nehru sent him the message, "Visit Mother Anandamayee."

The English Esquire came to India and after finishing his official assignments, he left for Varanasi to see Ma. When he reached the ashram, he found Her seated in the courtyard. A few visitors offered garlands and fruits to Ma. She exchanged a word or two with them. The new gentleman was sitting behind the public in the gathering. He didn't understand a single word said by Ma or the visitors. He was as if hypnotised by the divine charm of Ma. Later he had some talk with Ma which was interpreted by Atmanandaji and received prasad from Her. Before leaving the ashram he said to Atmanandaji, "We train the heir to the throne to be perfect in every aspect since the baby is born. But to err is human, it cannot be perfect totally. If it was possible at all for a human being, I am noticing that perfection is embodied in Mother Anandamayee.

32

Passing Away of My Mother Kulalakshmi Devi

After the family reached Kashi in the year 1944, my mother Suhasini (Kulalakshmi Devi) used to get up early in the morning and visit all the prominent nearby temples as a routine. She also performed the 'Panch Kosi Parikrama'. One day, early in the morning my mother was calling out for my sister and me from her bed in a meek and frail voice. We rushed to her. She seemed very weak and was not able to get up from her bed. Her face was ashen and eyes were sunk.

Suhasini Chakraborty (Kulalakshmi Devi)

We got to know that she had vomitted once early in the morning.

At that time in Kashi there was a huge crowd of devotees, who had gathered for a dip in the Ganga on the occasion of 'Chudamani Yog'. In those days necessary medicines and injections for various ailments were not readily available. For that reason there was an outbreak of cholera amongst the huge gathering of devotees. A doctor came in, examined my mother and prescribed medicines for cholera, but in vain.

At dusk, the routine evening kirtan was performed before her. The Saints from Ma's ashram and the Ramakrishna mission often visited our home and had religious discussions with my father. That day, by co-incidence, Swamiji from the Ramakrishna mission–Shree Neelkantha Maharaj (my father's co-disciple), Swami Shankaranandaji, Swami Umeshanandaji, Brahmachari Keshav and my uncle (Govinda) were there. Later, Mahamandaleshwar Swami Hariharananda Giriji Maharaj came there. Realising that it was the last moment of my mother, all of them jointly did the rendition of the Vedas.

My mother never kept the cash, etc. in the cash box. Instead she used to keep it in a container on an open shelf. Pointing at that container she showed it to my father and said, "The cash, etc. is here". She probably knew that she would be leaving and must have thought that there would be requirement of money and my father would be harassed looking for it. Hence, she showed the place. My father asked, "Would you like to say something?" She replied, "No". She started feeling sick in the morning and within a span of 19 hours at about 9:42 p.m. she breathed her last.

Govinda uncle had been residing in Kashi for a long time. With the help of his contacts he made arrangements to take the body to the Manikarnika cremation ground in the night itself. One Shankaracharya used to reside near the Manikarnika cremation ghat. He was informed and convinced for the cremation during the night as a special case. During my mother's death the alignment of the stars and planets were so special that the priest commented that it was a very special and rare conjunction of the heavenly bodies. As it was the demise in the region of Kashi of a married woman, and to top it all, during the auspicious conjunction of heavenly bodies, the Shankaracharya permitted the cremation at that hour. What could be more auspicious than being cremated at the Manikarnika cremation ground where it is believed that the earrings of the Supreme Goddess had fallen. Thus liberation (Mukti) was assured as the scriptures say.

Shree Shree Ma was then at Vindhyachal. On hearing about my mother's demise, Shree Shree Ma said, "Exactly after a period of one year, one month, one day and one hour she had the fortune of achieving Kashi." After glancing through my mother's diaries my father confirmed that Ma had pronounced correctly.

During those days my paternal grandfather and grandmother, my aunts (wives of my father's elder and younger brothers), my father's sisters and my mother's sisters were all present. But Ma sent my maternal grandmother (Virajmohini Devi) from Vindhyachal back to our house to look after us. 'Jai Ma' for your ever present grace.

Standing Left to Right
Satyananda, Premananda's daughter (baby) on his lap, Nityananda, Nagendranath Chakravarty

Sitting on Chairs Left to Right
Mataji's Niece Geeta, Shraddha, Didima, Krishna, Vishuddha

Sitting on Ground Left to Right
Keshvananda and Vasudevananda

33

Passing Away of My Grandmother Virajmohini Devi, February, 1970

Smt. Virajmohini Devi

My grandmother Smt. Virajmohini Devi belonged to a highly educated and well to do family of East Bengal. It was heard that my grandfather decided to do Durga puja and prepared accordingly. Then Goddess Kali ordered him in a dream to do Her worship instead of Durga puja. Grandfather said it was too late as everything for Durga puja was already arranged.

But Mother Kali instructed him in details the name of the sculptor, the measurement of the idol, the name of the priest, wherefrom the articles for worship should be brought etc. He dreamt repeatedly and my grandmother saw him levitated on the bed while dreaming as such. Then he started the worship of Goddess Kali and till date it has been continuing in my maternal home.

Virajmohini Devi lost her husband early in life and survived with two daughters. Her parents-in-law were not there and being the eldest daughter-in-law, she had to look after the whole family at that young age. She arranged for higher education of her brother-in-laws, got them and her two daughters married and relinquished home to go to Varanasi. She spent her days in sadhana and pilgrimage. All over India she toured on foot to visit the main temples. She even went to Baluchistan to visit Goddess Hinguleshwari. She faced many difficulties but overcame them by her will power.

She went to Dhaka, Shahbagh to see Ma, and felt attracted consequently she stayed with Her. When the plot on the Ashtabhuja hills at Vindhyachal was bought, no brahmachari dared to stay and build the building on that place which was infested with scorpions, snakes, tigers and robbers. Then Ma engaged my grandmother for that difficult job. She stayed there all alone for a pretty long time and managed to build the ashram. We heard from her that she stayed in the cave downstairs and build the upper stories. Due to fear of thieves and dacoits she didn't keep any money with her. Every day she covered on foot the distance from the ashram to the post office at Mirzapur to withdraw money to pay to the masons. Since there was no arrangement of water nearby, she used to fetch water from a small spring flowing near 'Kalikho', which was quite a distance from the ashram. She ate only once a day and supervised the masons' work. After paying off the workers, empty handed she used to sit for her prayers till late night in the open verandah. Scorpions, snakes, etc. moved around freely. One night she was doing her jap when a robber with a long bamboo in hand came and moved to and fro, peeped into the cave and found a brass pot which was filled with water. He threw the water and went away with it.

Ma came to Vindhyachal ashram after it was completed. Wherever Ma went functions took place. Narain Swamiji told me that Ma wanted to feed sadhus and pandits. She asked Nepal da (Narain Swamiji) to invite sadhus and pandits from Varanasi. But they denied, as the Bengalis eat fish and Ma was from Bengal, the strict vegetarian pandits of Uttar Pradesh did not accept the invitation. Virajmohini devi was a Bengali but she was a widow and while staying at Varanasi had observed the strict vegetarian rules for long. Ma mentioned her name and sent Nepal da again to the pandits. At last they agreed but said that nobody should enter the kitchen except Virajmohini devi, not even Ma Herself. That was the first feast of sadhus and pandits in Ma's ashram.

It was in August 1936, from Shrirampur Ma sent away Baba Bholanath, Bhaiji, Swami Akhandanandaji and Gururpriya didi to different places and started by a night train for a secluded journey accompanied by Virajmohini devi and Kamal da (Swami Virajanandaji). Before going Bhaiji gave a copy and a pencil to Virajmohini devi and asked her to write down the diary of the unknown journey. Grandmother tried to write avoiding Ma's notice. But nearly at the end of the sojourn Ma asked her, "Ma, you write something, isn't it? Bring that book." Grandma understood she was caught red handed. You cannot hide anything from the omniscient Ma. So she brought the same and Ma asked her to immerse the copy into the river and said, "Let unknown remain unknown".

While Ma was moving through Uttar Pradesh, one Bengali station master happened to see Ma and was attracted to Her. He enquired about Ma and my granny said, "She is Goddess Bhagwati Herself." As it was not definite where Ma would go, the gentleman purchased two tickets up to the terminus. Seeing that they had simply nothing, he brought some utensils and a lantern for them. Ma boarded an ordinary third class compartment and just lay down. Granny kept the things hidden since she knew that if Ma could see them She would distribute the same to others. After a while she fell asleep. Later she awoke to see Ma sitting on the seat and talking with other passengers, mainly villagers. They asked Ma where was Her husband and how many children She had etc. etc. Ma laughed and answered mostly in gestures. She saw the utensils and lantern in the hands of the ladies and understood that her efforts to hide them, were in vain.

Once I was with Ma at Dehradun. The station Master, old and retired, came to Ma. He said, about 40–50 years ago he had visited Ma. He respected Virajmohini devi as his Preceptor because it was she who introduced Ma to him as Goddess Bhagwati. Then pointing towards me, Ma said to him, "She is the granddaughter of Virajmohini."

My maternal grandmother, Virajmohini Devi, was in a normal healthy state. She was of 91 years of age, had mild pain in the joints and had high blood pressure. She had no other ailments. Once she had gone to visit a doctor near our house. The doctor had gone out to see a patient on a house call. She was waiting with other patients, sitting on a bench and narrating stories about Ma. In the meantime the doctor arrived. All of a sudden grandmother fainted and in that condition she was carried back home. She breathed her last within few hours, in a state of unconsciousness.

At the age of 18 my maternal grandmother had lost her husband and the only son. She was like a guardian mother to everyone in the locality. In their difficult times they used to come to her. When her body was taken to the 'Keoratala' crematorium, many people joined the procession. When her body was being consumed by fire on the pyre, the whole place was aromatised. People around commented, "She must be a pure soul, thus the fragrance."

Shree Shree Ma was at Kashi ashram when the news of her demise reached Her by post. She said, "This is called the true determination. When this body had gone to 'Agarpara Ashram', in the crowd I noticed that Viraj Ma was standing there. I enquired, "Viraj Ma how are you?" She replied, 'By your grace I am fine. I have everything which one normally requires and have nothing to ask for. But during Agyatvas you mentioned that you are both my husband and son. If you are so, then bless me that I can go back walking on my legs.' On such requests, this body generally says, 'whatever God desires', but in Viraj Ma's case this body consented by nodding head. Look, she literally left her mortal frame without being dependent on anybody."

34

Agyatvas (As narrated by Gurupriya di)

In the month of July, 1936 Ma left for her sojourns of 'Agyatvas' (undisclosed hermitage) along with Viraj didi. That incident I heard from Viraj didi, after reaching Tarapeeth. I am narrating the same here.

In the afternoon of 3rd August Ma reached Shree Rampur. On reaching there, Ma took shelter in the Gauranga temple and all the devotees assembled there. Ma had already announced that before sunset the devotees from Kolkata would have to return to Kolkata along with Bholanath. In the evening Ma went for a stroll along the banks of the Ganga. Later on, Ma revealed that on reaching there (banks of Ganga) Ma saw the idol image of Jagannath and consequently She decided to go to Puri. Ma had left Kolkata with the only dress She had worn. When Triguna babu gave Ma a set of clothes, Ma discarded the clothes She was wearing and gave it to him.

At night Ma boarded the train to Kharagpur after purchasing the required tickets. Triguna babu handed over a blanket and a change of clothes for Ma's use, secretly to Viraj didi. While at Shree Rampur railway station, one person gave Ma a good saree, some sandesh and some vermillion. The sandesh was distributed there and the saree Viraj didi took along with her.

On reaching Kharagpur and not finding the connecting train to Puri, She hired a small room and stayed there for the night. Later, She boarded the train for Puri. On reaching Puri, She took shelter in Goenka's dharmashala. Since there was no vacant room, She stayed in the verandah.

In the dharmashala, there was an Oriya family staying in one of the rooms closeby. Viraj didi had kept the bundle of blanket and saree and gone to visit the temples of the area. On reaching the dharmashala, Ma said, "Give this good saree to them (Oriya family), I shall take a dress (saree) from them in exchange." Nobody other than Kamal knew about this. On returning after visiting the temples, when Viraj didi wanted to fetch the bundle of blanket and saree, the family members on their own said, "would you sell this saree? What would be the price?" Viraj didi responded, "I don't know the price, one devotee has presented this to Ma. I shall not sell it." Then the family members said, "Ma wears a saree with thin border. Ma wouldn't wear this saree." When Viraj didi narrated the incident to Ma, She smiled and asked to call the family members. She requested them to take the saree. But they just wouldn't agree to take the same without paying the price. On this issue there was a discussion for a long time. Ma cajoled the family members by addressing them as 'father' and 'mother' and with her sweet talk convinced them to take the saree and they left after taking the same. But after some time they came back again with a proposal of buying a thin bordered saree for Ma. She tried to desist them many times. Then on their repeated requests She agreed. They brought a thin bordered saree for Ma and presented it to Her. The secret which only Kamal knew when Ma had arrived was revealed.

In the evening Ma went out for a stroll along the seashore. On seeing Ma, suddenly a Vaishnav boy came and exclaimed, "I have seen you in Shahbag, aren't you the 'Mother' of Shahbag?" On saying this, he left and informed Makhan babu in the Vijay Krishna Goswami ashram. Ma was still strolling along the seashore and Makhan babu went to the dharmashala looking for Her and returned not finding Her there. When Ma was walking around in the verandah of the dharmashala after returning from the seashore, all of a sudden She informed, "I can see Makhan babu going around with a lantern in his hand." Soon after She had said this, Makhan babu appeared before Ma with a lantern in his hand. On seeing Ma unexpectedly, he was delighted. After having a conversation with Ma for some time, he returned.

The next day, in the early morning Ma was strolling along the seashore. There She met a boy from Navadweep who had seen Ma in Navadweep. He joined Ma and visited many places. In the evening Makhan babu escorted Ma to meet Shyamdas Babaji and took Her to places like 'Anandabajar' and many such places. On returning to the dharmashala he brought many dishes of prasad and fed Ma with his own hands and Ma also reciprocated by feeding everyone present there.

That day itself, after dusk Ma started for Bhuvneshwar. On reaching Bhuvneshwar, She stayed in a dharmashala. Next day in the morning, She visited many places and returned to the dharmashala in the afternoon. On hearing the news about Ma's arrival Shri Dinesh Bhattacharya came and met Ma. He conversed with Ma for nearly two hours and also sung some songs. On the same day, around evening hours She was on Her way to Gomo, Aedra, etc. and after visiting these places, She reached Agra. Staying there for one day and after visiting 'Shyam Kutir', She reached Mathura by car.

On reaching Mathura She stayed in a dharmashala for three days. None of the devotees had any information about Her stay. Since it was not allowed to stay in the dharmashala for more than three days, She left the dharmashala as scheduled. She gave instructions to Kamal to book tickets to return to Kolkata. Kamal resisted a lot, but Ma explained the circumstances and sent him off. She was accompanied by Kamal to the railway station. On returning from there She went to the Vishram Ghat and sat there. That day was the day when Ma ate only fruits. There was nothing left with them. Whatever little utensils Viraj didi had brought to Puri, were all given to Kamal to carry back. She cut out a piece of the blanket and gave away the rest to Kamal. There was nothing else left with Ma except a small pot, a piece of blanket and the dress She was wearing. They had a small amount of money left with them. Viraj didi bought some fruits with that little money and started feeding Ma. Looking at this scene many onlookers stood there. Looking at Ma in Her unkempt hair and someone else feeding Her they started laughing thinking Her to be a mad woman. Ma also started laughing with them.

The time of dusk was approaching. It wasn't certain that where would She go. Pointing at a place next to the road Ma asked, "Would you be able to stay there?" In the meantime a Kashmiri lady, a devotee, came and delightfully sat at the feet of Ma and paid her obeisance. She expressed her good fortune on being able to meet Ma. She wanted to take Ma to her house, but Ma wouldn't go to anyone's house. Then she said, "We have a temple in Vishram Ghat, come there." Then she took Ma along and made arrangements for Her stay in the temple. She bought milk, fruits, etc. for Ma's meal. The next day she prepared 'chapati' and vegetables at her home and brought them along to feed Ma. As she was about to feed Ma, one gentleman named Shivnarayan Pandit (Kashmiri) came there and was delighted to meet Ma. He mentioned, "After meeting you once, I looked for you in various dharmashalas, but couldn't find you. Now you come along with me. I have a temple where you could stay. There you wouldn't have any problem." Ma said, "It would not be possible now, we will see later on." That gentleman said, "I will accompany you."

On 14th August, Friday, that gentleman started for Vrindavan along with Ma. At around 2:00 p.m. in the afternoon Ma reached the dharmashala of the king of Vardhaman. The manager there, Shri Jogen babu knew Ma. He received Ma and took Her inside the dharmashala. After some time Ma asked Mr. Pandit to return back to Mathura.

Next day, i.e. 15th August, Ma left Vrindavan and went to Mathura railway station. After reaching there Jogen babu asked for Ma, "Ma where would you like to go? Which destination shall I procure the tickets?" Ma replied, "There is nothing certain about me. Along the way if anyone takes me along, I could go to that place. Now you purchase a ticket for Agra." The Manager purchased the tickets and gave them to Ma. Before She left for Mathura from Vrindavan, Ma had left a set of clothes with the Kashmiri lady and told her to 'keep them washed'. On hearing those words, the lady thought that Ma would visit Mathura again. Probably the lady didn't know that in a similar way Ma would give Her dress, blanket, bed sheet, etc. to many people only not to take them back. After descending at Agra Fort railway station, Ma asked Viraj didi to purchase tickets for Etawah and She waited on the platform. In the meantime two boys came along and surprisingly started talking to Ma and pleaded with Ma, "You come along with us to Agra. We shall make arrangements for your stay on the banks of Yamuna, you will have no difficulties in staying there." Saying this, they even gave their address.

Ma changed train at Tundla to reach Etawah. At Tundla railway station suddenly one boy saw Ma and came to Her and said, "Mataji, I have seen you in Sultanpur, would you like to go to Sultanpur? I am going to Sultanpur." Ma replied, "I have bought tickets for Etawah." The boy made efforts and got the tickets changed and got the tickets for Sultanpur.

Ma changed Her plan midway and instead of Etawah proceeded to Sultanpur. After reaching Allahabad while changing trains this boy was not traceable. While travelling to Sultanpur Ma and Viraj didi travelled in the ladies compartment. At Pratapgarh station one Muslim woman boarded the train. She asked Ma. "How many children do you have?" Ma replied, "I am also your child. How can I beget children?" On listening to these words, the woman got perplexed and emotional. Then after a small conversation she became quite friendly with Ma. Viraj didi had brought a small toy for Ma. For some time Ma kept toddling with the toy and then said to the woman, "Mothers usually have toys for their children; you take this toy and keep it with you." She gave her address to Ma and requested Her to meet again. While leaving she had tears in her eyes. Ma proceeded to Sultanpur along with Viraj didi. On reaching Sultanpur they took shelter in Kalu Malli's dharmashala. Rama Sharma (Sharada's sister) was the lady doctor in Sultanpur. Viraj didi went and met her. Rama came along and made all the arrangements for Ma. She had reached Sultanpur at about 9–10 a.m. in the morning. After staying there for the day, next day She set out to visit Gomti. On the way, on seeing a motor car going past, She asked,

"Where will this motor go?" Someone said it was going to Faizabad. Realising it She said to Viraj didi, "Come, let's go to Faizabad." After boarding the train at about 11:00 a.m. in the morning they reached Faizabad at around 4–5 p.m. in the evening. From the railway station in Faizabad they hired a tanga (horse driven cart) and started for Ayodhya.

At about 5–6 p.m. they reached Ayodhya. There they took shelter in the temple of Laldas Babaji. Rama was also with them. It was decided that they would shift to another temple. While strolling along the banks of Saryu river they heard the rendition of the Ramayan in Ahilyabai's temple and went and sat there. The temple was very beautiful. Rama inquired from the pujari, "Can Ma stay in this temple?" The pujari delightfully agreed and showed them two rooms. Then Ma stayed back at the temple and Rama left. Ma stayed in the temple for about seven days. Nobody came to know about Her whereabouts. In the morning hours She would be lying down in Her room. In the evening hours the rendition of the Ramayana used to be conducted in the verandah and Ma would go and sit there. After that Ma used to stroll around on the banks of Saryu and peep into the Kutis (huts) of monks and saints and look for something. She never used to utter a word. The monks used to finish their bath and ablutions early in the morning and come back to their huts and shut their doors. Ma used to peep through the apertures of the walls of the huts and look inside. Those seven days passed like this.

On the eighth day Satyanarayan puja was being conducted in the temple. In Faizabad this temple had a Kashmiri priest. Many Kashmiris of Faizabad were ardent devotees of Ma. During the event, one boy saw Ma from a distance and set out on his bicycle to Faizabad town and informed all devotees of Ma about Her arrival. On hearing about Her arrival, 2–3 motor vehicles, full of devotees and their families came over to the lotus feet of Ma. They also accosted and blamed the priest saying, since Mataji was here for so many days, then why didn't he inform them. After hearing all this, the priest was perplexed and surprised. He said, "I didn't recognize Mataji." Due to this incident the residents of Ayodhya also came to know about Ma's arrival. They also came over in great numbers. In turns everyone started paying their obeisance to Ma with flowers, garlands, fruits, sweets and by performing special aarti. There was a huge pile of clothes, offerings, etc. Ma distributed everything among devotees. It was like a festival of joy. Next morning again the devotees came together to do their obeisance to Ma. In the afternoon there was a photography session with Ma. In the evening the rendition of the Ramayana got over. After dusk Ma's photograph was positioned on the seat made for Lord Rama and the priests performed the puja and aarti. As Ma announced that She would be leaving Ayodhya that very day, there was a pall of gloom and tears being shed in torrents. But Ma's departure couldn't be stopped. That night Ma was taken to Faizabad railway station in the motor car of Sri Mankeshwar Raina. They had to wait at the station for two hours for the train. During this period, more than a hundred people assembled at the station. Till midnight, children, grownups, elderly men and women gathered around Ma and paid their obeisance with offerings.

At about 12 p.m. Ma boarded the train for Lucknow. In the train a lawyer from Barabanki requested and pleaded with

Ma to come to Barabanki. Ma replied, "As of now I am going to Lucknow, we shall see later." She disembarked at 5:00 a.m. at Lucknow station. There She got the tickets for Etawah and proceeded towards Etawah. After disembarking at Etawah She reached the doorsteps of Pitamber Panth (civil surgeon). He was taking his bath. As he got the news, he rushed to the door even without wiping himself and got surprised on seeing Ma in Her state along with a lady. He said, "Ma, What is it? You have come alone in this state?" He spread blankets in his lawns for Ma to relax. Later he made arrangements for Ma's stay in Dauji's house which was newly constructed, three miles away, close to the banks of Yamuna river. She stayed there for 25 days. Every day at 12 noon the civil surgeon used to send someone there to find out if anything would be required for Ma. Later, at about 5–5:15 p.m. in the evening he used to come to Ma in his car. He stayed there for a considerable time and as the days passed other devotees also started coming to visit Ma. All of them had discussions on spiritual matters. Everyone started enjoying Ma's company and conversations. The queen of Pratapgarh came to know about Ma's arrival and took Ma to their garden house. There she performed puja and aarti for Ma. Many people had gathered there on the occasion. Religious songs and kirtan were sung. Gradually the crowd around Ma started increasing. The poor people used to come with a handful of rice or pulses to offer to Ma. Ma used to happily accept the same. There was a photography session on the banks of Yamuna with Ma.

While at Etawah, one day in the afternoon, Ma sat under 'Ashwattha' tree. The tree had spread so much with its branches that the place was nearly dark. Viraj didi had carried some grapes along to feed Ma. There was a Shivalinga (a phallic stone representation) under the tree. Ma didn't eat those grapes, She said, "Give all these to Shiva." Viraj didi did accordingly. The place was very lonely. Ma used to go and sit on the ghats of Yamuna frequently. Everyone used to come there for Ma's darshan. There was a cremation ground nearby–hence the burning smell of dead bodies was always lingering.

On this location while strolling on the banks of Yamuna, one day Ma noticed, under a 'Neem' tree, there was a hutment in which lived a labourer's family. Ma reached there and met them. That poor man spread out papaya leaves to make a make-shift seat for Ma. "She put up Her prevailing daughter act and started addressing him as father." They (the family) started taking care of Her as an esteemed guest, gave Ma a raw Papaya and didn't accept any money in return. Ma used to go there often and spend some time. Many well-to-do and prominent people who used to go there for Ma's darshan, also used to sit on seats made of papaya leaves.

From Etawah Ma set out for Naimisharanya. The civil surgeon of Etawah bought the tickets for Naimisharanya and gave some money for further expenditure.

On the day She reached Naimisharanya, She again set out for Lucknow and on reaching there, took shelter in Sarojini Dharmashala. The manager there, Sati babu, had seen Ma previously. He took good care of Ma. Ma stayed in Lucknow for seven days. On the eighth day, Manik met Her on getting the news of Her arrival. On the ninth day Ma left for the banks of Gomti river. It was around noon. It was the day when Ma ate only fruits. Some fruits were carried along and they sat under the shade of a tree, spreading a blanket on the banks of Gomti. Some passers-by saw them and started thinking aloud amongst themselves, "May be some trouble has befallen these people, would it behove us to give them some help?" Such conversation was going on amongst them and in the meanwhile Ma kept sitting facing the Gomti river. Suddenly one Kashmiri gentleman, an old devotee of Ma, saw Her and literally jumped out of his motor vehicle, came near Ma and paid his obeisance at the lotus feet of Ma. After staying there for some time he left and informed other devotees. Next morning many devotees came and paid their obeisance at the lotus feet of Ma. Her ardent devotee Nani was also residing nearby at his daughter's place. He couldn't stop shedding his tears of joy on seeing Ma. That day itself at around 10 a.m. Ma shifted to a dharmashala on the banks of Yamuna. She reached the railway station at around 7 p.m. and kept sitting there till about 10 p.m. From there She boarded a train for Barabanki. Manik also travelled along with them.

Ma set out for Barabanki being attacked with fever. She had fever in Lucknow itself. She reached Barabanki at around midnight and sat in a vacant place in the station itself. She was in fever as high as 104°C. Next day, early morning She took shelter in a dharmashala and sent a message to a previously known lawyer. As soon as the lawyer got the message, he along with a few gentlemen came over to have Ma's darshan. In the meantime many devotees started visiting the place. A few accomplished pandits came over and were delighted to converse with Ma. On listening to Ma they were overwhelmed and chanted, "Glory be unto thee". There also many people made their offerings to Ma and did puja, etc.

After sending off Manik from there, Ma set off for Bareilly. Viraj didi was feeling feverish. After reaching Bareilly, She went to a dharmashala which was near the station. Ma walked up to the dharmashala, but no accommodation was available there. An arrangement was made in the verandah on a cot and spreading the piece of blanket over it, Ma kept sitting there. One wrought iron oven was procured and Viraj didi made some tomato soup over it for Ma. For herself she made sabudana and ate.

One Punjabi lady devotee (Maharatan), who was previously known to Ma was residing in Bareilly. Her husband Shri Yashpal was the registrar. Viraj didi went out looking for her. In the day even after her best efforts she couldn't locate her. At night she took along with her a Punjabi boy from the dharmashala and again set out to look for Maharatan. This time after searching for long she found out that Maharatan's house was close to the dharmashala. After reaching the house she enquired from the servant "Is Maharatan at home?" On overhearing the name Maharatan, she rushed out and hugged Viraj didi and asked, "Where is Mataji?" On hearing about Ma's arrival in Bareilly from Viraj didi, she couldn't control shedding tears of joy. Immediately she hired a horse-driven cart and carrying some milk for Ma, she set off to meet Ma along with Viraj didi. After reaching the dharmashala she arranged for the best room in the dharmashala. Next day Maharatan took Ma to the market place and bought Her warm clothing, blanket, etc. She wouldn't listen to any of Ma's resistance. She pleaded with Ma again and again, so Ma used them. But, Ma wouldn't discard her old piece of blanket. She would spread that underneath the new blanket. Maharatan also presented a blanket to Viraj didi. Ma was in Bareilly for nine days.

Maharatan spent most of her time along with Ma in the dharmashala. In the evenings she used to take Ma for outing in her car.

While in Bareilly, one day Maharatan took Ma to her house. She made arrangements outside the house for Ma to sit. That day Mr. Yashpal kept sitting at Ma's feet. In the meantime, another Magistrate (Mr. Dixit) along with his wife arrived at Maharatan's house in his motor car. He was delighted to see Ma. He heard a few words of Ma also. Then Mrs. Dixit narrated one story about herself.

The incident was as follows. In the recent past an astrologer on reading her palm predicted, "On the 9th day of October 1936, you will have a special 'Darshan'." On calculating from the lunar calendar, it was the same day. On meeting Ma on the exact predicted day of the astrologer, Mrs. Dixit was delighted and due to the incident she developed an affection for Ma. During the night she used to spend her time with Ma. Ma used to say, "Now go, it is late in the night. It is time for you all to have dinner." She used to reply, "I don't feel hungry, I wouldn't eat. Where would I find your company?" She would keep saying about leaving shortly, but she wouldn't just leave. Later, one day, many prominent people of the city came over and sang kirtan and devotional songs for Ma. In Bareilly all ladies used to go together on Sundays and sing kirtan and devotional songs. One day the ladies took Ma to that place and performed kirtan and puja of Ma with fruits and sweets. Ma had also mentioned, "In Bareilly the ladies do nice kirtan. While sitting at the kirtan they don't talk at all." In these few days many devotees became known to Ma. Everyone had great regards and devotion for Ma.

In Bareilly, one monk used to regularly do Japa in the Mahadev temple of the dharmashala. He heard that one Mataji had come. On approaching Viraj di with desire to meet Ma and on being confirmed that Ma met everyone, he went and met Ma and said to Ma, "After doing a lot of penance, I still can't control my mind and I can't rest in peace." Ma gave him some advice secretly and said to him, "Don't tell this to anyone. If you sow a seed and then keep plucking it out to see time and again, the seed wouldn't sprout. After sowing the seed in the ground it should be nurtured, it has to be watered. Then when the seed sprouts and grows into a tree, many seeds again are formed from the tree, as is the way of nature. So many flowers and fruits fall off." The monk was delighted by Ma's advice. Thus, gradually many more people came to Ma and received Ma's advice or instructions and were overwhelmed with gratitude.

After staying in Bareilly for nine days, Ma said to Viraj di, "Whence blanket and all have arrived, let's make good use of it and go to Nainital." While Ma was leaving Bareilly, many devotees clicked photographs of Ma and it seemed as if a festival had started at the railway station. People who were a little away kept looking in awe at this festival. The coupe in which Ma boarded was full of flowers and garlands offered by the devotees. Thus, bidding farewell to Bareilly, Ma set off for Nainital. Another surprising fact, at many places, many people mentioned that they had seen Ma previously in their dreams as a shadowed figure.

After reaching Nainital as Ma got down from the motor car at a place called Tallital She saw Krishnaram Panth, an old devotee who was previously known to Her, standing there.

He was also surprised to see Ma and with lot of enthusiasm he received Ma and said, "I don't come to this side of the town ever. Today somehow there was a great desire to visit this place and couldn't help but came here. Now I understand why there was this great desire. For the last few days my inner-self was crying for Ma. I had written to so many people at so many places to get some news about you and today you have taken the pains to give me darshan and come here." Saying this, he started weeping uncontrollably. He wanted to write to everyone and inform them but Ma stopped him from doing so and said, "There is nothing certain as to where I would stay and for how long, so for no reason people should come and be pained." The wife of the district engineer, Tarachand babu, was along with Krishnaram Panth. They arranged for a 'dandi' and took Ma to Nainadevi temple. There they made arrangements for Ma's stay. The incident turned out as if Panthji had gone there to receive Ma. She stayed at Nainital for nine days.

Five-six days after she reached Nainital, the Navaratri preceding Durga puja started. In these few days the devotees had their hearts fill in paying their obeisance and doing puja, etc. with so many types of offerings. All the folks used to come to Ma and sit there with eyes closed and pray. One day as Panthji was taking Ma to his house in a dandi all around Her a crowd moved along showering flowers and petals on Her. One person, with his palms joined and reciting the appropriate mantras, was preceding the dandi. It was very delightful to see the scene.

One day, one person (Devi Dutt) from that hilly region, took Ma to a monk's ashram. After reaching the ashram everyone did puja to Ma and performed kirtan, etc. The monk was observing vow of silence. He was sitting there with a small lit fire spiced with herbs and a gentle smoke emitted from that. He got up and gave Ma some fruits and flowers. On Ma's instruction Viraj didi distributed all the flowers and fruits among the monks and all present there.

Another day, group of maidens came and sat around Ma singing devotional songs and recited the appropriate mantras. That day was a Saturday dated 17th October, 1936. Ma asked the maidens to come next day also and said to Viraj didi, "Do you observe Navratri? Do you want to do the worship of the maidens during Navratri? Then arrange for the same. Ask someone to get one dozen handkerchiefs. Also arrange sandal paste, fruits and sweets, etc." About seven-eight maidens had come and sung songs. But it was surprising that the next day twelve maidens arrived. Previously Ma had asked to get a dozen handkerchiefs. Ma got the maidens presented with handkerchieves each with garland, fruits and sweets. She also got the aarti done for the maidens by Viraj didi.

From Nainital, Ma came to Bareilly again and stayed for three days and as decided earlier She sent a message to Manik at Lucknow. Manik joined Ma at Bareilly and they proceeded to Rajghat.

After staying at Rajghat for a day they went to a place called Kailash at Agra and took shelter in Shyam Kutir. While travelling to Agra, in the train, Ma had said, "It seems that someone will catch me." True to Her words, as they got down at Rajamandi railway station and were proceeding to Shyam Kutir, the son of Shri Birendra Chandra Mukherjee saw Ma sitting in the tanga (horse driven cart) and followed Her earnestly on his bicycle and on getting close the first words he uttered were, "This time I have caught you. Now where will you escape? Where ever you go, I will go along with you. Many a times while in Agra you hoodwinked me." Then, on Ma's advice he went back home and informed everyone. As soon as they heard of Ma's arrival, Shri Birendra Chandra Mukherjee along with his family came over and did puja, aarti, etc. of Ma. That day was Mahashtami. Dr. Bhargava was also in Agra. On getting the news he came over and had Ma's darshan. Ma also went to Agra city and visited the ailing son of Shri Birendra Chandra Mukherjee in the hospital. That day Ma got Kumari puja (worship of Maidens) for the two daughters of Shri Birendra Chandra Mukherjee done by Viraj didi and the next day, that was Mahanavami day, She asked Viraj didi to perform Kumari puja for Dr. Bhargava's daughter.

On the day of Vijaydashmi She set off from Agra and via Delhi reached Lahore early in the morning. She stayed at Lahore for a day in a dharmashala. That very day they visited a Kali temple complex. As Viraj didi was about to bow her head in obeisance at the feet of Goddess Kali; at that very moment and in the sequence of her movement Ma was positioned in such a way that Viraj didi bowed her head at the feet of Ma. As Viraj didi got up she saw Ma standing in front of her. At that moment it struck Viraj didi and she wondered, "Has Ma revealed Herself to me?" and she returned to the dharmashala from the Kali temple complex. They spent the night at the dharmashala.

Next day they started for and reached Amritsar at about 4 p.m. From there, they reached Garhmukteshwar via Meerut. After reaching Garhmukteshwar Manik was dispatched back.

One day while moving about in Garhmukteshwar, Ma reached at the place of an artisan and stood there saying, "Where else should I go? Let me sit here." Saying this She sat down there. The artisan was making earthen pots. Observing him Ma said, "The earthen material is undergoing a lot of pain, but still it has to be rotated to make the vessel. If a thing has to be made, such pain has to be undergone."

There are a few more incidents to be mentioned here. When Ma started She did not have any money for expenditure. But I heard there was never any shortage of money. Whenever She went anywhere, out of the blue people bought her the tickets etc. and gave some money to Viraj didi. About the food, many people think that they survived on poori, sabji, sweets, etc. bought from the market, but what I heard from Ma and Viraj didi later, it wasn't true. Even sweets were not bought from the market for regular consumption. Whatever was available, Viraj didi cooked the same and fed Ma and the remains were consumed by her as prasad. On some days it was just boiled vegetables. Sometimes it was just boiled tubers and sometimes rice and vegetables were cooked. On some occasions some devotees cooked food and fed the same to Ma. But Viraj didi was not allowed by Ma to have even the food cooked by devotees. She always cooked her own food.

After 15 days in Garhmukteshwar, they stayed at Sultanpur for nine days and then came to Ayodhya. They maintained their secrecy about their stay for 4–5 days while at Ayodhya. Suddenly one previously known sanyasini came and saw Ma and she informed everybody. Ma was staying at the Badrinarayan temple in Ayodhya. As the news spread around, devotees started coming in groups to the temple to have Ma's darshan. From Faizabad, Gopalji's uncle Shri Mankeshwar Nath Raina and his wife came over to have Ma's darshan. Raina's wife had mentioned that, "Just before she got the news, she saw Ma in her prayer room, in a shadow form and it seemed that someone was saying, 'Mataji has arrived'. Among the people present there in the temple, a few ladies had mentioned that they also had dreamt that Ma would be coming.

The devotees together took Ma to Faizabad from Ayodhya. There Ma stayed at the railway station. On the station itself the devotees arranged for puja, aarti and offerings of meals. One blind boy came over and repeated strotras. Ma asked someone to give him some fruits. From Faizabad station Ma proceeded to Devgarh. She stayed there for four days. Ma stayed there in secrecy. Previously known Prangopal babu was then residing in Devgarh but Ma didn't meet anyone.

At Devgarh a group of tourists came to stay in the dharmashala in which Ma was staying. Among them one lady, for some reason, was suffering from acute form of depression, and her health had deteriorated drastically. All of a sudden, seeing her condition, the manager of the dharmashala informed them, "One mataji is residing in this dharmashala, you may like to go to her." On hearing this, the husband of the ailing lady knocked at the door of Ma's room. Viraj didi opened the door and on hearing his story, got irritated and said, "Mataji does not deal with such ailments." Then the husband of the lady forcibly entered the room and submitted himself at Ma's feet and started weeping profusely. Then Ma on Her own told Viraj didi, "Come, we would go and look up the lady." Saying this, Ma along with Viraj didi and the gentleman went over and saw that the lady's condition was quite serious. The hands and feet had become cold and the body had turned bluish. Tears kept rolling down her eyes continuously but she couldn't open her eyes. After having a look, Ma got Viraj didi to get a pomegranate from Her room and got the juice made out of it and made her consume it. She told the manager to change their room. Ma also went to that room, got the windows opened and asked for the ailing lady to be put on a bed and She came back. Next day it was found that the ailing lady had absolutely recovered. They left Devgarh the same day along with Ma. Viraj didi told us that the recovery of the lady in such a short time had surprised her.

35

My father late Shree Nagendranath Chakravarty and my mother late Shrimati Suhasini Devi (Kulalakshmi Devi) were mantra disciples (spiritual initiation by mantra) of revered Swami Shivanandaji (Mahapurush Maharaj), who was a direct disciple of the revered Shree Shree Ramakrishna Paramhansa Dev and the second president of Belur Math.

The first President of the Ramakrishna mission, Swami Brahmananda Maharaj, while on his spiritual sojourn, came to Assam. The he visited our house and stayed for a few days. Swami Brahmananda had given the name Premananda to my elder brother. He was among the first batch of students for matriculation at Ramakrishna Mission Vidyapeeth, Deoghar.

My third eldest brother Dr. Satyananda Chakraborty presently has been a practicing doctor at Kashi Ramakrishna Mission Sevashram and a permanent resident of the Mission.

My maternal aunt's elder brother-in-law Shree Gyan Ranjan Brahmachari was the disciple of Shree Shree Sarada Ma and he was the first in the family who had met Shree Shree Ma Anandamayee. On hearing from him, my maternal grandmother Virajmohini Devi visited Dhaka and had the darshan of Shree Shree Ma Anandamayee and was blessed to submit totally at Her feet for her lifetime. As per the traditional and customary rules for receiving guests as prevalent in Bangladesh, Shree Shree Ma Anandamayee offered her Jal (water) and Paan (Beetle leaf) (probably the origin of the word *Jal-pan*). My maternal grandmother always used to say, "Ma is Bhagwati Herself."

Shree Nagendranath Chakravarty

The naming of my brothers and sisters were a very special event. I think it would be worth mentioning. My eldest brother's name was given by Shree Brahmanandaji as Premananda as mentioned before. When my second and third elder brothers joined Shree Shree Ma Anandamayee Vidyapeeth at Dehradun, in Ma's presence, their sacred thread ceremony was solemnized and Ma named them as 'Sanatan' and 'Purushottam' respectively. My eldest sister-in-law was the eldest daughter of Ma's younger sister Shrimati Hemangini Devi. When she was in Kanyapeeth, Ma named her as 'Krishna' and her father had previously named her as 'Parul'. But in our house she used to be called Krishna as named by Ma. When my elder sister Savitri and my maternal cousin sister Basanti joined the Kanyapeeth at Raipur, Dehradun, Ma was present there. When my sisters went to pay their obeisance the following was uttered from Ma's lips–"Shraddha, Shuddha".

My father decided to do the sacred thread ceremony of my eldest brother in Shree Shree Ma's presence. Hence, in the month of January, 1936 he travelled from Assam to Tarapeeth with my elder brother. Baba Bholanath was observing 'maun'. But on Ma's special instruction he broke his vow of maun and performed all the ritualistic ceremonies and conducted the whole sacred thread ceremony for my brother and thus he was the 'Acharya Guru' of my brother. For eleven days my brother stayed in a room in seclusion observing the ritualistic injunctions.

In the meantime Ma had a kheyal that during Her 'Sadhana Leela' the ritualistic ceremony of sacred thread had played out in Her body and then Ma gave instructions for the conduct of the sacred thread ceremony for Gurupriya didi and

Baba Bholanath's adopted daughter, Marani di. The role of the Acharya Guru for Gurupriya didi was performed by Shree Dinesh Shastri ji and for Marani di by Baba Bholanath. Gurupriya didi and Marani didi observed the ritualistic observance of staying secluded in a room for three days. Since that occasion Marani di used to treat my eldest brother as her own brother.

In would be worthwhile to mention here that during Basanti Puja in the year 1971, Ma was present in Kashi. As usual the Puja was being conducted in all its pomp and splendor. During the morning time when ritualistic obeisance 'Pushpanjali' was being conducted, Ma walked out of the Mandap and sat down in the courtyard. It was then the devotees were offering their puja. The bhog ceremony was to be done after the Pushpanjali. While proceeding to make arrangements for the bhog, I observed that the flowers and the Bilva leaves, etc. of Pushpanjali were all scattered over the make shift altar and around it till the priest's seat and if I had to clean all that I would inadvertently touch the altar. Nirvan da and Sailesh da (priest and brother) had gone back to their respective rooms– the thought came that what could I do now? I informed Narayan Swami ji and he made the arrangements to clean and get the space ready to lay out the bhog. He said, "You all are the Brahmacharinis and lead a pure life, you might as well take the sacred thread. There will not be any problems. During the bhog ceremony when Ma walked into the Mandap, Shree Narayan Swami ji narrated the incident to Her. Respected Narayan Swami ji was very well versed in Shastras and very strict in their observances. It was through him, Ma invoked the idea and made the proposal a reality–unfathomable were the ways of Ma's kheyal.

Arrangements were made for the sacred thread ceremony of two persons; Chandan di and I were the senior persons, so everybody thought that it was for both of us. In the meantime one day Ma was residing at Her room on the second floor and a few of us were standing next to the door. All of a sudden Ma came out of Her room and took me aside and asked, "Tell me what you should do?" I enquired on what issue. Ma said– "What do you want to do on the issue of the sacred thread ceremony?" The words that came out of my lips were–"Ma, I have come to you and submitted myself, in whatever guise you decorate me will be not an issue. I have nothing to say but my inner self says 'No'. On hearing this Ma went back to Her room the way She had come. On 3rd June, 1971, the sacred ceremony was conducted for Chandan di and Geeta. The

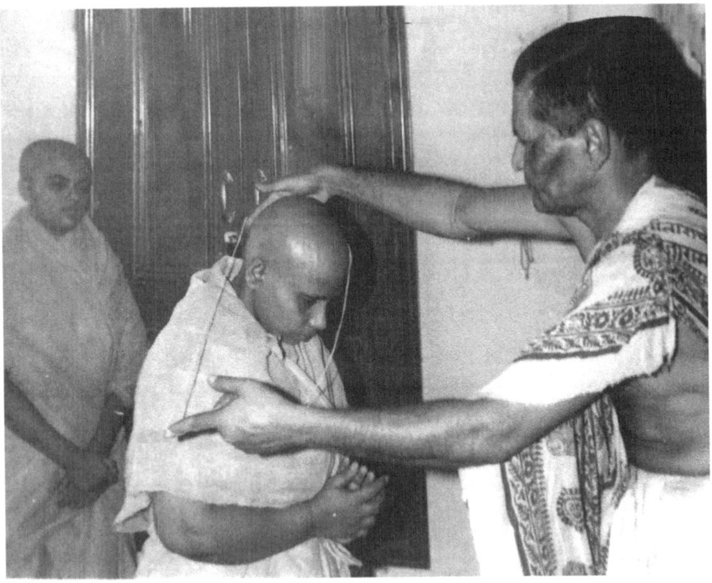

Shri Jadunath Bhattacharaya (Shree Shree Ma's Brother) giving the Sacred Thread to Chanan di and Geeta Banerji

brother of Ma, Shree Jadunath Bhattacharya was the Acharya Guru of both Chandandi and Geeta.

As my sacred ceremony was not done, there were many adverse, unpleasant and unsavoury comments made by many–she was not a worthy one and that was why her thread ceremony was not done etc. I used to rue the fact that when Ma asked me, without giving any thought to it, why I replied, "My inner self says no." I used to be quite upset about it. Later on I recollected, a year after I joined the Kanyapeeth, Ma gave me the 'Sanyas mantra'. After Sanyas the sacred thread ceremony could not be done, that was why Ma got these words out of me. Mahamahopadhyay Dr. Gopinath Kavirajji had said, "Whatever Ma says is the Shastras. Even in Her gestures nothing happens which is contrary to the Shastras. On 5th March, 1973 the sacred thread ceremony for

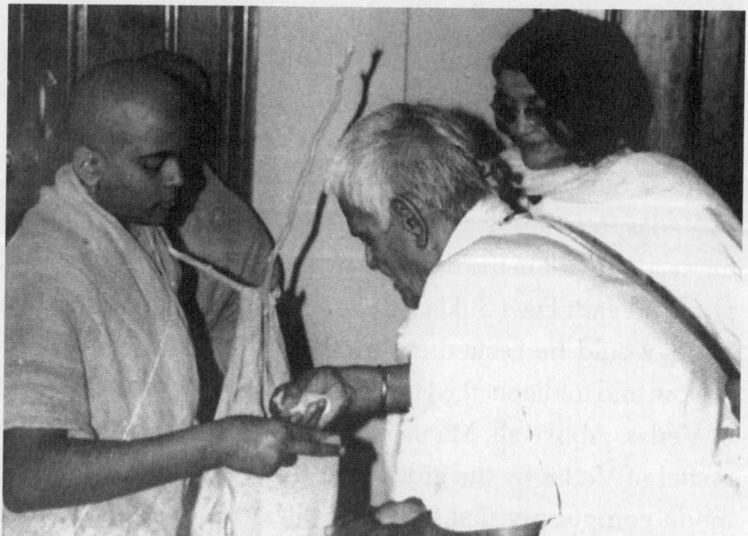

Bhiksha after Upnayan of Chandandi and Geeta Banerji

Jaya was conducted at Haridwar. Later Shantaji took sacred thread in front of Ma.

There are many views these days as to the subject of sacred thread for the maidens. But the investiture of sacred thread for maidens was prevalent in the ancient Vedic lore and the proof can be found in the Vedic literature.

Even the reading and contemplation of the Vedas is not accepted and encouraged by many. But Pandit Madan Mohan Malaviyaji with the help of the eminent Pandits of the Vedas started the curriculum of the Vedas in the women's college of the Banaras Hindu University.

Ma asked me to do B.A. in Sanskrit. Pandit Triyambakam Atmaram Bhandarkarji used to teach me. He had said that in ancient India women used to read Vedas and there were Acharyas who had the vision of the Ved mantras and among them Apala, Ghosa, Lopamudra, etc. were prominent. Their references are given in the lore. I was very fond of reading the Vedas. I requested Panditji to teach the girls of the Kanyapeeth how to recite from the Vedas. He taught the girls Purusha Sukta and Devi Sukta. As per the rules of the study of Vedas, utterances and recital should be done regularly. I made a rule that in the morning in our prayer room after Ma's puja and aarti Devi Sukta should be recited and the Purusha Sukta would be recited at Annapurna mandir. As per the custom and tradition, the girls even now regularly do the recital of Vedas. Above all, Ma used to be delighted listening to the recital of Vedas by the girls. After that it was customary and made compulsory that during the festivals the recital from the Vedas would be done by the Brahmacharinis of Kanyapeeth in our Ashram.

36

The Demise of My Father–Shree Nagendranath Chakravarty

In the month of May 1979, on the occasion of Ma's birthday celebrations we had gone to Bangalore along with Ma at the invitation of the Governor Shree Chenna Reddy.

My father was then residing with my eldest brother in Kolkata. After reaching Bangalore I informed my father by post. Later I heard from Pranab (my nephew) that because my letter had the mention of Ma's well-being, etc. he touched the same on his forehead in salutations, read it a number of times and kept the same next to where his head would rest in his bed. My father never did japa sitting on the bed, but sitting on an easy chair next to the bed. On that fateful day he didn't use the easy chair, instead he sat on the floor next to his bed with his knees folded and asked Pranab to hand him over the multi-framed and foldable photo frame which had pictures of Shree Ramakrishna Deva, Ma Saradamoni, Swami Vivekananda, Mahapurush Maharaj and Shree Shree Anandamayee Ma. After that he did pranam to each of the figures in a customary way from feet upwards towards the face and back downwards from face to feet and asked Pranab to keep it back on the shelf where it was usually kept.

In the shelf where the photo frame was kept a bottle containing Ganga water was also kept. He used to sip Ganga water everyday believing that the water washed the feet of Shree Narayan. That day, as usual he took the water from the bottle and drank it. Afterwards, he handed the bottle over to Pranab to keep it on the shelf.

Then he kept sitting in that posture stretching out his hands towards God in a stance of salutations. Pranab felt concerned on seeing his grandfather sitting on the floor. He called his mother (Shree Shree Ma's sister's daughter). My sister-in-law rushed in and asked, "Father, are you feeling unwell? Shall we put you on bed?" My father gestured not to do it. My sister-in-law stood watching for some time and sent Pranab to call his father (my eldest brother). My brother came and saw my father sitting in the kneeling position and in a posture of doing pranam. He also asked my father whether they would place him on the bed. Father refused. Then my brother sent Pranab to call the doctor. Doctor Debnath came and examined my father and pronounced that just a few minutes back he had breathed his last.

My father was the disciple of Swami Shivanandaji, the second President of the Ramakrishna mission. Having instructions from the Mission, the last rites and cremation were done in the Kashipur (Dum Dum near Kolkata) ashram premises.

My eldest brother informed Swami Paramanandaji of my father's demise by a telegram. Ma broke the news to me. I thought Ma would send me to Kolkata. But Ma asked to send a message to the priest to procure and get proper vessels to conduct the ritualistic rites for my father. The dhoti etc. was provided by Ma Herself.

By coincidence the dates of the ritualistic rites of my father coincided with the dates of tithi puja of Shree Shree Ma. As a part of the celebrations 'Shat Chandi' (one hundred renditions of Chandi Path) and other rituals like hawan, etc. were conducted. After the completion of Chandi Path and hawan, Ma was informed, requesting Her presence at the venue. Some important persons had come to visit Ma and hence Her arrival was getting delayed. Observing the same, the priest Bhola da asked me to complete the ritualistic rites of my father. Due to paucity of space, I sat down to do the rites of ritualistic offerings close to the venue where the Chandi Path was conducted. I had just started and Ma came and stood at the door and observing that Bhola da was worried, She signalled him to complete the ritual and stood at the doorway in such a manner that the cloth wrapper of Ma was touching my back. Till the ritual was over, Ma kept standing there in the same way with the garment touching me. After the completion of ceremony, the Chandi Path was conducted.

My father would do the Chandi Path everyday with devotion and used to say, "By doing the Chandi Path nothing untoward could happen." He did the Chandi Path for nearly throughout his life. May be because of that he had the grace of Shree Shree Chandi Incarnate.

Some people enquired if I could participate in the conduct of various rituals during Ma's tithi puja as I was still under the spell of a death in the family. In front of Ma, Swami Paramananda pronounced, "Firstly, Vishuddha is a maiden, secondly, her Guru is present here. Hence, she is not under the influence of the spell and there is no embargo on her to carry out the ritualistic rites of the puja."

After the celebrations Ma sent me to Kolkata by aeroplane with the help of the Governor Reddy. After reaching there I wrote back to Ma about the details of my father's demise. Ma wrote back–"The state that your father was in is reflected in the events associated with your father."

37

The Demise of My Younger Brother–Keshavananda, Feb. 2017

After the demise of his wife, my younger brother Keshav used to stay in the Shree Ram Krishna Mission home for the aged name 'Barisha'.

My father and all my brothers and sisters were sports enthusiasts and were connected to the world of sports in varying measures. At some point of time my father used to play lawn tennis. My eldest brother was a table tennis player and Secretary of the 'Tollygunge Agragami' club. The fourth eldest brother Basudev had won 6–7 gold, silver and bronze medals in swimming. My elder sister had won the 'Championship Cup' from the Uttar Pradesh Sports Board and many other awards. My younger brother Keshav was well acclaimed and accomplished in chess, karate and table tennis.

In February, 2017 the Indian Premiere League was on. In the old age home it was forbidden to have television sets in the room and everybody used to watch the matches in dormitory. Keshav watched the match till late in the night and went back to his room.

He used to get up early in the morning and practice Yoga and Pranayam. That day also he must have done his routine. When he was absent at the breakfast table in the morning, the in-charge of the old age home opened Keshav's room and found his dead body on the cot, with a smile on his face and the tape recorder was playing the song–"How far still is that Ananda dham (the abode of happiness)". On observing this the Maharaj (monk in-charge) said–"what I see looks like a death on one's own calling".

38

I thought of sharing a very personal experience of my life which bordered on a strange experience and remained unanswered even till date. Since I met Ma for the first time, whenever I used to do pranam to Ma, I had a feeling in my mind that my feet were touching Ma's bosom. It was indeed very embarrassing and I couldn't share this feeling with anyone.

In the year 1961 once Ma was in Varanasi ashram in Her room on the first floor. Dadabhai was distributing prasad. She asked me to go and see if Ma had any visitors in Her room. I ran upstairs and as I was at the door of Ma's room, I saw Ma alone and seated on the bed facing West. She suddenly turned Her head towards me and said in a loud voice, as if proclaiming something to the world, "Remember, Narayana Himself accepted Bhrigu's feet in His bosom." I was stunned, could make nothing of it except for an answer to the strange feeling in my mind. I quietly paid my obeisance and walked back downstairs.

I informed Dadabhai that there were no visitors in Ma's room. But I still couldn't tell her what Ma had pronounced. It was the usual feeling of guilt and a possibility of embarrassment that stopped me from narrating the incident to others.

In my twilight years I am provoked to let the world know about the incident and that too seems strange to me. I have heard and read about the story of Sage Bhrigu and I have to admit that I tried relating the incident but my thoughts were not related with Ma even in trace in my subsequent associations and of course the fear or guilt of self-praise in the hearts of people always bothered me.

I have come to a conclusion that like infinite other instances my Ma had Her own way of conveying what was desired. All this is for the good of mankind. As individuals She is always with us and constantly guiding us on our path and more so if the belief and prayers are intense. Now I pray to the reader and the knower of this episode to pray in real earnest so that Ma gives every soul and Ma's child what is required of them.

Jai Ma

Vishuddha

Appendix

A Story of Ma's Leela by Rama Guha

My father, Late Shree Manamohan Ghosh (better known as Mana da among devotees of Shree Shree Ma) was a reputed engineer and steward of Dhaka University. Our family had shifted to Varanasi from Dhaka in 1946 as per Shree Shree Ma's instructions following widespread riots in Dhaka. We settled at a house within stone's throw of the ashram at Varanasi.

The tale I am about to relate is a manifestation of Shree Shree Ma's infinite kheyal with Mira didi, one of my elder sisters. I was quite young and Mira didi was in her teens, when once she accompanied our father along with others to railway station when Ma was leaving Varanasi. As per Ma's kheyal, my father was asked to entrain and accompany the party to Patna and some other places. Mira di followed later and joined the party at Vrindavan. Mira di was very much attached to Shree Gurupriya didi and used to help her while she cooked and performed other chores for Ma. On this trip, Ma instructed Gurupriya di to give Diksha to Mira di, but this affair was kept secret.

When Mira di was 18, she fell ill with beri-beri, which was endemic at that time. Her heart was affected and her condition worsened steadily. She was invalided in a ground floor room of our house; her bed was placed near the window overlooking the street for better light and ventilation. One day while nursing her late night my mother heard her talking to somebody across the window. When queried, Mira di replied that she was talking to Shree Shree Ma. My mother looked out and indeed Shree Shree Ma was standing outside the window at that late hour. She had come to enquire about Mira di's health and soothe her distress.

Later in the day Mira di was laying her head on our mother's bosom looking out of the window when Shree Shree Ma arrived with Gurupriya di and others. Ma remained at the window, focused on Mira di, while Gurupriya di was sent into the room to prepare and administer medicines to the patient as per Her instructions. Everybody could sense that the end was drawing near. As was Her wont, Ma never stayed at the time of death, and here too She turned to Mira di and said, "Mira may I leave now?" Mira di had lost the power of speech by then, but she gesticulated with her hand "Two minutes". Ma was compelled to wait as within those two minutes Mira di breathed her last, having full darshan of Shree Shree Ma.

Mira's head was resting on my mother's lap when she breathed her last. On this incident, it was later heard that Shree Shree Ma had mentioned–"One person made this body stand in front of her and left her body in presence of this body."

The day when Mira di breathed her last, my father as per his regular routine had gone to ashram to supervise ongoing construction work. Normally, he would not meet Shree Shree Ma every day, and would return home after concluding his duties. On this day he was summoned to Ma's presence and Shree Shree Ma repeatedly lashed and whipped him with a stripling cut off a neem tree, all the time intoning, "Will you do it again?" Incomprehensible as Ma's action seemed then, in retrospect it seemed, by lashing my father so harshly Ma prepared him for the oncoming shock and lessened his grief.

Matri Kripa by Rama Guha

The mentioned incident is an example of Shree Shree Ma's ever present grace.

My mother was involved in the incident, hence I am mentioning a few lines about her. She was of a calm and composed nature. She spent her whole day looking after her mother-in-law, faultlessly and tirelessly discharging her duties of looking after her husband and children and after completing all this, after about 9 pm she used to pay her obeisance to Shree Shree Ma.

My mother had a great quality; she used to prepare various types of food dishes. Also, whenever Shree Ma was in Kashi she used to prepare various sweet dishes to be offered to Her for Her bhog. Shree Ma was a very frugal eater, but She used to accept the food prepared by my mother, specially sweet pancakes made of semolina. Shree Ma often called the girls of the ashram and showed them the presentation of the food offerings and said, "Look, how nicely the food has been presented on the plate." She also asked the girls to learn the art of presenting food from my mother. On special occasions like 'Annakut' or Basanti puja and when saints and eminent people visited Kashi, She sent coconuts to my mother to prepare the 'Bhog'.

I don't remember the date or year–one day Shree Ma gave a rosary to my mother to do her Japa. The rosary was made of white conch shells. By Shree Ma's grace my mother used to do her Japa twice a day with the rosary.

Then, a few days had passed since the demise of my father Shri Manamohan Gosh, popularly known as Mana da in the ashram. A few months before this my elder brother Shri Saroj Kumar Ghosh had also passed away. We were passing through a phase of mourning.

One day during dusk my mother was doing her Japa in the Puja room with the rosary and after completing that she put the rosary in a small container and then she proceeded to do the other part of her evening prayers. Kashi is known for the monkey menace, though they were generally not seen during the evening hours. That day suddenly I heard my mother wailing, "My rosary has been taken away by the monkeys." Surprisingly during those hours of dusk and in near darkness the monkey had come and selectively taken away the rosary from the container. Now my mother was wailing and praying to Shree Ma, "Ma I have lost everything. I have even lost the rosary given by you."

I rushed downstairs and informed my second eldest brother Shri Shakti Ghosh, "Brother, the monkey has taken mother's rosary." My younger brother was an ardent devotee of Shree Ma. At that moment itself he wrote a letter to Shree Ma about the incident and about my mother's misery.

We had resigned to our destiny. A few days later, one afternoon, my sister-in-law saw a spectacle and exclaimed loudly, "O God, the rosary is around the neck of a monkey!" We rushed to the place and saw that monkey would sometimes put the rosary around his neck and sometimes remove it. And then jumping around for some time he proceeded towards the 'Benaras Water Works' close to our house. Noticing this, my nephew, Shri Indranath, rushed ahead to retrieve the rosary. Though the 'Water Works' was close to our house, the route to reach there was circuitous via lanes, main road, descending the ghat on the Ganga and then climbing up the stairs towards the structures of the 'Water Works'.

Indranath ran towards the ghat on the Ganga. There he saw the monkey drop the rosary on a mound on the bank of the Ganga. There the children of the 'Mallah' (boatman) community were playing around. They picked up the rosary immediately. Indranath approached them and asked for the rosary. They said, "Give us money, then we will give." Indranath gave them whatever money he had in his pocket and procured the rosary. While returning he was counting the beads of the rosary. He found that not even one bead was lost, only due to the biting of the rosary one bead had got elongated. He returned and said, "Here grandmother, take your rosary." My mother finally got back her rosary.

This incident was informed to Shree Ma. When Shree Ma came to Kashi the next time, She gave my mother a rosary of 'Rudraksh' beads for doing her Japa. Shree Ma used to narrate this story to the devotees. She used to say, "Have you all ever heard about such an incidence, an animal of the wilderness, a monkey, comes and returns a rosary?"

Related to the incident, I would like to mention–the widows don't have the right to do Japa with a rosary made of sea (conch) shells. My mother didn't know about the injunction. It was a rosary given by Shree Ma and hence she would do her Japa with the same.

The retrieved rosary was kept with a lot of care by my mother. On special occasions when we used to do our pranam to her, she used to touch the rosary to our heads as a symbol of blessing.

Reviews

'Opinions of a few readers of this book after reading Bengali and Hindi version'

(1)

I can't express in words how glad I am after going through your book, 'My Mother Anandamayee'. My heartfelt congratulations to you. The illustration of the incidents and the simple lucid language of expression, both are wonderful. I give an example to clear it that I started reading this book in the midst of terrific heat of this place and finished it without break and totally unaware of the heat. I acquired pure bliss. Ma's endless grace is showering on you and being bathed in that continuous grace, the physical illness never overpowered you. Due to the stored fortunes of your previous births this impossible was possible. The anecdotes mentioned by you are mostly known to me yet your presentation made them anew. Everything is Ma's leela.

The characterization of your grandmother is extra ordinary, such persons are rarely to be found. Though her description, in your book, is relatively small but the essence of her character is very evident.

Those who have seen Kshamadi could realize easily her selfless service, but even for those who didn't have the chance to meet her, would be surprised to know that such people exist. It was of course important to highlight these aspects. All this is of course Ma's leela.

I am proud of you. I pray whole-heartedly at Ma's feet that you keep fit and serve Ma. This book will make me happy always and remind me of Ma.

Km. Sati Dutta Gupta
Ex-Principal of Kanyapeeth
(Daughter of Shree Amulya Kumar Dutta Gupta—
The writer of Shree Shree Anandamayee Prasanga)

(2)

Dear Vishuddha, I liked your book immensely and don't have words to express. While reading this book, those days which were spent in the company of Ma in profuse happiness come afresh. I wonder where those days have gone! At night when I can't sleep I read your book again and again.

Bubadi (Mrs. Ira Mukherjee), Mumbai

(3)

While reading the book 'My Mother Anandamayee' written by you, I am seeing Ma in front of my eyes and hearing Her voice. I feel that you have very cautiously and without exaggeration painted the delightful ever laughing picture of Nirmala Sundari Devi (Ma).

Ms. Malaya Sengupta, Jamshedpur

(4)

With the exchange of pure emotions it is a unique homage to Ma indeed. I am charmed after going through your book 'My Mother Anandamayee'. Once I finished it in one breath and now reading it again and again. I am seeing Ma and you together and then Ma's voice and the way of talking echoing in my ears. These are true anecdotes hence so hearty. Those who have got the company of Ma will appreciate this book forever.

Mrs. Basanti Moitra, Kolkata

(5)

My Dear Vishuddha, I read your book, 'My Mother Anandamayee' in one breath. I enjoyed it very much and felt as if I am seeing Ma again amidst us. Also the clear and easy language of your book also impressed me. You have related your heartfelt and eye-witnessed incidents with Ma which cannot be forgotten. Ma is inside you and inspiring you to write these true anecdotes. I have gone through other books on Ma but yours is quite different and it opens a new door to Ma.

While reading your book I forgot about my illness, pain and the troubles of my body. I was so happy that it healed up my body.

That reminds me the song of Tagore—"When I played with you, who knew who you are. There was no fear no shame." You are the most fortunate one to play with Ma. Glory to you and your attempts to write them. May Ma give you a happy long life.

With love and good wishes.

Chitradi (Ms. Chitra Ghosh), Kolkata

(6)

For the one whose lifetime was spent in the close proximity of Shree Ma, Bramhacharini Vishuddha's book 'My Mother Anandamayee' is a depiction of her love and indebtedness towards Shree Ma.

Vijayananda, Kankhal

A French doctor, Doctor Adolf Winstrolbe in his quest to learn philosophy and spiritualism and become yogi, toured Sri Lanka, Pondicherry and other places. When he was rather disenchanted and made up his mind to return to his native place, he chanced to meet a Canadian lady, from whom he heard about Ma. He travelled to the ashram at Kashi. As soon as he saw Ma, he exclaimed— 'I am wholeheartedly and totally attracted by the presence of Ma'. Since then he settled in India permanently. Subsequently Ma presented him the ochre robe and re-christened him as Vijayananda. As per Ma's instructions, he spent many years in Almora and Dhaulchina ashram and practiced the aspects of spiritualism.

(7)

Vishuddha, who had the unending opportunity to stay in the close proximity of Ma has written a wonderful and enchanting book 'My Mother Anandamayee' which got highlighted by Ma's companionship and divine insights.

Ram Alexander, Kankhal

In 1971 Alexander came to India from America and heard about Shree Shree Anandamayee Ma from a friend who was a devotee of Ma. He met Ma in Naimisharan. Ma christened him as 'Ram'. By Ma's grace he stayed in ashram and as per Her instructions carried out his spiritual practice from 1973 to 1983.